The world's largest collection of visual travel guides

MOROCCO

Edited by Dorothy Stannard
Editorial Director: Brian Bell

APA PUBLICATIONS
Part of the Langenscheidt Publishing Group

Although within sight of Europe, Morocco has the exciting diversity of a country that is much further afield. Two vibrant cultures – Berber and Arab – dramatically beautiful scenery ranging from towering mountains to lush oases, and a rich architectural and culinary heritage reward detailed exploration.

Morocco was therefore an obvious country to include in the 190-title *Insight Guides* series, a pioneering style of travel guide created by **Hans Höfer** in 1970 which aims to provide readers with real insight into the people and culture of their destination and not merely point them towards the best restaurants and hotels (though the guides do this too).

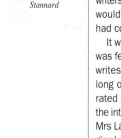

Höfer

To achieve this end in the case of Morocco, Höfer commissioned project editor **Dorothy Stannard**, a regular visitor to Morocco since her first adventurous trip there at the age of 25, when she and a girlfriend travelled the length and breadth of the country on local transport. An editor and writer based in Insight Guides' London office, Stannard, assembled a team of writers and photographers that she felt would do justice to the country she had come to love so much.

It was in Tangier that she met (and was fed by) **Anne Lambton**, who here writes about Moroccan cuisine – for long one of the world's most underrated cuisines but recently receiving the international attention it deserves. Mrs Lambton lives in a quarter of Tangier known as The Mountain, a leafy suburb long associated with English expatriates. She is full of enthusiasm for present-day Tangier, not in the least sorry to have missed the international era. Her friend, however, the late **David Herbert**, writer and second son of the 16th Earl of Pembroke, experienced

Stannard

Tangier in full swing. He was often described as its "unofficial social arbiter". For this book, whose first edition was published before his death, he recalled the famous parties given by his friend Barbara Hutton, the Woolworth heiress, who for many years owned a house in Tangier's medina.

Like the literary captain of Morocco, novelist Paul Bowles, **Stanley Reynolds** grew up in New England. Walking into a bar in 1957, met, and a little later married, a young Englishwoman, and in 1958 he left the US to settle in her hometown of Liverpool. As a young journalist, he graduated from the *Liverpool Echo* to *The Guardian* to *Punch* magazine, where he became literary editor. Here he writes about the draw of Morocco to the novelists of the 1950s – Paul Bowles and beat writers William S. Burroughs, Jack Kerouac and Brion Gysin.

Another contributing literary man is **Nicholas Shakespeare**, books editor of London's *Daily Telegraph*, novelist and son of a former British Ambassador to Morocco. Between 1988 and 1991 he travelled repeatedly to the Spanish enclave of Ceuta to glean information for his second novel. He said of his trip: "I had gone there in high hopes that I might find it a suitable place to set a novel. I was not disappointed. But while prepared to make Ceuta home to a number of paper characters, I would not willingly despatch any flesh and blood creature to the Cafeteria Nizi in the Plaza de los Reys."

Stephen Ormsby Hughes, author of the history section, has witnessed the whole compass of Moroccan affairs since Independence. Formally an RAF Coastal Command pilot, he first went to Morocco in 1953 to edit a news-

Ormsby Hughes

paper in Casablanca. Two years later the paper closed down but he stayed on as correspondent of the Associated Press. He also worked for the *New York Times*, *Time* magazine and the BBC until joining Reuters. In addition to the history section, he contributed a feature on the subtle definition of the Moroccan refrain *"In sha'Allah"*.

Also living in Rabat, **Reg Veale** worked as the Director of Studies at the British Council Language Centre there. He has spent all his working life overseas – in Fiji, Malaysia and Morocco – teaching English as a foreign language and managing language schools. In conjunction with his friend **Tiina Britten**, born in the Ivory Coast and educated in French Lycées in West Africa and Morocco, he wrote the chapters on Rabat, Casablanca and the southern coastline.

Veale

Marrakesh and Fez are at the top of every visitor's list of priorities. To capture the unique flavour of the great city of Marrakesh, the project editor enlisted the talents of **Alan Keohane**, a writer and photographer based in Marrakesh, who has also acted as a mountain and desert guide. Keohane, whose books include *The Berbers of Morocco*, a stunning photographic study, also wrote the chapter on The South and updated the chapters on the Atlas Mountains, the Southwest Coast and the Deep South.

Phillimore

Polly Phillimore, author of the chapters on Fez, Meknes and Moulay Idriss, is another longstanding visitor to Morocco, though she travelled all over the world in her capacity as a researcher and writer for the British Consumers' Association's travel publication *Holiday Which?*. She now lives in Ireland, but returns to Morocco whenever she can.

Robin Collomb is an established expert on the Atlas Mountains. From the age of 11 he misspent his youth potting mountain peaks around the world. He arrived in Morocco in the 1970s, some 1,700 summits and 35 years later, and duly published a guidebook to the Atlas for mountaineers and trekkers. That's just one of nearly 40 titles he has chalked up.

Collomb

Short features have been contributed by other enthusiasts. **John Offen**, writing about architecture, is a Paris-based interior designer who has written a book on Moroccan style. **Dave Muddyman**, covering music (the beauty of which Brion Gysin thought reason enough to become a Muslim), is a musician who regularly travels to Morocco to record and accompany musicians performing in the cafés of the medinas. Asilah, on the northwest coast, is his favourite haunt.

Mark Griffiths, writing about the film location business in Morocco, is a young filmmaker who between assignments dabbles in freelance journalism, turning experiences of exotic locations into travel features.

The Travel Tips section was compiled by **David Dickinson**, who served a tough travel research and writing apprenticeship on *Holiday Which?* magazine before becoming editor of the Consumers' Association health magazine. He escaped the fact-checking and information hauling involved in compiling the Travel Tips to fly to Agadir and cover the long coastal stretch down to Layounne.

Dickinson

The project editor would like to thank her brother **David Stannard**, who accompanied her on some of her research trips and, uncomplaining, undertook most of the driving, and **Said M'samri**, a constant source of inspiration in Tangier.

CONTENTS

Preceding pages: southern architecture; the Draa river.

CONTENTS

Maps

TRAVEL TIPS

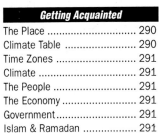

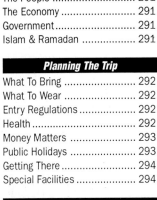

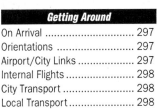

For centuries Europeans have enjoyed explaining the character of the Moor. Early visitors to Morocco, convinced of their own superior, civilised values, considered it their right, even their duty, to warn of the dark, lazy, deceitful and polygamous infidels on Europe's doorstep. Sir John Drummond Hay, Britain's consul in Tangier for the last half of the 19th century, wrote: "They combine all possible vices."

A popular image: Even these days, some of these Western prejudices and clichés remain, albeit tempered by praise of Moroccan hospitality or family values. In the popular imagination, Moroccans, like other oriental people (though in this case well west of London), are described as "chauvinists", "fatalists", and "hedonists" – simple stereotypes when one considers Morocco's eclectic racial origins.

Broadly, Moroccans may be divided into the urban and rural populations. The Berbers, the indigenous race, are still more likely to live in the mountainous *bled*, or countryside, where they migrated in the face of the first Arab invaders; and the Arabs, in the towns and cities of the plains. The Berbers are of three main types (sub-divided into countless tribes): the Riffians of the north; the Chleuhs from the Middle and High Atlas; and the Soussi, found in the southwest. Their origins are uncertain; theories include the possibility of European derivations, probably based on the not unusual occurrence of fair colouring and blue or green coloured eyes.

But the so-called Arab/Berber divide is now generally dismissed as a myth propagated during the French and Spanish protectorates to help justify colonial policies and undermine resistance. Today many Moroccans are of mixed ancestry: Berber, Arab and even black African (the latter originating from the black slaves imported from Mali during the Saadi dynasty), as can be seen from the variety of faces, even within the

same family. In the countryside, pockets of pure Arabs in regions that are otherwise Berber – for example, Erfoud in the Tafilalt and Tamgroute in the Draa – are the exception rather than the rule. Here the women are shrouded in heavy black *haik* and reveal only one eye to the world, in contrast to their brightly-attired Berber neighbours. Nonetheless, Berber – either *Shilha*, *Soussia* or *Riffia* – are totally different languages from Arabic, with many dialects. Whereas a Berber usually understands Arabic (and in order to

write, must use it), Berber remains incomprehensible to most Arabs.

But the two races have developed much in common. When the Berbers embraced Islam, they adapted it to include favourite pagan customs which were then absorbed into the Moroccan culture as a whole. For example, although Islam is not supposed to accept any intermediary between an individual and God, Morocco is littered with the white-domed tombs of holy men, *marabout*, to which the troubled and the sick – especially women – make pilgrimages.

In fact, a woman is more likely to visit the tomb of her favourite holy man (or even a

Preceding pages: crossing the courtyard of the Kairouyine Mosque, Fez; a young population; desert places; discussing the date harvest. **Left,** Berber girl from the Dades Valley. **Above,** a water seller poses.

supposedly sacred stream or tree) than go to pray at the mosque. She may camp for weeks at a *koubba*, where she will pray, grieve and just pass time.

Magic, too, is a fecund and potent force. As Paul Bowles, the American novelist and composer living in Tangier, wrote in his autobiography *Without Stopping*: "Sorcery is burrowing invisible tunnels in every direction, from thousands of senders to thousands of unsuspecting recipients." Every medina contains a *shouaf* to which not only the gullible and uneducated go to purchase weird concoctions or to seek advice; the apothecaries in the markets trade in dried bits of animal skin and pickled reptiles; benevolent and

evil *djin* (spirits) are thought populous; and the power of the so-called "evil eye", meaning the spells cast over one by a jealous ill-wisher, isn't taken lightly. The newspapers are full of lurid tales of revenge through witchcraft, and mothers give their children talismans to protect them – a "hand", a leather pouch containing fragments of Koranic verses, or perhaps a blue bead. Too much beauty or good fortune are often thought to provoke the evil eye. For this reason the most splendid carpet design is never entirely symmetrical or too perfect.

Again, Islam doesn't endorse the use of magic, but that it can tolerate it is another indication of its flexibility as a religion. In theory, Islam recognises both the other "written" religions, i.e. Judaism and Christianity, and in spite of the colourful accounts of Christian slavery in the 17th century and the departure of most Jews at Independence, Morocco claims historical respect for both. Many Jews emigrated to Morocco from Spain to escape the Inquisition.

King Hassan II, in his autobiography *The Challenge*, is proud of Morocco's history of religious tolerance. He claims the Jewish quarter, the *mellah*, was always built close to the palace in a city so that it should benefit from royal protection.

Islam is forgiving towards Muslims themselves. There are five "pillars" to the faith: *Shahada* (the testament that there is no god but God); *Salat* (the observance of prayer five times a day); *Saum* (fasting at Ramadan); *Zakat* (the giving of alms to the poor); and *Hadj* (the pilgrimage to Mecca at least once in a lifetime). But the Koran (the direct word of God given to the Prophet) and the Hadith (the sayings of the Prophet on Islamic conduct in everyday life) make generous allowance for the frailty of the flesh. Indeed, sexual intercourse, providing it is within marriage, is considered beneficial to the holiest of men.

Blessed with *baraka*: Equally, the strand of Islam known as Sufism has adapted Islam to include elements of mysticism – such as asceticism and meditation – which have more in common with Roman Catholicism than they do with orthodox Islam. At one time, those claiming *baraka*, a blessing supposedly bestowed by Allah on any direct descendants of the Prophet (quite a marketable asset), acquired the status of saints, deemed capable of miracles. Some of the cults that evolved around these saints inspired trance and self-mutilations in their followers – behaviour not recommended in any obvious way by the Koran.

Now outlawed, such extreme practices have died out or gone underground, but some remnant of their spirit is still alive in the trance music of the *gnaoua*, black African musician-healers in hats and waistcoats trimmed with lucky cowrie shells, a group of whom are often present on the Djemma el Fna in Marrakesh. At a more mundane level, *baraka* is claimed by *faikirs*, itinerant holy men (often deemed quacks), who offer herbs and prayers to the sick in country areas.

Traditionally, *baraka* also endowed its possessor with more civil authority than anyone else – which, in a country of constant tribal feuding, provided at least some kind of independent jurisdiction. Thus it has also helped determine and preserve the succession to the sultancy. Mohammed V's claim to the throne in 1956 was helped by the fact that his lineage can be traced back to the Prophet via Ali (the Alaouite dynasty), even though, according to the Koran, there should be no religious hierarchy in Islam and King Hassan's authority is ultimately rooted in a feudal system, not a "Divine Right". The people offer allegiance in return for the sultan's protection, symbolised by the giant

gurated in 1993) costing five billion dirhams built in Casablanca. Generally, the project was supported by the people, who were each asked by house-visiting officials to contribute to the expense of building it – their 60th-birthday present to their King.

French legacy: International consensus is that Morocco has done well since independence – all things considered, including problems of earthquake and droughts. Certainly, arriving in Rabat for the first time or driving into Casablanca along the residential Anfa road, one is struck by the sense of established prosperity. The French civic architecture and the elegant patisseries along Boulevard Mohammed V in Rabat create an

umbrella which the King carries on ceremonial occasions.

Naturally, following independence there were deep social and economic problems and Mohammed V and his son Hassan were able to draw strength from their claim to descend from the Prophet. In his autobiography, King Hassan stresses his Alaouite ancestry, and his dramatic accounts of escapes from would-be assassins do rather suggest a charmed life.

In the 1980s King Hassan chose to underline his piety by having a new mosque (inau-

impression of a town bourgeois enough for Madame Bovary to kick against.

France has left its legacy in the country's administration: in common with Europe rather than other parts of the Muslim world, Friday is a normal working day and Saturday and Sunday a weekend holiday; administratively the country is divided into provinces (or *préfectures* in the cases of Rabat and Casablanca) and sub-divided into communes; when conducting business the educated frequently talk to one another in French rather than Arabic; and until recently bright students were assisted by the Moroccan government to attend foreign, usually French,

Left, the sacred. **Above**, the profane.

universities. Inevitably, such students sometimes returned to Morocco with outlooks that had altered.

Superficially, therefore, Morocco can seem European rather than North African. But, in fact – unlike other Arab countries, whose cultures bear the heavy-handed stamp of their colonisers, the Ottomans – it retains much of its pre-Protectorate variety of character. Its Europeanisation is only a façade, even in the cities.

The *bidonvilles* of Casablanca, shantytowns built by those who, following World War II and the rapid industrialisation of Morocco, migrated from the country to towns, exist in conditions that have never improved

promote national pride, foster useful relations with Europe and America, encourage a popular reaffirmation of faith (while guarding against fundamentalism), and watch his own back, all at the same time.

The 1990–91 Gulf Crisis illustrated his expedience. The Moroccan Government was one of the first to demonstrate support for Kuwait and the West (major donors of aid to Morocco) and dispatched 1,500 troops to join the build-up of allied forces in Saudi Arabia. However, when war broke out in January 1991 and Moroccan public opinion rallied round Iraq's Saddam Hussein, King Hassan was forced to moderate his stance. Pro-Iraqi demonstrations in Rabat and Fez

– theirs is not the kind of poverty captured on postcards or promoted by the Tourist Office.

National pride: In the l970s a delayed reaction to the colonialism of the first half of the century heralded a mood of Moroccan nationalism. Groups of musicians, notably Nass el Ghiwane and Jilala, revived a popular ancient folk music known as El Malhoune, incorporating anti establishment, leftist lyrics. It degenerated into popular commercial music before it had much political impact, but it didn't go unnoticed in high places. King Hassan, conscious of skating on thin ice at times (and ever mindful of the demise of the Shah of Iran), has been careful to

were of a size not seen since the Green March into the Western Sahara. In the very speech banning such demonstrations, the King began referring to Saddam as "brother".

By Arab and African standards Hassan has produced a liberal kingdom. It is a country, though, where royal contacts are tantamount to success (though it should be remembered that nepotism has a long tradition in the Muslim East), and it is a monarchy in its full sense; constitutionally, the monarch can overrule any decision. Hassan's authority is underlined at all levels. In every public building, be it an ever-so-humble sandwich shop, a framed portrait of King Hassan hangs.

Since the attempted *coups d'états* in the 1970s particularly, press and broadcasting have been carefully controlled. Riots erupting in Algiers in the autumn of 1988 made headline news in Europe. In Morocco they were not reported at all, partly because Morocco was then engaged in delicate negotiations with Algeria over their support of Polisario guerrillas, but also because it was feared they might spread there. In December 1990 Morocco had its own bread riots, resulting in death and injury.

The danger is one of an educated proletariat who have little or no work. The level of full-time employment is low; a high percentage of people are engaged in casual,

seasonal or itinerant work. Meanwhile the country has seen the sudden growth of a *nouveau riche* class whose wealth is often founded on drugs, contraband or speculation. One of the first things to strike visitors arriving in Tangier – an important base for all these activities – is the number of brand-new Mercedes. Inevitably huge disparities between rich and poor cause social unrest.

A population of 24 million and an accelerating birthrate exacerbate difficulties and have at last prompted timid attempts at birth

Left, intimate dialogue between females. **Above**, a participant in a *moussem*.

control. In recent years King Hassan's speeches have made frequent references to the need for contraception – something which would have been condemned as anti-religious in the past.

Chronic unemployment must also account in part for the surprising number of male and female brothels, particularly in Marrakesh and Casablanca. Although prostitution's claim to be the oldest profession in the world is as true here as anywhere, it proliferated in Morocco under the French and Spanish protectorates. Military brothels were set up to cater for the French armies.

Western homosexuals still find a ready supply of catamites in Tangier and Marrakesh, while rich Gulf Arabs, escaping their own strict regimes, take advantage of Morocco's more liberal attitudes to establish private female brothels. These are not apparent to the average tourist, whose impression is of veiled women and sexual seclusion.

On the home front: On a more domestic note, social and family traditions, national and regional, are fervently followed. As well as the big religious festivals (the birthday of the Prophet; Ramadan; the feast of the lamb – Aid el Kebir – commemorating Abraham's sacrifice of a sheep in place of his son, and held 70 days after Ramadan) family events such as births, circumcisions, marriages, the *hadj* (pilgrimage to Mecca) and burial are loaded in ritual. After the birth of a child a lamb is slaughtered – two lambs if the baby is given two names. If the family is poor, it may be just a chicken that is killed, or if they are impoverished, a rabbit. For the circumcision of boys at the age of around four – these days aided by a local anaesthetic – another feast is held and the boy is plied with money.

Arranged marriages are still fairly common, especially in the low and high class families, and lavish weddings, usually 15-day affairs, are still the norm. But an increasing number of brides and grooms are opting for a simple ceremony, and many couples are living and sleeping together after the "engagement", an official ceremony – actually equivalent to the wedding ceremony in the West – which happens a year or two before the wedding (if they do, however, there is no turning back short of divorce or death). Probably more than in any other Arab nation, in Morocco traditionalists and modernists comfortably coexist.

Over 50,000 years ago Neanderthal man lived in Morocco. A specimen of his remains was found in caves at Tamara beach near Rabat in 1933. The so-called "Rabat man" seems to have been a boy about 16 years old. He lived at a time when the country was physically very different from what it is today, covered with dense forests full of wild animals.

Clues to the history of these people and their descendants are written on rocks. Engravings on flat slabs of rock – some can be seen near Tafraout southeast of Agadir – show that besides prehistoric man the area was populated by lions, panthers, giraffes, ostriches, elephants and antelopes.

There is evidence that there may have been some sort of civilisation about 5,000 years ago, as indicated by the discovery of rock carvings representing a ram with a solar disc between its horns similar to the god Ammon Ra of Thebes in Egypt.

The Greeks have left legends. Fabulous Atlantis is said to have sunk into the sea somewhere west of Spain and Morocco. Then there is the myth of Hercules forcing apart Europe and Africa to create the Straits of Gibraltar, a feat remembered in the Caves of Hercules near Tangier, and in the "Pillars of Hercules" – the rocks of Gibraltar and Ceuta. Some say the Garden of the Hesperides was also in Morocco and that the golden apples Hercules found were in fact oranges – an unlikely tale because oranges originated in Asia and were introduced into Morocco long after his time.

The Phoenicians: We know slightly more (but not much) about Morocco from the 12th century BC onwards, thanks to the Phoenicians who set up trading posts along the coast. Punic remains have been found at Russadir (Melilla), Tamuda (Tetouan), Ceuta, Tingis (Tangier), Lixus (Larache), Thymiaterion (Mehdia near Kenitra), Sala (Rabat) and Karikon Telichos (Essaouira). They were probably trading posts rather than settlements, although a number of Punic tombs

have been found near Tangier and Rabat. There is a record of how the Phoenician navigator Hanno sailed between the Pillars of Hercules in 460 BC and down the African coast, perhaps as far as the Equator, founding on the way another trading post at Cerne, which may be Dakhla in the Western Sahara.

We know practically nothing of the people who lived in Morocco in Phoenician times up to the fall of Carthage in 140 BC. There is no evidence that the sailors or traders of Carthage ever penetrated inland. Perhaps

they were not interested in colonisation, or perhaps the Berbers were a fierce warrior race and the traders were unable to conquer them. At all events, the Romans, who dominated the area for over four centuries until AD 429, found the Berbers, or the Barbarians as they called them, an intractable race who gave the Legions constant trouble when they were founding permanent Roman settlements. Among these outposts of the Roman Empire were Tingi (Tangier), Zilis (Asilah), Lixus, Valentia Banasa on the Sebou River near Kenitra, Sala Colonia and Volubilis.

Ruins can be seen today in Rabat at Chella, the Roman Sala Colonia. The name survives

Preceding pages: *Fantasia in front of Méknès* by Eugène Delacroix. **Left,** Volubilis. **Above,** bronze head of Juba II.

in Salé, Rabat's sister town on the other side of the river, still called Sala in Arabic. The most impressive remains are at Volubilis, 19 miles (30 km) north of Meknes, which was probably the capital of the Roman province of Mauritania Tingitana encompassing northern Morocco.

The most remarkable local figure of the Roman period was undoubtedly King Juba II who ruled Mauritania Tingitana for perhaps half a century. He died in AD 23, in his seventies. He had three claims to fame: he married Cleopatra Selene (the Moon), daughter of Anthony and Cleopatra; he was one of the most prolific writers of his time in Latin, Greek and Punic and he founded a purple dye

works at Essaouira.

The highly-prized purple dye was extracted from shellfish, each of which, it was said, had a drop "no bigger than a single tear". It was used to make the imperial purple robes of the Caesars. On the wind-swept islets near the coast of Essaouira deep deposits of seashells are thought to be evidence of this industry.

Juba's successor, King Ptolomy, came to grief because of the dye. He is depicted as a vain man who spent his 17-year reign in extravagance. On a visit to Rome he wore a robe of imperial purple of such magnificence that it aroused the jealousy of the malevolent

Emperor Caligula. Incensed that a "Barbarian kinglet" should dare to wear imperial purple, Caligula had the provincial upstart assassinated.

The Romans also exploited fish factories in Morocco to make *garum*, a sauce used in cooking. The remains of two of the factories can be seen at Lixus near Larache and at Tangier close to the Caves of Hercules, where the Romans, and probably the Phoenicians before them, used to quarry mill stones.

In the third century, Christian evangelisation of Rome's African provinces began. It seems that many Berbers embraced the new religion since there were numerous bishoprics including four in Morocco. In some cities the Latin and Christian ways of life survived the fall of the Western Empire of Byzantium. Latin inscriptions in Volubilis are dated as late as the seventh century.

In this period there were also Jewish communities, founded after the Exodus from Egypt. These form the oldest religious denomination to survive without interruption in the country down to the present day. Though many Jews left Morocco following the founding of Israel in 1948, there are ??

A dark age: The Vandal invasion of 429 wiped out what was left of Roman Catholic civilisation. King Genseric of "Vandalusia" in southern Spain set out from Tarifa with 80,000 people, including 15,000 troops, who swept through Morocco and along the North African coast, destroying everything in their path in an orgy of looting and burning that culminated in the sack of Rome in 455.

It is thought that Vandal depredations were such that the North African Berbers were forced to become nomads, helped by the camel, which had been introduced to Morocco in about the third century.

Although Emperor Justinian restored Catholicism to North Africa after the Vandals (considered to be Christian heretics) were defeated by Belisarius in 533, Morocco and indeed most of North Africa entered a period of obscurity in the next century. And then, 3,000 miles away in the east, a new fire of religious fervour burst into flame which was to sweep along the Mediterranean coast and bring Islam to Morocco.

<u>Above</u>, mosaic from Lixus, now in the archaeological museum in Tetouan. <u>Right</u>, invasion of the Vandals.

El Maghreb El Aksa (the "Farthest West") as Morocco is known in Arabic, was seen in Arabia, the birthplace of Islam, as a reservoir of misguided infidels who needed to be converted to the new faith *besiff* (by the sword). The first of these military missionaries was one of the greatest of North African heroes, Sidi Okba ibn Nafi.

Inspired by fervent dedication to the teachings of the Koran, Okba left Arabia in AD 666, 34 years after the death of the Prophet Mohammed, at the head of an Arab cavalry force. By all accounts, admittedly written by Arab historians centuries after the event, the expedition was a splendid sight as it drove westwards, the curvetting steeds and their scimitar-wielding warriors sweeping through deserts and mountains to spread the divine revelation.

Converting pagans: In fact, Okba made three expeditions, apparently covering over 5,000 miles on horseback to convert pagans, Christians and Jews. He paused for a time to found the city of Kairouan in Tunisia and finally arrived in Morocco on his third thrust westwards in the year 684.

In Tangier he met the Count Julian, a shadowy figure who was the Christian Visigoth governor of territory on both sides of the Straits of Gibraltar. Okba considered the possibility of invading Spain, but Julian told him it was well-defended and advised him to go instead into the pagan regions of southern Morocco.

Arab chroniclers say that in the Sous valley near Taroudant he defeated a Berber army so big that "Allah alone could count them", an oriental hyperbole frequently used to describe the exploits of the Arab invaders.

Somewhere later, perhaps on the curving sands of Agadir bay, he rode his charger into the waves and cried: "Allah! If this sea did not stop me, I would go into distant lands to Doul Karnein (where the sun sets), forever fighting for your religion and slaying all who did not believe in you or adored other gods than you!"

Left, removing shoes – a practical measure rather than a mark of respect. Above, *Religious Fanatics in Tangier* by Eugène Delacroix.

Okba made no attempt to rule Morocco, evidently happier on a horse than on a throne. He quickly withdrew to be slain in a battle with Berbers in Algeria, where his tomb is still revered. Thirty years later another Arab conqueror, Musa ibn Noseir, arrived to subjugate Moroccan tribes between Tangier and the Tafilalt oases in the name of the Umayyad Caliph of Damascus.

Zealous Berbers: The commander of Musa's forces was a Berber chieftain, Tarik ibn Ziad, a glorious hero enshrined in history and

literature as the man who led the Muslim invasion of Spain. With an army of Berber warriors he routed the Visigoths in 711 to begin seven centuries of brilliant civilisation at a time when the rest of Europe lived in the Dark Ages.

Tarik's army landed on the bay of Algeciras, near the limestone pinnacle which was named after him, Jebel Tarik or Tarik's mountain, today known as Gibraltar. From this foothold the Muslim armies were to spread with spectacular speed across Spain and into France, where they were finally halted by Charles Martel at the battle of Poitiers in 732.

It seems certain that these armies were composed almost entirely of Berbers rather than Arabs. They had voluntarily embraced Islam and, like many recent converts, were the most fervent if not fanatical supporters of the faith, whose simplicity and conquering spirit suited their temperament. In Morocco they also revolted against attempts at Arab domination and the greedy exactions of the eastern caliph's tax collectors.

In Morocco they founded several independent Muslim kingdoms of the Kharijite sect, which emerged following one of numerous schisms caused by bloody quarrels in the east over succession to the caliphate after the Prophet's death. The heretical king-

Arabian migrants: These three groups of Arabs were expelled from Arabia by the caliphs because they were too troublesome. The historian Ibn Khaldoun likened the Hilalis to "an army of locusts destroying everything in their path". Desert bedouins with an insatiable appetite for plunder, they streamed into North Africa but were halted by the Almohad dynasty.

The powerful Almohad monarch Yacoub el Mansour, who had created an empire comprising Muslim Spain and most of North Africa, deported the more turbulent Hilali tribesmen and settled others in the Gharb, Haouz and Temesna areas on the coastal plains of Morocco where they would form

doms already existed when another Arab hero arrived in 788, accompanied only by an ex-slave to establish what was to be the first orthodox Muslim dynasty in Morocco.

Idriss, a descendant of the Prophet, was fleeing from the Abbasid caliphate and he took refuge in Walili (Volubilis), where the local Berber tribesmen proclaimed him sultan. His reign was short-lived and the dynasty expired in 974 (*see page 41*).

The next three Moroccan dynasties were all Berber. There were still very few Arabs around until the invasions of the Beni Hilal and Beni Solaim in the 11th century and the Maaqil in the 13th century.

only tiny Arab islands in a Berber sea.

In the 13th century the Maaqil bedouins from southern Arabia migrated rather more peacefully along the northern edge of the Sahara. As the Merinid dynasty declined, they crossed the Atlas mountain passes to settle in the Sous and Draa valleys and one group, the Zaers, pitched their tents at the gates of Rabat.

These movements of Arab invaders were slow but irresistible in times when Morocco was in turmoil between the fall and rise of different dynasties. They left a lasting imprint. Firstly, they Arabised the countryside and, secondly, composed of pastoral nomads they tended to disturb the Berbers' sedentary agricultural ways.

The last two Moroccan dynasties, the Saadians and the Alaouites, described themselves as *shorfas* , or pure Arabs descended from the Prophet. The Saadians and Alaouites both originated as Arab families from the East who settled in the 12th century in the Zagora and Tafilalt oases, where they lived modestly for centuries before seizing power.

In reality the two "Arab" dynasties ruled over a predominantly Berber nation and it remains highly questionable whether Morocco can be truly described as an Arab country if the term is taken to mean its racial origin. As Galbraith Welch Dwyer wrote in

Still, many Moroccans say they are Arabs, proud to belong to the conquering race of the Prophet, and some speak with a certain disdain of the Berbers as if they were an inferior race. This has led to the misconception that Morocco is divided between Arabs and Berbers, an idea that was espoused in colonial times by the French, when in fact if there is any division it is simply the same as anywhere in the world: between the urban and rural populations.

Nevertheless the Arabic-speaking Muslims of Morocco feel quite at home as members of the Arab League and of the Islamic Conference Organisation founded by King Hassan II. They have no identity problem,

an excellent book for the general reader, *North African Prelude*, "The heroic blood of the original conquerors is today diluted almost out of existence."

Arab/Berber divide?: The Arab conquerors came in relatively small numbers a long time ago and most of them were males. The Hilali and other invasions had almost petered out by the time they reached Morocco, where through inter-marriage they melted into the Moorish family.

<u>Left</u>, how to wear your beliefs on your heart – badges inscribed with words from the Koran. <u>Above</u>, Arab or Berber? It's difficult to tell.

and their nationalism is a natural heritage handed down through a dozen centuries of independent Muslim rule.

Just as Europeans went west across the ocean to found Christian nations composed of many races in the Americas, so too the Arabs several centuries before them went west over the sand seas of the Sahara to El-Maghreb El Aksa to bring Muslim civilisation to Morocco.

If the people of the New World are Americans, then there can be no doubt that "Moroccans" is the proper word to describe the patriotic people of Africa's equivalent to the Far West.

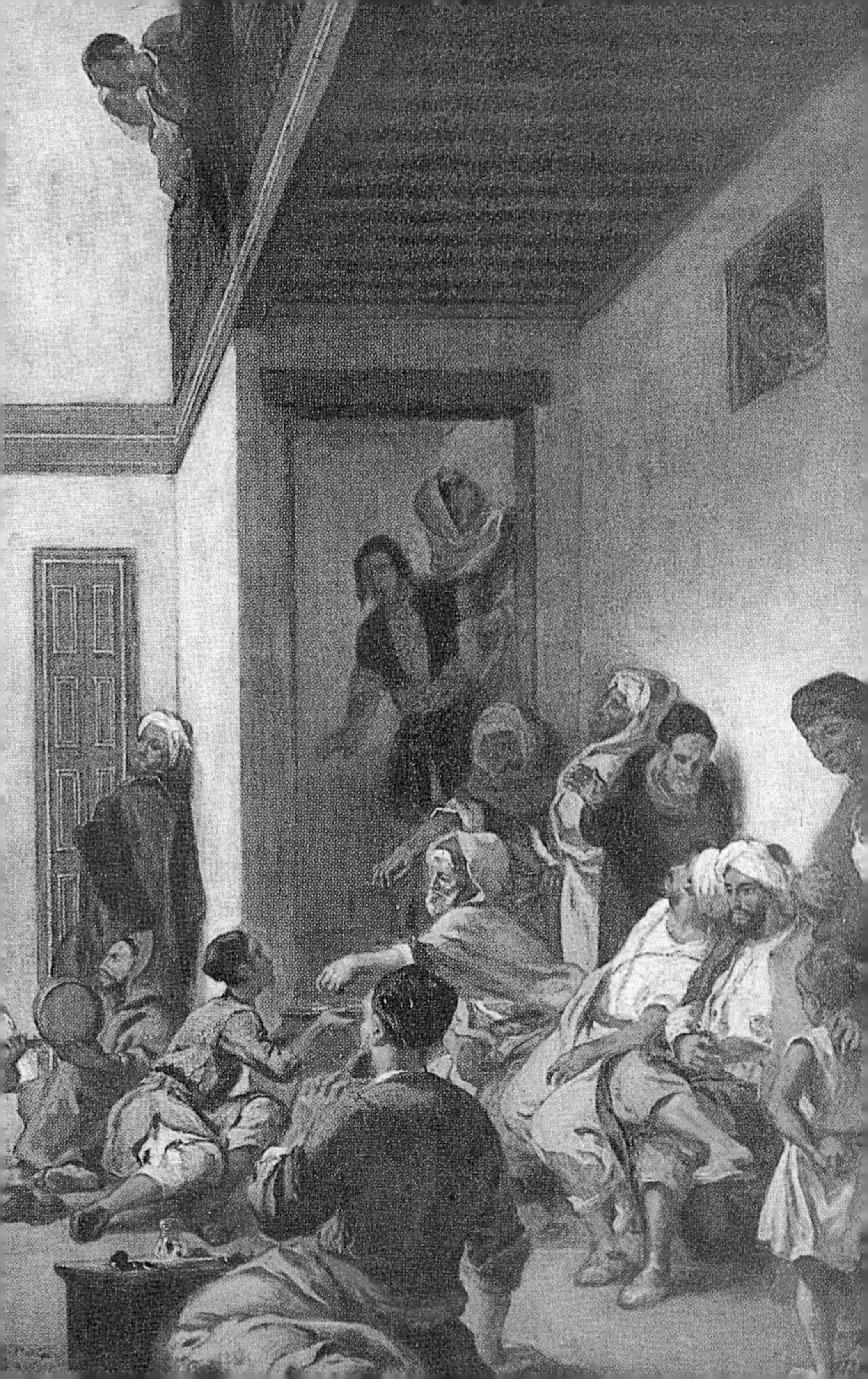

Harun er Rashid, the magnificent Caliph of Baghdad, hero of *The Thousand and One Nights*, was unwittingly responsible for the creation of the first Muslim dynasty in Morocco, the Idrissids, who ruled in the time of England's King Arthur and the Knights of the Round Table.

Idriss ibn Abdullah, a descendant of the Prophet Mohammed through his daughter Fatima and son-in-law Ali, was among a group of rebels who disputed the legitimacy of the Abbasid caliphs, of whom Harun er Rashid was the fifth.

The revolt was one of many due to the fact that the Prophet did not designate a successor and had no surviving son. Consequently Islam was plagued for centuries by discord over the legitimacy of its rulers. As we shall see, the lack of a clear-cut tradition, such as primogeniture, to establish succession, and the fact that polygamous rulers often had numerous sons, were to be the cause of anarchy many times in Morocco as rival pretenders fought for the throne.

Harun er Rashid sent his army to crush the rebels, and they were massacred near Mecca in 786, but Idriss escaped. After a two-year journey accompanied by only a faithful ex-slave, Rashid, he arrived in Morocco to take refuge in Walili, the former Roman town of Volubilis. Impressed by his erudition and piety, the superficially Islamicised Berbers made him their leader.

Hearing that the rebel had set up a kingdom, Harun er Rashid sent a Judas-like envoy, who killed Idriss with a poisonous potion in 791. But two months later Idriss's Berber concubine Kenza gave birth to a son. Nurtured by Kenza and the faithful Rashid, the boy became Sultan Idriss II and the dynasty was established.

The Idrissids founded the city of Fez where they were joined by hundreds of rebel families from Cordoba and Kairouan, bringing with them a sophisticated Arab civilisation which led to the creation of the Kairouyine

Preceding pages: *Jewish Wedding in Morocco* by Eugène Delacroix. Left, a painting of Sultan Abderrahmen (1822–59) outside Meknes, also by Delacroix. Above, a Moroccan Emir.

University, today the oldest in the world.

On the death of Idriss II in 828 (probably also assassinated on orders from Baghdad) Kenza divided the small state between their 10 sons. This led inevitably to the decline of the dynasty and it expired in 974.

Moulay Idriss near Volubilis, the holiest city in Morocco, shelters the tomb of Idriss I, who is considered a saintly man. His son's shrine in Fez is also the object of pious devotion. Each year a *moussem* (pilgrimage) is made to their tombs to honour the founders

of Muslim Morocco and of the only dynasty which did not have to impose itself by force of arms.

Veiled Sultans: Youssef ibn Tashfin, a Berber from Adrar in what is now Mauritania where the men wore veils, was a religious zealot. He set up a *ribat* or hermitage in the desert from which to propogate the true faith. His movement was known as El Murabetun (people of the *ribat*), deformed by Europeans into Almoravides, the first of three Berber dynasties.

In an incredibly short time, the veiled Almoravide sultans created a Berber empire which covered northwest Africa as far as

Algiers and southern Spain. While the murderous Macbeth was king of Scotland, the Normans were invading England, and the first Crusade took the city of Jerusalem, the Almoravides led by Tashfin swept up from the desert, founded Marrakesh in 1060, captured Fez in 1069, and then pushed on into Spain.

Muslim Spain, in the time of the romantic *Cid Campeador* Rodrigo Diaz de Vivar, was divided into 23 *Taifas*, or petty principalities. The Almoravides had little difficulty in dominating them on the pretext of helping to defeat Christian armies, as they did at Zallaqa near Badajoz in 1086. They took Granada, Cordoba and Seville in the south, Badajoz, Valencia and Saragossa in the north, although they were unable to hold them for long. Tashfin's son Ali ruled the empire from 1120 to 1143 and with him the fierce and austere Almoravides abandoned the veil to become luxury-loving potentates in Andalusia.

The Almoravide dynasty disappeared almost as quickly as it had arisen out of the desert void, but not before spreading Andalusian culture throughout the Maghreb. Among their few remaining monuments are the mosque at Tlemcen in Algeria and ramparts – which they were the first to build – around Fez.

The greatest of all Berbers: Ibn Toumert, popularly known as "the Torch", was another radical religious reformer who emerged at the beginning of the 11th century to preach a unitarian (*tawhid*) doctrine. His followers became known as *El Mowahhadidoun* or the Almohads. By the time the fiery Toumert died in 1130 he had gathered numerous Berber tribes around his banner.

The torch was passed to Abd el Moumin, an able warrior chieftain who proclaimed himself Caliph and Amir el Mumineen ("Commander of the Faithful"). Oriental historians called him the greatest of all the Berbers. Moumin seized Marrakesh and Fez, controlled all Morocco by 1148, moved into Spain when called in by anti-Almoravide rebels, and raced across North Africa, defeating the Hilali Arab hordes at Sétif.

By the time he died Moumin had forged an empire even larger than that of the Almoravides', extending as far as Tripoli. Most of Muslim Spain was reduced to vassaldom under his son Yacoub Youssef.

His grandson, Youssef Yacoub, consolidated Almohad power and won the title El Mansour (the victorious) when he crushed the Christians under King Alfonso VIII of Castile at the battle of Alarcos on 18 July 1195.

Yacoub el Mansour's reign was the zenith of the Almohad dynasty, a golden age of Andalusian brilliance. He surrounded himself with distinguished poets and philosophers, such as the Jewish thinker Maimonides, the court physician Ibn Tofail, and Ibn Rashid (Averroes, after whom the main Casablanca hospital is named), who commented on the works of Aristotle and introduced him to Christian monks.

In Morocco he founded Rabat, then known

as *Ribat el Fath* (the camp of conquest), a vast enclosure ringed by ramparts that still stand with the Oudayas kasbah on a bluff overlooking the sea, and the monumental Bab er Rouah (gateway of souls). The camp was used to assemble troops for military expeditions into Spain.

In the period of their glory between 1160 and 1210, the Almohads built a number of other famous landmarks, such as the Giralda in Seville, the unfinished Tour of Hassan in Rabat, and the Koutoubia mosque in Marrakesh. But, like their predecessors, the Almoravides, the reforming zealots inevitably sank into silken civilised ways. In their time Alicante boasted 800 looms making silk cloth and the minting of fine gold coinage. Paper mills were set up in Ceuta and Fez.

Towards the end of the dynasty, Sultan el Mamoun, in 1230, was reduced to accepting 12,000 Christian cavalrymen from King Ferdinand of Castile and Leon in order to retake Marrakesh from local dissidents. As part of the bargain he allowed the construction of a Catholic church in the city. A Marrakesh bishopric subsisted until the 14th century to serve foreign mercenaries.

The Black Sultan: The Beni Merin was a nomadic Berber tribe from the Sahara pushed westwards by the Hilali invaders. It settled northeast Morocco in the period when King

His son Abou Youssef crossed the Straits of Gibraltar four times to help the Muslims reconquer lost territory, notably after one memorable battle on 8 September 1275 in which the army led by the Christian hero Don Nuno Gonzales de Lara was routed, a black day for the Cross.

Abou el Hassan, son of an Abyssinian mother and known as the Black Sultan, who ruled the Merinid empire from 1331 to 1351 (during the Hundred Years' War in Europe), was a prodigiously powerful and active man. He reorganised the empire between the Atlantic and the Gulf of Gabes in Tunisia and held it with an iron hand. He was less successful in Spain, where his army was beaten

John was forced by the English barons to sign Magna Carta in 1215, and the infamous Spanish Inquisition began in 1238 to persecute Muslims and Jews.

The Beni Merin took part in the battle of Alarcos and were aware of the rewards of the *jihad* (holy war) which they began waging – with the help of Christian mercenaries – against the Almohads. By taking Fez on 20 August 1248, their leader Abou Yahya established the Merinid dynasty.

<u>Left</u>, the Koutoubia Mosque, built by the Almohads in Marrakesh. <u>Above</u>, Chella, near Rabat, fortified by the Merinids.

at the battle of Rio Salado near Tarifa in October 1340.

Hassan died a disgusted man and was buried in Chella near Rabat. His own son Abou Inan had rebelled against him to rule until 1358 when he was strangled by a vizir in favour of a five-year-old pretender. Inan had lost control of what is now Algeria and Tunisia, the Maaqil Arab invaders started to move in, the Spanish connection was finished, and the Christians began their encroachments. The gangrene of anarchy set in under various infant sultans.

Although their political achievements could not be compared with those of the

Almohads, the Merinids left a substantial cultural legacy in the shape of *medersa*, or colleges, in delicate Hispano-Moorish style, which can be seen in Fez, Meknes and Salé. The Bou Inania *medrassa* in Fez, finished in 1357, is one of the most remarkable, with a clepysdra water clock in the narrow street outside that at one time told the time with 13 brass gongs.

Christian encroachments: At the beginning of the 15th century, piracy became a way of attacking Christians and an excuse for the latter to intervene in Morocco. The Spanish kings were undoubtedly motivated also by a spirit of revenge after seven centuries of Muslim domination which was to end with the fall of Granada in 1492.

While Muslim and Jewish refugees began flooding into Morocco to escape the Inquisition, Spanish and Portuguese kings sent armies and navies after them. Henry III of Castile took Tetouan and massacred the population in 1399, Portugal grabbed Ceuta in 1415 and, after three attempts, finally took Asilah and Tangier with a fleet of 477 ships and 30,000 men in 1471.

After *Los Reyes Catolicos* Ferdinand and Isabella ousted the Muslims from Grenada, Spain occupied Melilla in 1497 with a fleet originally intended to take Columbus on his second voyage of discovery, while the Portuguese established fortresses on the Atlantic coast at Agadir, Azemmour and Safi, and the Ottoman Turks arrived on Morocco's doorstep at Tlemcen.

They were dark days for Morocco, enfeebled for a century by anarchy under the Wattasid dynasty (1465–1549), but they were a prelude to another glorious era. The renaissance came as a reaction to Christian intolerance: the bloody excesses of the Inquisition were matched by Moroccan xenophobia and fanaticism caused by the presence of infidels on the soil of *Dar el Islam*, the sacred House of Islam, calling for a holy war.

The spirit of the *jihad* coalesced around the Saadians, who overthrew the last of the Wattasids in 1557 and astounded Europe when they annihilated a Portuguese army of 20,000 at the Battle of the Three Kings on 4 August 1578.

Members of the Arab tribe of Beni Saad arrived in the 12th century to settle in the Draa valley near Zagora and later in the Sous near Taroudant. Claiming descent from the Prophet, they founded the Arab dynasty by taking Marrakesh in 1525. After being driven out of Agadir in 1541, the Portuguese also abandoned the ports of Safi and Azemmour.

These reverses inspired 24-year-old King Sebastian of Portugal to seek revenge by launching a crusade against the "barbarians", albeit against the advice of his Jesuit mentors. But historians tell us Sebastian was a mystical fanatic who thought apparent anarchy in Morocco presented a golden opportunity for personal glory in the name of God.

Sebastian was joined by one of the Saadians, Mohammed el Mutawakkil, who was sultan for a brief period until he fled to Spain after being overthrown by his brother

Abd el Malik. Mohammed hoped to regain his throne. The cream of Portuguese nobility was assembled and embarked with a large fleet to land at Tangier and Asilah. The men marched southwards slowly and ponderously, lugging 36 bronze cannon.

Their progress was so slow that Abd el Malik was able to muster a force of 50,000 cavalry. The two armies met near Ksar el Kebir where the Portuguese suddenly found themselves trapped in a fork between the Loukos river and its tributary the Oued el Makhazin.

The tide rose, making it impossible for the men to ford the streams, while wave after wave of charging Moroccan cavalry cut them to pieces. Sebastian and Mohammed were drowned and Sultan Abd el Malik died of sickness before the battle was over. The disaster was complete for Portugal, who later lost to Spain both its crown and its African possession, Ceuta.

The victory had a tremendous impact in Morocco after the death of the three kings, giving enormous prestige to Abd el Malik's brother Ahmed, proclaimed sultan on the battlefield. He became known as Ahmed el Mansour el Dehbi (the victorious and golden) after extracting huge ransoms for the Portuguese nobles captured in the battle.

Since Spain was too powerful for him to

haustion on the way. The rest arrived at Timbuctoo after marching for 135 days in probably one of the most gruelling gold rushes of all time. An offer made by local emperor Ishaq Askia to buy them off with 100,000 pieces of gold and 1,000 slaves was spurned by Ahmed as "insulting".

The Songai empire was destroyed and Ahmed named pashas to rule it. Goaded by greed, the pashas were unscrupulous (there were 149 of them between 1612 and 1750). Their unruly troops massacred the population or sent them into slavery in caravans carrying gold back to Marrakesh.

Laurence Maddock, an English trader in Marrakesh, counted 30 mule loads of gold

attempt any exploits on the Iberian peninsular, Ahmed instead set out to conquer the salt and gold mines of the Songai empire on the banks of the Niger river. A ragtag army of 3,000 Christians, Kabyles, Ottomans and negroes, led by the Spanish renegade Jouder and trained by Turks, trekked across the Sahara Desert. To paraphrase the Duke of Wellington, it was the scum of the earth enlisted for lucre.

Half of the troops died of thirst and ex-

Left, piracy off the Atlantic coast. **Above**, cannons in Essaouira are a reminder today of a defensive past.

dust arriving in the city in a single day. The historian El Ifrani said court officials were paid in gold and there were 1,400 hammers at the palace to strike gold ducats.

To match his great wealth, Ahmed built himself a sumptuous palace, El Badi, with Italian marble bought kilo for kilo in exchange for sugar produced by Christian and Jewish renegades in the Sous valley. Foreign visitors marvelled at the magnificence of court ceremonial à la Turk, for Ahmed had spent his youth in Constantinople and had tasted Ottoman refinements.

His notoriety spread throughout Europe. He corresponded several times with England's Queen Elizabeth I, proposing an Anglo-Moroccan alliance against Spain after the defeat of the Spanish Armada by Sir Francis Drake in 1588.

He organised the Makhzen government, which survived with little change into the 20th century. Of the rest little remains. His palace was razed by the next dynasty. Among the few notable relics are the Saadian tombs built by Ahmed's son Moulay Zidan, which were walled up by his successors until the French came to Morocco.

One consequence of the Saadian era was that the influx of thousands of black slaves, white renegades and mercenaries changed the racial composition of the country. The

Moulay Ismail: The next remarkable sultan was Moulay Ismail, whose 55-year reign was one of the longest and most brutal in Moroccan history. He was a cruel and profligate megalomaniac reputed to have had a harem of 500 women, over 700 sons and uncounted daughters.

Ismail was the brother of Moulay Rashid, the founder of the Alaouite dynasty and the scion of an Arab family which had emigrated from Arabia to the Tafilalt oasis in the 13th century. The family was descended from El Hassan, son of Ali and the Prophet's daughter Fatima.

Ismail's reign is well-documented by Arab historians and also by European diplomats,

LE GRAND CHERIF MOVLEY-SEMEIN ou ISMAEL
Roy de Maroc, Fez, Tafilet et autres Provinces, Ports et Villes Maritimes dans la Mauritane en Afrique, Frere et Successeur de Muele Aratid Son Plaisir de respandre le Sang Coupable ou Innocent, il regne plus par la crainte que par Sa douceur, &c. il a envoyé en France en 1682, un Ambassadeur nommé Hadgy Mehemed Temmin, pour faire Amitié avec le tres-Puissant Monarque Louis le Grand, et pour l'Establissement du Commerce entre'eux, &c.

result can be seen in the faces of Moroccans today, ranging from ivory white to brown and ebony black.

Ahmed died in August 1603, at a time when Shakespeare was writing his plays. He was undoubtedly the greatest of the 11 Saadian sultans, eight of whom were assassinated. Three of his sons fought over the succession for seven years, and for a time Morocco was divided into two states ruled from Fez and Marrakesh. A third proclaimed in Rabat-Salé was an independent corsair republic led by *Moriscos* expelled from Spain, the "Sallee Rovers" mentioned in Daniel Defoe's *Robinson Crusoe*.

monks and the slaves they came to redeem from captivity at the hands of the corsairs. Some 2,000 Christian slaves and 30,000 other prisoners were employed for half a century in an orgy of building in Meknes, which he made his capital.

A hotchpotch of gigantic structures was built, mostly of adobe but also with some marble looted from Volubilis and Ahmed el Mansour's palace in Marrakesh, which Ismail had razed to the ground. The city was ringed by ramparts 15 miles (25 km) long. It included palaces with vast colonnaded courtyards, huge gardens, a zoo, stables for hundreds of horses, granaries, barracks for large numbers of troops, and of course a harem where his legitimate wife the Sultana Zidana, a giant negress, cracked the whip over hundreds of concubines.

Each time he granted his favours to one of the oiled and perfumed women she was paraded through the palace on a litter accompanied by singers and dancers. At the age of 30 she would be pensioned off and sent to live in Fez or the Tafilalt.

When Ismail visited the building sites he would personally run his lance through slave labourers if he thought they were shirking, or crush their skulls with bricks he considered badly made. The French diplomat Pidou de Saint Olon saw him dripping with blood after

slitting a slave's throat.

The French remember the despot for his plan to marry the Princess Conti, the illegitimate daughter of the Sun King Louis XIV, a proposal that caused hilarity in the Palace of Versailles and not a little bemusement in Meknes when Ismail was turned down.

Ismail's power rested on an army of blacks, the Abids, formed from the remnants of slaves brought into the country by the Saadians. They were placed in a stud farm at

Far left, Moulay Ismail. **Left**, his heart's desire, Princess Conti, daughter of Louis XIV. **Above**, accounts of Christian slavery were graphic.

Meshra Er Remel on the Sebou river and made to increase and multiply, all the boys being pressed into military service at the age of 15.

Considered more reliable than Arab or Berber warriors, the blacks were garrisoned in kasbahs built at strategic points around the country. They were also used to retake Larache and Asilah, to lay siege for years to Ceuta and Melilla, and to evict the Turks from Tlemcen. The English left Tangier of their own accord after occupying it from 1662 to 1684.

Ismail's death at the age of 81 in 1727 was followed by a period of chaos such as Morocco has never seen before or since. His numerous sons and the Abids fought over the succession for 30 years. One was proclaimed and dethroned six times and in a generation there were 12 sultans. A contemporary wrote that in this period "the hair of babes in arms turned white" with terror.

In contrast, Sultan Mohammed ibn Abdullah (1757–90) left memories of a pious and peaceful man. He built Mogador (Essaouira), designed by the French architect Cornut of Avignon and finished by an English renegade named Ahmed el Inglesi. He forced the Portuguese out of their last stronghold at Mazagan, which he renamed El Jadida, but failed to evict Spain from Melilla. He was the first leader in the world to recognise the infant United States of America and Washington, called him "Great and magnanimous friend".

There was a bloody two-year interlude under his son Moulay Yazid (born of an English or Irish renegade mother), a sanguinary demon who among other excesses had Jews crucified in Fez by nailing them to the doors of their houses. Mercifully he was killed in 1792. He was followed by his brother Moulay Slimane (1792–1822) and Moulay Abderrahman (1822–59), who were pious and benign.

In the last half of the 19th century, Morocco isolated itself, became poor and weak, and was plagued by dissidence in the *bled essiba*, the parts of the country outside the *bled el-makhzen* controlled by the government. The last notable Alaouite sultan, Moulay el Hassan (1873–94), spent most of his reign in the saddle trying to subdue rebellious tribes while European imperialists began gnawing away at the country's fragile fabric.

In the "last scramble for Africa" at the beginning of the 20th century, Britain, France, Germany and Spain vied with one another to dominate Morocco, one of the few remaining parts of the African continent outside the colonial grasp.

It had escaped colonialism not because it was considered worthless – on the contrary, it was and remains strategically very important – but because it was an old independent nation with an organised society capable of resisting invasion. That made it different from the rest of the "Dark Continent" with its archaic tribal systems and maps featuring "elephants for want of towns".

Also, Morocco had existed as a Muslim nation for more than 1,000 years. It had a long history of dynastic rule, its own culture and civilisation, ancient cities such as Fez, Marrakesh and Tangier, and a record of fierce resistance to invasion.

Until the turn of the century, Morocco had survived by playing one European power off against another. But gradually the rivals were eliminated. In return for a free hand in Morocco, France agreed to allow Italy to colonise Libya and then, as part of the Entente Cordiale, struck a similar deal with Britain, which in return was given carte blanche in Egypt.

This left two contenders: Germany, whose Kaiser Wilhelm landed in Tangier and later sent a gunboat to Agadir to demonstrate its "interests"; and Spain, which, because of her centuries-long occupation of the Ceuta and Melilla enclaves on the coast, claimed "historic rights" in Morocco.

When European plenipotentiaries met at the Reina Cristina hotel in the Spanish seaport of Algeciras in January 1906 to discuss Morocco's future, Britain and Italy supported France. The Act of Algeciras proposed a plan of reforms and recognised France's "privileged position" in Morocco.

Germany withdrew as World War I loomed, after receiving from France the "gift" part of Cameroun in West Africa. Spain signed a secret accord with France delimiting their respective "spheres of influence" in Morocco. The European claimants to the Moroccan cake were now reduced to two.

The Prodigal Son: This coincided with a crisis in Morocco. Sultan Moulay Hassan, a strong monarch who spent most of his reign in the saddle fighting rebellious tribes, had died suddenly in 1894. He was succeeded by his son Abd el Aziz, who emptied the treasury with extravagant spending on frivolous pursuits. Unscrupulous Europeans sold him

solid gold cameras, pianos no-one at court knew how to play, a German motorboat, with its own German engineer, and a magnificent gilded state coach even though there were then no roads.

To solve the financial crisis, large loans were contracted with a French bank consortium. To repay them, Morocco had to forfeit its customs dues, leading to revolts against the growing influence of the "infidels" and the encroachments by French troops in areas bordering Algeria.

One revolt, backed by powerful tribal chiefs of the south, resulted in 1908 in the overthrow of Abd el Aziz by his brother Hafid.

Left, conference members at the Reina Cristina hotel in 1906. **Above**, Abd el Aziz, one of the more profligate sultans.

But the new ruler was unable to assert his authority over a debt-ridden country assailed by external pressures and internal dissent. He was forced to sign the Protectorate Treaty in 1912, under which France became responsible for foreign affairs and defence and undertook to enact reforms. Hafid immediately abdicated in favour of his half-brother, Moulay Youssef. As the American historian Edmund Burke III remarked, "Morocco stumbled into the modern age."

France took over "useful Morocco", the main cities on the central plains and all the territory bordering on Algeria. Spain received the crumbs – the rugged Rif mountain area adjacent to its enclaves, and in the south the

the independence movement gained momentum, the post offices proved useful to independence workers from the French and Spanish zones, who used them to gain uncensored news of what was happening in the rest of Morocco.

Penetration of Morocco by France and Spain met with bloody resistance. As soon as the protectorate treaty was signed in Fez, the walled city was besieged by warrior tribes and it was not until 1934 that France was able to pacify the whole of its zone.

Spain's occupation of the northern zone was marked by the 1920 revolt of the "Emir" Abd el Krim, whose Berber warriors routed a Spanish army of 60,000 at the battle of

enclave of Ifni, the Tarfaya strip and beyond the Western Sahara, Rio de Oro.

International city: Because of its strategic location, Tangier and its immediate vicinity became an "International Zone". For some time diplomats had been extending their influence in the town. They had been responsible for the building of the Cap Spartel lighthouse and had set up a sanitation programme. Good works, they thought, would foster good relations. No-one, and particularly Britain, wanted Spain to control both sides of the Straits of Gibraltar. Each nation within the international zone had its own currency, post offices and banks. Later on, as

Anual. It was a remarkable achievement. Abd el Krim set up an independent republic in the Rif, with an education programme, a State bank and much of the administrative infrastructure of a modern country. He was finally defeated by a combined Spanish and French army commanded by the "saviour of Verdun" Marshal Philippe Pétain, and he surrendered to the French rather than face Spanish execution. He was exiled to the French Indian Ocean island of Reunion and later died in Cairo.

Lyautey's way: Marshal Hubert Gonzalve Lyautey, the first French Resident-General, or chief administrator, was an experienced soldier but also an audacious idealist. His "maxims" are still current in independent Morocco: for instance, "Not a drop of water should reach the ocean" and his warning, "Morocco is a cold country with a hot sun."

He believed the protectorate concept should be scrupulously respected: in other words, that all actions must be taken in the name and with the consent of the sultan in cooperation with the "makhzen" government, or traditional Moroccan élite. From the start, he realised the importance of preserving Moroccan culture, and made sure the new French-built towns were built some distance from the medinas. He also insisted that the younger Moroccan generation should take

mirers remarked, the sultan reached the point where he had to read the French newspapers to find out what was going on in his own country.

Exactly as Lyautey had predicted, intellectuals formed a nationalist movement in Fez to spearhead resistance just as the "pacification" ended in 1934. Some of them were French-educated and inspired by "*Liberté, Egalité et Fraternité*", others, trained in Fez's old Kairouyine University, were strongly influenced by Middle-Eastern politicians.

The movement was amply fuelled by resentment over two grievances. First, the influx of French settlers (which Lyautey had opposed) took over the best farmland and

an active part in all stages of the country's modernisation, otherwise they would become frustrated and rebellious. This proved prophetic.

After Lyautey departed in 1925, succeeding Resident-Generals (there were 14 in 44 years) turned the protectorate into a virtual colony with direct administration that sidelined the traditional ruling classes and left few outlets for the talents of ambitious young Moroccans. As one of Lyautey's ad-

Far left, European encroachment. **Left**, Marshal Lyautey. **Above**, the Rif presented the most determined resistance to France and Spain.

monopolised the economy. Second, a heavy-handed bureaucracy (which had a mania for regulating everything, including the profession of snake charmer!) made sure that Moroccans were given only subaltern jobs.

Desirable property: While development of the Spanish zones was minimal because of the civil war and the poor shape of the Spanish economy under Generalissimo Francisco Franco, France poured resources into Morocco, building roads, railways and ports, laying out modern, efficient farms, opening up mines, and setting up education, public health and justice systems on the French pattern, in short transforming the country.

Ironically, in nationalist eyes, the French protectorate made Morocco even more worth fighting for than before.

When Sultan Moulay Youssef died in 1927, he was replaced by his third son Mohammed, who was 18 and had led a cloistered life. The French thought he would be more amenable to their interests. This was to prove a grave miscalculation. What was later seen as a serious political mistake was the publication by the French of the Berber *Dahir* (decree) in 1930 to which the young and inexperienced monarch set his seal. The decree was intended to apply tribal custom law to the Berbers instead of traditional Islamic law. It incensed the Berber tribes, arousing charges that its underlying purpose was to convert the Berbers to Christianity.

Disorders broke out and nationalist leaders such as Allal al Fassi, Mohammed ben Hassan Wazzani, Ahmed Balafrej and Mohammed Mekki Naciri were arrested. With many others, they were in and out of jail or in exile for the next 25 years.

In the Spanish zone, meanwhile, nationalists were tolerated – more to exasperate the French than out of idealism, since Madrid was still angry at being given the poorest parts of the country. The Franco regime encouraged rivalry and in-fighting between four nationalist groups to divert attention from the fact that Moroccan troops had been recruited for the "anti-communist crusade" in the Spanish Civil War.

The Glaoui: To counter nationalist agitation, the French enlisted the support of the "Grand Caids" or Berber tribal chiefs of the south led by Thami el Glaoui, the Pasha or governor of Marrakesh, surnamed "The Lion of the Atlas", and other personalities with grudges against the sultanate. The religious leader Abdelhay el Kettani, whose brother Mohammed was flogged to death on orders from Sultan Moulay Hafid in 1909, was one.

Sultan Mohammed ben Youssef had espoused the nationalist cause by the time the nationalists who had formed the Istiqlal (independence) Party issued a "Manifesto" in January 1944 demanding for the first time not just reforms as hitherto but outright independence. This move was said to have been inspired in part by President Franklin D. Roosevelt's advice to the Sultan when they met at the Anfa conference near Casablanca during World War II.

Seething unrest: As agitation grew, the French reacted by arresting the ringleaders. Riots and demonstrations followed, and finally the Sultan went "on strike" by refusing to seal protectorate decrees.

When General Augustin Guillaume, the 10th French Resident-General, took over in Rabat in July 1951, he found an uncooperative Sultan and seething unrest among nationalists. He also found a protectorate apparatus ready to defy the government in Paris and give in to the demands of the diehard leaders of settlers, who by then had grown to nearly half a million.

El Glaoui, Kettani and other Moroccan "collaborators" decided, in March 1953, that

Sultan Mohammed ben Youssef must be deposed. The idea received active support from settlers and their lobby in Paris, where ephemeral French governments of the Fourth Republic were coming and going at dizzying frequency.

In May Guillaume, accompanied by Marshal Alphonse Juin, a former Resident-General born in Algeria, reviewed tens of thousands of Berber tribesmen assembled near Azrou in the Middle Atlas mountains. Many were French army veterans who had served valiantly under Guillaume and Juin in the final stages of World War II. They were generally seen by settlers as "good Moroccans", in contrast to the "bad" ones represented by the urban nationalists. The latter considered the Azrou parade as a dress rehearsal for a march by massed Berber tribesmen on Fez and Rabat to force the Sultan off his throne.

French Foreign Minister Georges Bidault in April had told Guillaume clearly: "The French government will not accept being placed by anyone before a *fait accompli*…I ask you to oppose without hesitation any new progress towards a situation in which we shall have no choice but between deposing the Sultan and using force against our friends."

But El Glaoui and 300 of his fellow plot-

doubtless under the impression they were on their way as usual to attend the Muslim feast day ceremonies of Aid El-Kebir, due to start on 21 August that year, when the sultan would perform in public the traditional sacrifice of a ram.

The French founder: In an atmosphere of hysteria whipped up by the plotters and echoed in the colonial press, French Prime Minister Joseph Laniel gave the green light for the Sultan's deposition, apparently believing that the only alternative would be civil war in Morocco. His Interior Minister, François Mitterrand, did not agree and resigned in protest.

A grim-faced Guillaume went to the pal-

ters met in Marrakesh on 13 August, 1953 (while Guillaume was in Vichy taking the waters for his liver) and planned to depose Mohammed ben Youssef and proclaim Sidi Mohammed ben Arafa as sultan instead, an obscure 70-year-old who was a distant relation of the monarch.

Despite another Bidault message warning of the "incalculable consequences of such a *pronunciamento*", contingents of tribes began to march on Fez and Rabat, some of them

ace in Rabat on Thursday morning, 20 August 1953, to demand that the sultan abdicate in favour of his younger son, Prince Moulay Abdallah, whom the French thought would be a more "flexible" ruler than the elder son, Prince Moulay Hassan, the settlers' particular *bête noire*.

When the Sultan refused to comply, he and his sons and daughters were immediately whisked away in a fleet of black cars to the old Rabat airport, today the site of the Hyatt Regency Hotel, and flown into exile, first in Corsica and then Madagascar.

His departure was cheered by the Moroccan plotters and their settler friends of the

"*Presence Française*" association, but their "victory" was short-lived. Only three weeks later, on 11 September, puppet-sultan Ben Arafa narrowly escaped death when Allal ben Abdallah (after whom numerous Moroccan streets are now named) crashed an open car into a royal procession on its way to the mosque in Rabat, then tried to knife him.

This signalled the start of violent popular protests against the exiling of the legitimate sultan. It quickly snowballed into an urban terrorism campaign coupled with the emergence of a "liberation army" in the Rif and Middle Atlas mountains.

Resistance fighters, who were not necessarily controlled by the nationalists but were often small independent groups of patriots, shot French leaders and Moroccan "collaborators" and set off bombs in crowded cafés or markets. On Christmas Eve 1953, in Casablanca's central market, Mohamed Zerktouni (one of the city's main boulevards is named after him) planted a bomb in a shopping-basket that killed 20 people and wounded 28. The choice of the Christian holiday was symbolic: the Sultan had been exiled on a Muslim feast day.

The terrorists enjoyed the silent support of the population at large, some of the simpler people swearing they could see their Sultan's face in the moon or saying he was "*chez* Madame Gaspar" on that faraway island in the Indian Ocean.

Extremist French settlers reacted by organising terrorist campaigns of their own, at times shooting indiscriminately from cruising cars or murdering French personalities they suspected of pro-nationalist sympathies. There was evidence that they were being helped by the French police.

The campaign reached a climax on the second anniversary of the Sultan's departure into exile, on 20 August 1955, when tribesmen descended on the small farming town of Oued Zem, southeast of Casablanca, and savagely butchered 49 French people, including eight women and 15 children. The French Foreign Legion was sent in on a punitive expedition. According to Moroccan sources, 1,500 tribespeople were slain, raising tension at a time when the latest Resident

General, the liberal civilian Gilbert Grandval, was trying to solve the crisis while being physically attacked and insulted by outraged French settlers.

In Paris, meanwhile, Prime Minister Edgar Faure called a conference of nationalist leaders in Aix-les-Bains, urged on by fears that a *jihad* (holy war) was about to be launched against France in Morocco and Algeria. The uprising broke out in the Rif mountains on 1 October when the "Moroccan Liberation Army" attacked three French outposts on the border of the Spanish zone.

The Aix-les-Bains conference was designed to form an interim Moroccan government and hammer out a compromise solu-

tion to the dynastic problem in the shape of a "Throne Council". But the Council formula was contested by none other than Thami el Glaoui himself, who astounded everyone by announcing on 25 October that the solution was to bring back Mohammed ben Youssef to his throne.

In the circumstances, France could hardly do otherwise. The legitimate sultan was flown back to Rabat on 16 November 1955 to receive a hero's welcome, whose scale and fervour has not been seen in Morocco since. He announced to massed crowds assembled in front of the palace that the protectorate had come to an end.

Left, Ben Arafa is installed as sultan by the French. **Above**, three weeks later he narrowly escapes assassination.

Sultan Sidi Mohammed ben Youssef changed his title to King Mohammed V in 1956 when Morocco regained its independence. The change symbolised the additional prestige he had acquired as "The Liberator" of the country. His great popularity, together with his religious prestige as Amir el Mumineen (commander of the faithful), enabled him to rule with uncontested authority during a crucial period when an élite had to be assembled to run a modern nation.

Although he had been humiliated by the French, he proved a moderate and magnanimous monarch. Foreigners were kept on to advise inexperienced Moroccan officials so that the transition would be fairly smooth. Many French settlers fled of their own accord, but others ran farms and industries until as late as 1973 when "Moroccanisation" measures were taken.

Morocco joined the Arab League, was a founder-member of the Organisation of African Unity (OAU), and cultivated cordial relations with France and Spain, who helped create the Royal Armed Forces and supplied aid for economic development. New industries sprang up based on agriculture and phosphates.

Restive people: The number of schoolchildren grew from a few thousand to over 3 million in 25 years; at the same time improved health conditions stimulated rapid population growth coupled with the emergence of a restive urban proletariat. Providing work, housing and social services became (and remains) an arduous, uphill task.

A crisis erupted in October 1956 when the French in Algeria forced down the aircraft carrying Algerian nationalist leader Ahmed ben Bella and his associates from Rabat to Tunis. Rioters attacked French settlers in a violent protest organised by nationalists in support of the Algerian Front de Libération Nationale. Relations with France were strained further because Morocco was channelling arms to the Algerian revolution.

The former Spanish and French protectorate zones and the Tangier international zone

were quickly abolished, but it took several years to convince Spain to evacuate the Tarfaya strip and the enclave of Ifni in the south, in the latter case only after local tribes staged a revolt.

King Mohammed V's main domestic problem was dealing with the old-guard Istiqlal Party, whose leaders considered themselves the real architects of Moroccan independence, deserving to monopolise power in what they called "homogenous governments", i.e. excluding other political parties.

The Rif Rebellion: Istiqlal pretensions sparked revolts by other nationalist groups who felt deprived of the fruits of victory. One of the most serious broke out in 1958 in the Rif mountains after the Istiqlal ordered the arrest of Dr Abd el Krim Khatib and Mahjoubi Aherdan, two Moroccan Liberation Army (MLA) leaders who had led guerrillas against the French but also contested the Istiqlal party's ascendance.

Although the King ordered the release of Aherdan and Khatib, the Rif rebels defied Rabat until February 1959. There were heavy casualties when 20,000 troops commanded by Crown Prince Moulay Hassan were sent

<u>Left</u>, a young King Hassan II. <u>Above</u>, literacy is becoming the norm rather than the exception.

in to wipe out resistance. Nevertheless the King espoused the Istiqlal's territorial claims to large tracts of Algeria, the Spanish Sahara and Mauritania, claims which soon created diplomatic difficulties.

At the same time he tried to thwart Istiqlal attempts to dominate the government. Aherdan and Khatib were allowed to create a rival party, the People's Movement, representing the rural majority, which held office in all later governments, while by the end of 1962 the Istiqlal was eased out of power and went into opposition.

Hassan's accession: King Hassan II ascended the throne in February 1961 on the death of his father. As he told King Juan

In 1963 newly-independent Algeria rejected Moroccan claims to parts of its territory and a brief war broke out. Moroccan and Algerian troops fought over oases in a disputed area where the frontier had never been formally drawn. The conflict was halted by the Organisation of African Unity, but Mehdi ben Barka was sentenced to death *in absentia* for treason for taking Algeria's side in the dispute.

Just before the border war, Morocco's first constitution was promulgated. It outlawed the one-party regime, guaranteed basic democratic freedoms and provided for an elected parliament, but the king retained substantial powers. The first parliament elected in May

Carlos of Spain 25 years later: "When I ascended the throne, people said I would not last more than six months."

By this time the Istiqlal Party had split. A radical left-wing, led by Mehdi ben Barka, emerged with distinctly republican leanings regarded by the palace as a serious threat to the throne. Ben Barka's breakaway faction, which came to be known as the *Union Socialiste des Forces Populaires* (USFP), agitated for radical political and economic reforms, attacking the king's "personal power" and accusing the monarchy of being feudal or even fascist – views shared by the socialist regime in Algeria.

1963 comprised five parties who spent their time in petty bickering.

The King dissolved the parliament in June 1965 because of the "contradictory and irreconcilable demands of the parties" and he declared a "state of emergency". For five years he ruled by decree with a government of independence. He was the Prime Minister.

Plots and coups: Faced by what they saw as the King's autocratic rule, left-wing militants resorted to violence. Many were arrested in connection with five plots against the monarchy between 1963 and 1977; on two occasions, in 1965 and 1973, armed infiltrators entered the country from Algeria;

in 1965, 1981 and 1984 there were serious street riots fomented by leftists.

The agitation was severely repressed and there were mass trials resulting in death sentences. Mehdi ben Barka, who had been living in exile and was suspected of inciting the agitation, disappeared in Paris in mysterious circumstances on 29 October 1965. He was certainly assassinated. General Mohamed Oufkir, Moroccan Minister of the Interior at the time, was convicted by a French court of master-minding ben Barka's abduction (he was in Paris at the time of the incident), and sentenced to life imprisonment in his absence.

France recalled its ambassador in Rabat

where the Islamic Conference Organisation was created. This enhanced his own prestige and helped to forestall criticism from Islamic fundamentalists. The King now had his hands free to return to more democratic rule.

He decided to rescind the state of emergency, and a second constitution was adopted by referendum; but it was boycotted by the parties, who complained it had been drafted without their consent and was therefore an imposition.

The parties also boycotted the general election so that the second parliament was a colourless assembly with over 90 percent of its members so-called independents. The opposition claimed the vote was rigged.

and for three years relations were frozen as the King steadfastly refused to admit Oufkir's guilt, rejecting suggestions that the General be dismissed. Relations with France were resumed after De Gaulle's death and French financial aid began to flow again.

At about the same time cordial relations were established with Algeria and Mauritania after the King abandoned the Istiqlal's claims to their territory. He also convened Muslim leaders to a meeting in Casablanca

Left, after the death of Mohammed V, mourners cover their heads in respect. **Above**, women queue to cast their votes.

Elected for six years, parliament was a rubber-stamp affair plagued by absenteeism.

In an unsettled atmosphere, senior officers of the Royal Armed Forces staged an abortive *coup d'état* by storming the royal palace at Skhirate on the beach near Rabat on 10 July 1971 while the King was celebrating his 42nd birthday. Nearly 100 guests were gunned down by 1,400 non-commissioned cadets but the King escaped by hiding in a bathroom in a corner of the sprawling palace.

The army's motivations were mixed. Some coup leaders like General Mohammed Medbouh, Minister of the Royal Military Household, who was killed during the raid, were outraged by corruption and extravagance. They believed corrupt ministers should be brought to trial and made an example of and not just dismissed. Others were doubtless less idealistic and simply out to seize power in what would probably have been a right-wing military dictatorship.

The Defence Minister, General Oufkir, had the rebels rounded up with the help of loyalist troops. Ten officers including four generals were summarily executed. Just over 1,000 of the troops stood trial in the following February, but only 74 were convicted.

The verdict appeared surprisingly lenient, but the King's contention was that the coup was the work of only a fraction of the armed forces and so it seemed politic to avoid alienating loyalist officers and troops. If this was in fact the royal thinking, it proved misguided because, on the following 16 August, the pilots of three Air Force jets tried to liquidate the King and his entourage by pumping cannon shells into his airliner as it was flying home from France.

Once again the King escaped unscathed. As he related later, he spoke to the fighter pilots on the airliner's radio in a disguised voice to tell them "the tyrant is dead", whereupon they called off the attacks.

General Oufkir's alleged suicide during the night after the attacks was at first thought to be the act of a dedicated senior officer who felt he had failed in his duty to protect his sovereign. The official version revealed days later was that he had master-minded the attack and was a despicable traitor who planned to rule Morocco using as a puppet the King's elder son, Crown Prince Sidi Mohammed, then aged nine. His original plan was to shoot down the royal airliner over the sea and camouflage it as an accident.

At their trial Air Force officers said Oufkir had persuaded them that the King had to be liquidated to save the country from chaos. The truth is difficult to ascertain. The 11 ringleaders were all executed, so their real motives and the loyalty of other officers remain the subject of speculation.

In an apparent effort to defuse discontent, six former cabinet ministers and four accomplices were brought to trial for corruption. Eight were sentenced to prison terms ranging from four to 12 years for taking bribes totalling over $2 million, but three years later they were all released.

The two abortive military coups convinced many, including apparently the CIA, that the Moroccan monarchy's days were numbered. This may help explain why, in the following year, on 3 March 1973, several hundred armed men infiltrated the country from neighbouring Algeria with the intention of touching off a "popular uprising" on the 12th anniversary of the King's accession.

The "uprising" also failed, reinforcing the popular belief that the King enjoyed *baraka*, or divine protection. Perhaps misled by their own propaganda which claimed that only a spark was needed to set off a revolution, left-wing USFP activists who led the infiltrators found that, instead of welcoming them as "liberators", peasants in border areas tel-

ephoned local security forces. During the trials, at which 22 were sentenced to death, it was revealed that the plotters had also planted bombs at US offices in Rabat and Casablanca and at the main theatre in the capital. None exploded, apparently because the myopic activist who had made them got his wires crossed.

In 1974 the non-party government led by Prime Minister Ahmed Osman, the King's brother-in-law, decided to more than double phosphate rock prices to $64 a ton and borrow money on the strength of this to finance capital-intensive development projects. But the higher price held for only a short time because of a world-wide recession.

A sudden surge in the price of crude oil when Morocco had to import at least 75 percent of its energy, combined with substantial increases in dollar and interest rates which imposed severe constraints on debt-servicing, and later a series of serious droughts which made it necessary to import millions of tons of grain, placed Morocco in an uncomfortable financial position.

But these problems were overshadowed, albeit aggravated from 1975 onwards, by the Western Sahara problem. When Spain announced plans to give her desert colony internal autonomy and hold a referendum there, the King revived Moroccan historic claims to the territory and launched a campaign to recover it for the "motherland".

arch constituted sovereignty. With extraordinary speed and great efficiency he organised the spectacular Green March.

Some 350,000 unarmed Moroccan men and women were mobilised and on 6 November, led by Premier Osman, they marched south across the frontier waving flags and copies of the Koran. They camped for three days under the guns of the Spanish Foreign Legion, which held its fire, and then withdrew when the King announced that they had "accomplished their mission".

The Green March succeeded mainly because Generalissimo Francisco Franco was gravely ill. In their disarray at the prospect of the dictator's imminent death, Spanish lead-

The Green March: Asked to decide whether the area was a *terra nullius* before Spain colonised it, the World Court found that West Saharan tribes had paid allegiance to Moroccan monarchs but that this did not constitute sovereignty, which should be decided by self-determination. The King interpreted this as vindication of Moroccan claims, arguing that in a Muslim society, and particularly in Morocco, allegiance to the monarch constituted sovereignty.

Left, anti-government demonstrators are rounded up and arrested. <u>Above</u>, the Green March into the Sahara Desert.

ers were desperately anxious to avoid a colonial war. Thus on 14 November they transferred the administration of the disputed territory to Morocco and Mauritania.

The Algerian President, Colonel Houari Boumedienne, who until then had supported Moroccan and Mauritanian claims to the Western Sahara, suddenly came out in open support of the Polisario Front – a group of left-wing guerrillas led by a former member of the Moroccan communist party, Mustapha el Ouali, who began campaigning for independence of the Spanish colony.

Algeria trained, armed, financed and gave sanctuary to the guerrillas, who proclaimed

IN SHA'ALLAH: YES, NO OR MAYBE

They tell the story of a poor father of a large family whose landlord ordered him out of his tiny house in the old city for non-payment of rent. Luckily, as frequently happens in Morocco, he knew a man who knew a man who knew an important dignitary who could intervene in his favour.

After weeks of patient contacts, he found himself in the august dignitary's presence. There were the usual courtesies over glasses of mint tea before he explained his predicament, pleading for an "arrangement" that would prevent him and his family from being thrown into the street.

On his return home, his anxious wife questioned him closely. The husband related the encounter in detail and told how he had asked respectfully for the favour. So what did the dignitary say? "He nodded his head and smiled and said *In sha'Allah,*" the husband replied.

Immediately the wife burst into tears, and rolled about on the divan in great distress; because she realised that the dignitary had meant no, he would do nothing.

This apochryphal story illustrates the fact that *In sha'Allah* can mean many things: literally "If God wills" or "God willing", but also many nuances between yes and no, including possibly, perhaps, maybe, of course, absolutely, or why not?...if God wills it. The intended meaning can often be detected by the intonation.

Strictly speaking, the phrase is part of Islamic culture, where the name of God is constantly invoked. Before starting a meal or a journey, the Muslim will say *Bismillah er-rahman er-rahim* (In the name of God, the clement and merciful), which is a way of giving thanks for the meal, or praying for a safe journey. The King always pronounces it before starting a speech.

El-Hamdu Lillah (Praise be to God) is also heard frequently to express satisfaction, pleasure or simply give thanks to the Almighty for benefits such as good health, rainfall or prosperity. In times of trouble, the phrase used may be *Allah u Akbar* (God is great), the implication being that the deity is above human tribulations.

Thus *In sha'Allah* is primarily a devout religious invocation signifying that man's fate is in the lap of God and "the best laid plans of mice and men gang aft awry". In colonial times foreigners regarded it as an example of Muslim fatalism.

When in the early 1970s the state television network began broadcasting weather forecasts, they drew a protest from the *Ulema,* or doctors of Islamic law, who said it was outrageously pretentious, if not sacrilegious, to say it was going to rain tomorrow without adding the phrase *In sha'Allah*. Now all weather predictions are peppered with the phrase.

In sha'Allah is never contracted, each syllable is always pronounced clearly with varying degrees of emphasis, even by the Berbers who use it when they are speaking their native Shilha, Tamazirt or Tarafit dialects. This begs the question of what does it really mean in current Moroccan conversation. According to Abdullah Stouky, an author and publisher, "It means anything, everything or nothing."

Usually it means the speaker accepts a proposal, but if anything happens to prevent an agreement or a meeting "it is not my fault".

Another factor necessary in evaluating common Arabic expressions is what Abdullah Stouky calls "the phenomenon of ambivalence". For example, the word for blind man is *bassir,* which means literally "he who has lucid vision", and the word for kettle is *berred,* which means "the cooler". It should not be surprising, therefore, that *In sha'Allah* can mean the opposite of what one thought was intended.

Tourists need not venture much further into the intricacies of Arabic, one of the most complex and subtle of languages, unless they want to spend a few years learning it properly. But they can usefully remember handy phrases like *Allah y Jib* (God will provide) when accosted by a persistent professional beggar (that's what most locals tell them), or *Allah y Henik* which literally means "May God give you calm", an approximate equivalent of goodbye.

The last word on the topic is from Godfrey Morrison, late correspondent in West Africa of *The Times* of London, who said, "*In sha'Allah* is rather like the Spanish *mañana,* except that it does not have the same sense of urgency." It thus fits in with a popular Moroccan saying: "slowness comes from Allah and haste from the devil." ∎

the Saharan Arab Democratic Republic (SADR) just as the last Spanish troops withdrew at the end of February 1976.

The war dragged on for more than a decade and imposed a heavy burden on the Moroccan treasury while Boumedienne was able to finance it out of his petroleum resources. Aggressive Algerian diplomacy enabled the SADR to get official recognition from over 70 non-aligned or so-called "progressive" states, among them Libya and the communist regimes of North Korea, Vietnam and Cuba, prompting the King's supporters to say there was a "worldwide communist conspiracy against Morocco".

In the event, the war took on some of the

principle" of self-determination and equated the Polisario's struggle with its own bloody independence war against France.

However, a major difference was that while the Algerian war became increasingly unpopular in France, and ultimately forced political settlement, the Sahara war produced unprecedented cohesion in Morocco. Far from weakening the King, it created national unity as all political parties from left to right rallied around him. In this atmosphere, the King held new elections in 1984 which resulted in a credible parliament.

The small but vocal Party of Progress and Socialism based in Casablanca became the only communist party in the world to oppose

aspects of an East-West conflict, the Polisario were armed with Soviet weapons while pro-Western Morocco received military aid from France and the United States.

The Moroccan view was that Algeria was bent on creating a satellite state in the Western Sahara which would give it access to the Atlantic coast, that Polisario believed its guerrilla war would bring Morocco to its knees, and perhaps that the monarchy would eventually collapse. Algeria on the other hand maintained it acted on the "sacred

Above, in 1981 Morocco placed electronic sensors along its frontiers.

the Polisario; leaders of the socialist USPF were even jailed briefly for criticising the King's decision to accept a self-determination referendum at a summit of the OAU in Nairobi in 1981. The irredentist Istiqlal Party not only approved the takeover of the Western Sahara but also continued to press Moroccan claims to various parts of Algeria and the whole of Mauritania as well.

Finally, the King had to restrain his armed forces, many of whose field officers believed that the quickest way to end the war would be to launch a major strike into Algeria and attack the Polisario's rear bases.

The King warned several times that he

would exercise the "right of hot pursuit" into Algeria as the guerrillas withdrew, but he never carried out the threat because of the risk of a devastating war.

The turning point came in 1981 when Morocco began building defence lines composed of ridges of sand and rock studded with electronic sensors to give forewarning of guerrilla attacks. Gradually the lines were extended eastwards until they ran for 1,610 kilometres (1,000 miles) along the Algerian and Mauritanian frontiers. The army gained control of four-fifths of the territory and forced a military stalemate. By this time Algeria, where Colonel Chadli Benjedid had succeeded Boumedienne, had decided

that the war could not be won and it was time for a political settlement.

Truce achieved: After mediation by King Fahd of Saudi Arabia, Algeria and Morocco restored their relations in May 1988. Morocco and the Polisario accepted a peace plan drafted by the United Nations. The plan proposed a ceasefire to be followed by a self-determination referendum, under international control, to give the people of the thinly-populated area a choice between independence or remaining part of Morocco.

Toward the end of the 1980s reconciliation with Algeria paved the way for realisation of the old North African dream of economic union, "The Grand Arab Maghreb", composed of Algeria, Libya, Mauritania, Morocco and Tunisia.

Into the 1990s: Many of the promises of the late 1980s have yet to come to fruition. The *Union du Grand Maghreb* has been abandoned, not least because Algeria is facing grave internal problems caused by fundamentalist violence, which makes both Morocco and Tunisia keen to keep their distance. So far, King Hassan has been successful in keeping Islamic extremists at bay, though there have been riots by young fundamentalists in Fez.

In the Western Sahara, the promised referendum has yet to take place, though the ceasefire still holds. The first attempt at a vote, in 1992, was postponed due to US disquiet and Polisario objections when the Moroccan government moved 37,000 Moroccans into the region on the grounds that their familes had originated in the area. While Morocco continues to frustrate the referendum, UN peace-keeping forces sweat it out in the desert and *Saharwi* refugees, who fled the Western Sahara when the Moroccans moved in in 1975, face another year in camps. UN mediation in the Western Sahara is estimated to cost £2.4 million a month, a sum which many UN members, including America, are reluctant to sustain.

On the homefront, Morocco is pressing ahead with an extensive privatisation programme involving over 100 enterprises (including two breweries, a wine-making company and 11 luxury hotels), risking the wrath of fundamentalists in the process. It is vigorously seeking foreign investment and generally upping its international profile, with Marrakesh in particular becoming a popular international conference centre. There are hopes of increased EU aid to North Africa and the creation of a European-Mediterranean economic free trade zone by the year 2000.

Liberalisation is not confined to the economic sphere. In 1993 Morocco held its fairest election to date, albeit five years later than scheduled and amid inevitable accusations of vote-rigging. Though the two fundamentalist parties were banned, and the bulk of the other parties firmly supported the king, the election showed firm commitment to increased democratisation.

<u>Left</u>, Hassan II today. **<u>Right</u>**, King and country, linked in lights.

The Spanish do not hesitate to call **Ceuta** the pearl of the Mediterranean, but they should. One can think of few towns – Lima, perhaps, and Kinshasa – which have inspired more odium.

"Ghastly place," the writer Rupert Croft-Cooke was told in the 1970s.

The odium attracted him so much he decided to settle there, in a flat overlooking the Plaza de Africa.

Nor can the charges levelled against Ceuta be described as new. Not even Thornbury in his *Life in Spain* had a pleasant word to say about the place. "I see nothing in Ceuta – the town of Seven Hills, the little decayed Rome from whence the Berbers shipped to conquer Spain, slay Don Roderick and furnish matter for that promising epic of Southey's – but rows and angles of decaying ramparts and a slope of houses which seem slipping off into the sea."

Ceuta is more interesting for its past than its present. With Gibraltar, which lies like a shark's fin opposite, it is reputedly one of the Pillars of Hercules – and the straits between them *finis terrae*, the end of the world.

But Ceuta was an important place 2,000 years before Gibraltar became a beam in Spain's eye. Abyla of the Phoenicians, Julia Trajecta of the Romans, Lissa, Exilissa, Septem, Septa, Cibta – it has changed names as many times as it has changed hands. It is also one of the sites claimed for the garden of the Hesperides, the seven daughters of Atlas whose task was to hang golden apples on the evening sky. Ceuta's history is chequered with this kind of legend. Another is that Ulysses drank its water for seven years when he felt himself captivated by Calypso. More likely to be true is the claim that it was the first place in the west where paper was manufactured (under the Almohads).

The Moors won it from the Goths, who are meant to have bestowed the governorship on a woman with one eye. In AD 1001 another governor crossed the Gibraltar straits with his private army only to be strangled by his own eunuch at Jaen. But its importance as "the key to the whole Mediterranean" came in 1415 when it was seized by an expedition from Portugal which included Henry the Navigator.

The capture of Ceuta from the Moors (who had used it as a point of embarkation for their conquest of Spain) took five hours, "to the amazement of all men", after which Henry was knighted by his father in the mosque they had just desecrated. Their expedition had been billed as a crusade against the Infidel, but it broke the geographic bounds of Europe. Its success not only encouraged expansion into Africa but also the great expeditons that were to uncover India and the Americas.

Ceuta kept loyal to Spain when Portugal

seceded in 1580. Most of the time was spent in a state of siege. The first governor lived for 16 years inside a chain-mail coat in case of attack. One siege lasted 26 years.

A Spanish possession long before Morocco ever became a nation, Ceuta continues to embarrass both Morocco, which wants it back, and Spain, which doesn't want to give it but which also realises that its own continued presence there – and in Melilla, its second enclave futher along the coast – rather erodes the argument for wresting Gibraltar back from the British.

Such friction has meant that crossing into Ceuta can be an exercise in frustration. When, after the war, it belonged to the International Zone, it was not uncommon for passengers to be stripped and their cars taken apart. Then you would have to rely on the kindness of the Spanish governor's Titian-haired English mistress. Things are a little easier now.

As a rule, visitors to Ceuta do not stay more than a few hours. Most come from Spain on the ferry from Algeciras. Crossing the narrow straits like Yeats's heron-billed pale cattle birds, they flock to the duty-free shops. At night you can see their car head-

the Hotel Murilla in the Plaza de Africa.

In the Plaza de Africa is the church containing the statue of the Virgin after whom the town is consecrated. The 15th-century wooden effigy of Our Lady of Africa was apparently found on the beach by a Portuguese sailor. The antique baton on her arm is borrowed sometimes when a dignitary takes up high position. She has several of these herself.

Apart from Patron Saint, the Virgin combines the role of Officer Commanding the Garrison and, oddly, Mayoress – this last

lights sweeping away from the port where the poet meditated on death.

Nor is there much to keep them. In their architecture, the buildings resemble grey wedding cakes. The mountain where the Hesperides hung their evening apples, Monte Acho, is a military fortress and its slopes flap with garbage.

Hotels are few and expensive: the Ulysses, in Calle Camoes, which is like the inside of a marble stomach; the Pension Rosi, which looks over a small square with an alarmed statue of Ruiz, and the smartest of the lot,

office granted in perpetuity by a unanimous vote of the 70,000 strong municipality.

A stroll about Ceuta relieves one of the desire to visit Spain's other enclave, Melilla, which lies half a day's drive to the east. Again, the character of a modern duty-free garrison town (Franco served here as a colonel in 1925) drowns out a proudly bugled past. Melilla was Spanish 192 years before Le Roussillon became French and 279 years before the birth of the United States. These years have condemned, not enhanced, the place. Apart from a few wider streets, a bull-ring and some gardens, it has little to offer.

Rupert Croft-Cooke liked it, though.

Left, Our Lady of Africa. **Above**, Ceuta's harbour.

The wave of fundamentalism spreading through the Muslim world is not much more than a ripple by the time it reaches Morocco. King Hassan himself, who in the past liked to portray himself as a bit of a swinger, isn't keen to over-encourage the zeal of the Eastern mullahs.

From the start, King Hassan was keen to promote Morocco as a progressive state and, along with Tunisia, it has always been one of the more socially liberal Muslim countries. Alcohol is freely available, Western women's magazines are sold intact (without the rude bits cut out) and those who choose European lifestyles are happily accepted.

Veiled faces: The majority of Moroccan women still wearing the *l'tam*, or face veil (the Morocccan version covers the nose, mouth and chin), do so out of tradition rather than because they have been influenced by the born-again Muslimism emerging in Algeria and Egypt. More common, and more likely to be to do with religious principles is the simple headscarf.

Generally, in the north of Morocco, use of the *l'tam* is confined to older matrons and rarely do they wear the all-enveloping black *haik* worn in the south. Frequently women attired in a traditional manner – *djellabah* or kaftan, often slit at the sides – will be seen with their jeans-clad, or even short-skirted, daughters. Men keen to marry a committed Muslim don't find it easy to find a young woman prepared to express devoutness in a covered face.

In the countryside, Berber women have always shouldered a large share of agricultural work – they are *under* those walking thorn trees you see in the Rif and Atlas Mountains – and therefore don't wear restrictive veils or *haik.*

Nonetheless, certain Islamic laws on marriage laid down by the Prophet in 7th-century Arabia continue to be applied and King Hassan has shown no intention of interfering with them. Polygamy, now prohibited in Tunisia, is still legal in Morocco. (Indeed,

outside the Royal Circle it is not known how many wives King Hassan has.) Similarly it is still legally permissable for a Moroccan man to beat his wife.

In theory, a male Muslim may take four spouses; he may also marry a Jew or Christian: neither of which a woman is entitled to do. In practice, polygamy isn't quite so easy. A man who wishes to take another wife must prove to the *adiil,* the Islamic judge in civil matters, that he follows the five requirements of Islam (*see page 24*) and therefore has the

right to benefit from Islamic law.

Female propriety: Until a few decades ago it was common for a woman not to have seen her husband before the first stage of the wedding, an official ceremony conducted a year or so before the wedding proper and known as "the engagement". Even now, arranged marriages where there will have been negligible contact between the bride and groom are not unusual. In a society where sexual relations are a potential minefield and the honour of the family is paramount, many men still delegate the delicate task of choosing a bride to their mother and sisters.

Women are still governed by strict codes

Preceding pages: boys, still the favoured sex. Left, young women in Fez. Above, veiled threats, at least to outsiders.

of propriety, especially prior to marriage. For example, while it is perfectly acceptable for an older woman to take snuff, kept inside the neck of her kaftan, it is positively indecent for a young woman to smoke in public. And the late-night presence of a group of unchaperoned girls in even the most upmarket *salon de thé* will still raise eyebrows. A woman's place, at least after the evening promenade and the market's closing-time, is in the home.

With such protective attitudes the norm, it is easy to see why Morocco was shaken to its core when, in 1993, it was revealed that a national police commissioner was being charged with raping more than 500 women and girls over a seven-year period and re-

cording their ordeals with hidden video cameras. But while all Moroccans were horrified that such a terrible thing could happen in a country which prides itself on its lack of sexual crime only a few chose to connect the seven-year silence of the victims with society's paranoia about female virtue.

Married bliss: Once a couple decide to marry, preparations are made for the engagement. Like the wedding, it is an elaborate affair, traditionally beginning with the groom proceeding to the bride's home with donkeys laden with marriage offerings – bolts of fabrics, cones of sugar, baskets of candles and spices – and a fattened calf bringing up

the rear. Such gifts now have symbolic importance rather than material value and sadly the tradition is disappearing.

The wedding itself is a 15-day occasion of gender-segregated feasts and visiting, regulated by strict protocol. For two months prior to the occasion, the bride is attended by a *negaffa*, who acts as a personal beautician – supervising depilation, coiffeur and the application of henna to hands and feet in delicate, lacelike patterns – and instructs the bride in the arts of being a wife. During the wedding celebrations, the *negaffa* flanks the bride at all times, announcing her when she enters a room and attending to her needs (traditionally the bride would sit motionless, with her eyes closed). Until a few years ago the *negaffa*'s most important job was to witness the consummation of the marriage to confirm that the bride was a virgin.

Changes afoot: Morocco's feminist movement has been most feisty over issues relating to work opportunities, to most effect during the 1970s, the decade when women worldwide struggled to be heard. On the question of polygamy their approach is tentative – unsurprising when their organisation has been headed by one of the royal princesses – leaving it to the political Left to do the real chiselling.

The use of such pressure groups is in preparing a climate for change rather than producing change itself. They are helped by economics: most men can afford only one wife these days, and she will probably go out to work – the development most likely to produce dramatic change. In the meantime many women have to hold down a job and run a home, in a country where a minimum of four children is still the norm, washing machines are rare, convenience foods are almost non-existent and the midday meal – a full-blown affair with two or three courses – is still taken at home. Men, meanwhile, do little to help with childcare or housework. Their only contribution to housekeeping is to do the shopping, traditionally a male chore on account of the desire to protect women from the cut and thrust of the market. However, these days even shopping is being packed into the increasingly busy schedule of Morocco's women.

<u>Above</u>, country women have always worked. <u>Right</u>, mother and daughters in Dades Valley.

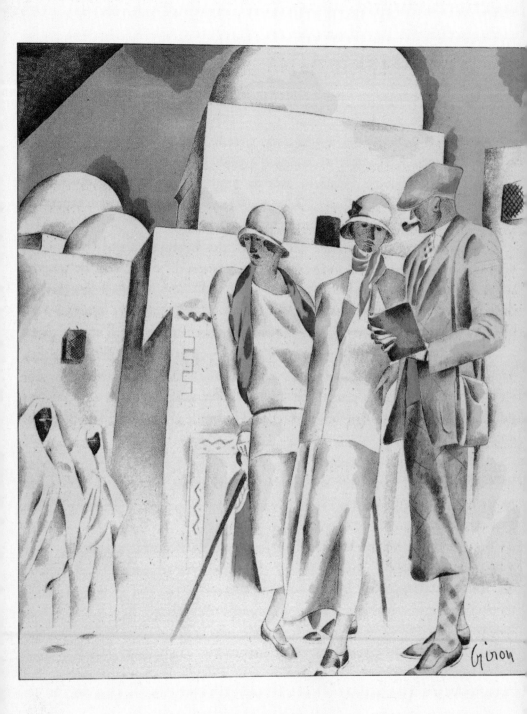

The Novelist as Tourist

Paul Bowles, Tennessee Williams, Allen Ginsberg, William S. Burroughs, Joe Orton... Morocco has attracted more than its share of 20th-century writers.

"Morocco appeared again in a dream one balmy night in May in New York just after the 1939-45 war," said Paul Bowles, the most long-standing, sympathetic and distinguished of infidels who have come to the royal desert jewel of North Africa to live. He had first been there in 1931, with Aaron Copland, with whom the young Bowles was studying music in Paris, and – we are, apparently, to believe – Morocco was never much more in his mind until it stole into his Manhattan dreams more than a decade later.

For such a romantic, of course, Morocco is going to come in a dream, and such a romantic American will also, of course, then immediately – or, at least, next door to immediately – pack a bag, kiss his pretty wife Jane goodbye and sail for dreamland. (In those days one still sailed across the Atlantic – it was half the cost of flying.)

Golden age: Lucky, romantic Bowles: he found Morocco as dream-like in daylight as in the deep-sleep spring night-time of Manhattan. In fact, Morocco, the real thing, was better. There had been no scented desert winds in the dream. In the dream he had loved the noise of Tangier, and Tangier was indeed noisy and exotic. Fez was in her golden age – the traffic sounds of the 1940s were limited to the jingling bells on the horses (the horses and the carriages that now appear in the "Visit Old-fashioned Morocco" adverts in glossy magazines).

All the world, after 1945, had been rushing to New York City, the Imperial City of the new Atomic Age, but Paul Bowles sat in his room at Bab el Hadid in Fez and looked across the dusty valley of the Oued el Zitoun, listening to the wind rattling the high canebrake. "The food was good," he said, in a matter of fact, dry New England Yankee manner, "and I began to write my novel."

Previously he had written only short sto-

ries; this was his first novel, *Sheltering Sky*, the first of many of Bowles's Moroccan novels and short stories. A collection of his stories that came out as recently as 1989, *A Thousand Days For Mokhtar*, are largely about his adopted home.

Like all the great Arabists – like Lawrence, who spoke of the glamour of strangeness and turned himself into a sort of Sheikh of Araby, like the fun-loving Burton and even the indefatigable, bustling Victorian Doughty – there is a touch of the mystic about Bowles, a

Western man from a long line of Westerners who came by choice to live in the gorgeous cities of Islam.

It is surprising to learn from Bowles, an upright, energetic, old New Englander, a strange combination of aesthete and East Coast America prep school master, that the unusual title of his exotic first novel came from that jolly, old music-hall song, "Down Among the Sheltering Palms (Oh, honey, wait for me)". The idea was, Bowles said, that in the desert there was only the sky to give shelter.

How odd that such a tinny old turn-of-the-century song obsessed such a serious student

Left, the glamour of strangeness. **Above**, William S. Burroughs – with a drink, of course.

and composer of music; odd, too, that the non-European noise of Morocco should give such pleasure to Paul Bowles's musically-educated ears. In *Who's Who*, in fact, Bowles lists himself as a composer first, and a writer second. The music of Morocco had come to him in the big, life-changing dream, and, he claimed, the next day, while he was riding on the top of an open bus in New York, the actual plot of the Moroccan novel started to come to him.

What it is to be a mystic and have the music of Morocco come to you in dreams, and plots spring from the traffic's roar of New York City! No wonder Bowles loves Morocco.

But his Morocco is not all poetry and

not really play the piano, was setting industrial Manchester to music; indeed, he would seem to be inventing the jazz piano of the progressive school; round about the same time in New York, Thelonius Monk was also banging the piano with fist and elbow in order to make music out of the sounds of industrial society.

But what a treacherous lure the exotic is for the literary fish and how Morocco has reeled them in: Tennessee Williams, Gore Vidal, Truman Capote, Allen Ginsberg, Jack Kerouac and that great grey ghost of sex and drugs and bebop writing, William S. Burroughs. One is out of sympathy with them. They are the artist as tourist, the writer

mysticism. In his autobiography he tells a funny story of a "musical evening" spent in the bosom of a Moroccan family which possessed an uncle who had, rare for this time, travelled to the north of England. Towards the end of the evening the Moroccan uncle sat down at the piano and proceeded to pound it with his fists and both elbows.

This went on, according to Bowles's wristwatch, for a full 11 minutes, whereupon the musical uncle leapt to his feet and, beaming a big smile, announced that the title of the musical composition was "Manchester". Obviously the glamour of strangeness works both ways. The Moroccan uncle, who could

as day-tripper. Morocco was that best of all combination, both chic and cheap.

Hadn't Barbara Hutton, the original poor little rich girl, the lady who owned all those five and dimes, set up house there? And hadn't smart, lavish, decadent parties been thrown there, with such a chi-chi number as the elegant Cecil Beaton himself giving a beach party by the Caves of Hercules, with one cave filled with champagne and another filled with hashish?

But the poor New Englanders. Unlike the old Englanders, they didn't have a Raj. They had to go to an old French colony. After all, they couldn't go to an English one: the English would laugh at them if they picked up the wrong spoon. Besides, the Yanks never could understand the social rules by which the British played. They couldn't understand why an Englishman laughed at one thing and didn't laugh at another.

Morocco was French. The French were more free about everything. And the idea of French Morocco, the Morocco of Beau Geste and all those French Foreign Legion forts, how romantic it was. And when you had enough kif it got mystic.

They were also, in the main, homosexual. They came to Morocco for the boys. And the dope. Plus it was cheap, if you had dollars, if you had money from home.

The novels and stories of Paul Bowles give a truer image of Morocco, although when they first started to appear in the United States they were wildly misinterpreted. Libby Holman, the American singer who was married to Smith Reynolds, the American tobacco millionaire, told an amusing story of their precocious, teenage son Christopher being asked in 1949 what he wanted to do during his school holiday that summer. Christopher Reynolds's head was full of Paul Bowles's stories of wild, exotic Morocco. The archetypal New York rich kid, sounding like a brat in a *New Yorker* cartoon, said: "I want to go to Africa with Paul Bowles and have my tongue cut out."

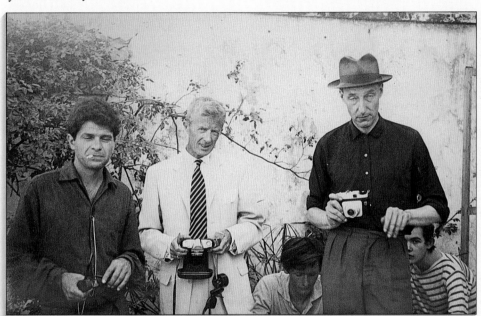

The exotic when Paul Bowles came to Morocco was far more exotic than it is today because you did not see it on television; and when you did see it at the cinema it was movie melodrama; not shot on location but done in Hollywood or Pinewood backlots. One thinks of *Casablanca*, with Humphrey Bogart, Ingrid Bergman and Claude Rains; and even the newsreels presented a bogus picture-postcard image.

Left, Bowles's novels, including *The Sheltering Sky* which attracted film-maker Bernardo Bertolucci. **Above**, Paul Bowles (centre) with Gregory Corso (left) and William S. Burroughs.

Morocco was a *Boy's Own Paper* story, full of adventurers, white men in pith helmets and devilishly dangerous but funny foreigners. It was, after all, the land of kif, the kasbah, old narrow-gauge railway lines with steam-drawn coaches marked *IVième Classe* travelling over the high plateaux between Oujda and Colomb-Béchar, where, completely astonishing the tourist, the line could be blocked by snow.

When Paul Bowles arrived, Morocco was, most of all, still a French colony, like its neighbour Algeria – like, indeed, Vietnam, which no-one actually knew as Vietnam but merely as French Indo-China. It was this

Frenchness of Morocco which Paul Bowles seems to love most of all, although he doesn't dwell on it. It appears merely as shading on the colourful native Moroccan backdrop before which Bowles's fictional characters play.

In his autobiography, however, Bowles lets slip that things have never been the same since the French left. At one point he speaks of the glamour of French Tangier and then says Tangier is now only "a vast slum". That seems unkind, and untrue. First-time tourists returning from contemporary Morocco speak of it in much the same way as Paul Bowles did in 1947.

In 1947, no doubt, there were Europeans, old hands in Tangier, who spoke of the

wonders of Morocco in 1937. William S. Burroughs, for example, a late arriver to the joy of Morocco by Paul Bowles's calendar, was able to find the same music in the street noises as Bowles had heard in 1931. Burroughs had come to Morocco because drugs were cheap, because he was less likely to be arrested for using drugs than he would be in New York or London at that time, and yet, however base these motives, he fell under the musical spell of Morocco. "The whole Muslim world," he said in an interview, "is practically controlled by music." Burroughs started recording the local street music.

Brion Gysin was another. He said he would probably have become a Muslim because of the music of Morocco, particularly the ecstatic music to which the secret brotherhoods danced. He opened a restaurant instead, the 1001 Nights Restaurant in the wing of a Tangier palace that belonged to a Moroccan friend. Gysin introduced the Rolling Stones to the ancient village music of Morocco. In 1971 Brian Jones made a record, *The Pipes of Pan*, at Joujouka.

Morocco, which was "very Sixties" as far back as the Forties, became a hippie heaven. There was all that music and *majoun*, cannabis jam, and, of course, there was Marrakesh, where all the terribly smart French dress designers from Paris now have homes.

Of the serious writers, only Paul Bowles stayed. Ginsberg blew in and out. Jack Kerouac treated Morocco like a day out at the seaside in Long Island. Gore Vidal, Tennessee Williams and Truman Capote were likewise on holiday. Silly as they might seem on the surface, underneath they knew that the exotic was for journalism and the ordinary for literature.

James Joyce, who lived most of his adult life surrounded by the exotically foreign and yet continued to write about the everyday life of ordinary Irish people, knew this. Paul Bowles seems not to have known it. Or perhaps he was too precious a New England flower, too mystic to remain in crass, commercial America.

All the writers used Morocco because it was a cheap place to live. Like some sort of wily old desert lizard or salamander, Bowles took on the protective colours of Morocco's Muslim world without being the thing itself. One wonders if he knows. In his 1989 collection of stories, there is an outstanding one, "A Distant Episode", in which a visiting American professor is captured by North African nomads and then displayed as a performing animal. The story ends with the professor, all decked out in beautiful, jingling ornaments, being led off into the Sahara Desert.

Perhaps Bowles, the novelist as tourist, has also been enslaved by the glamorous strangeness that first beckoned him in the dream.

Above, Brion Gysin and his Dream Machine. **Right**, Barbara Hutton, Woolworth heiress and the ultimate poor little rich girl.

A WILD TIME WAS HAD BY ALL

The late Honourable David Herbert lived through, and was a major protagonist in, what many have rightly or wrongly called Tangier's golden era – the time when the internationally famous and infamous descended upon the town to make hay while the sun shone and publicity blazed. Before his death in 1995, he recalled the parties thrown by his friend Barbara Hutton, the Woolworth heiress.

Barbara's house was in an overcrowded part of the medina surrounded by small Moroccan houses. Originally it had belonged to the holy man Sidi Hosni, whose tomb is buried here; it had then become the property of Walter Harris, correspondent of the London *Times*; and after that the home of the American diplomat Maxwell Blake. Barbara's bid beat that of Generalissimo Franco.

It was actually more of a palace than a house, with a warren of staircases, rooms, mezzannines and terraces. As the parties took place on the terraces, we would be in full view to the outside world. The Moroccans of the neighbourhood enjoyed themselves just as much as the guests. They loved the lights, the music, the ladies' lovely dresses. They always stayed until the party ended.

The usual form was for Barbara to receive guests seated on a gilded throne surrounded by Thai silk cushions. People were brought up to her as though she were a lady of royal birth. They would practically sit at her feet on the lovely cushions and worship at her shrine. Pretentious, perhaps, but for Barbara it was pure theatre, the staging of a tale from the Arabian Nights.

As soon as she had a large enough entourage, she would spring to her feet and dance the night away with all and sundry, and, this being the international era, that included cabaret artists, hairdressers, and pianists from the current nightclubs as well as the Tangier élite.

Her most notorious parties, among the ones which attracted exaggerated headlines back in the American and British press, were those where guests came dressed and behaving as members of the opposite sex. Straight-laced diplomats, bankers and respectable Moroccan businessmen would come in full make-up and decolleté, in spite of moustaches and hairy chests. Their wives, the elderly and the young, wore dinner-jackets or business suits and flattened their hair with brilliantine plastered over nets. In contrast to such spectacles, Barbara would come dressed exquisitely as a girlish Robin Hood.

There would be entertainment, including Flamenco singers and Moroccan acrobats. Belly-dancers would be hired from the Koutoubia Palace; and on special occasions, such as the annual ball when guests were invited from all over the world, the Blue People from the Anti Atlas Mountains would show in Tangier – on camels and carrying loaded rifles – to perform their ceremonial dances.

But although Barbara's parties were beautifully staged, to say they were always a success would be an exaggeration. If she was in a good and happy mood, Barbara was the perfect hostess. If she was tired or sad or had had too much to drink, they could be a disaster.

On these occasions she would not appear the whole evening. If she had sent a message saying, "I am not well, but do enjoy yourselves and have a lovely time," all would have been fine; but she didn't. The orchestra would play on in a dreary fashion, and there might be a little desultory dancing, but when we realised that Barbara would not emerge, the party died and little by little people drifted home.

Her parties generally finished late, usually at dawn. Then Barbara would say goodnight to her guests, looking incredibly lovely with her emerald tiara sparkling in the early morning sun. There was always a present for each one.

In Tangier Barbara remains a legend to this day. The poor Moroccans have no feeling of resentment against her or her wealth, or the fact that she had certain streets in the kasbah widened in order to accommodate her Rolls-Royce; they remember her kindness. Guides proudly point out, to tourists of every nationality, who have probably never heard of her and so do not know the difference, "You see over there, that was the Palace of the Woolworth heiress Barbara Button." ∎

No less an international culinary guru (and part-time Marrakesh resident) than Robert Carrier has pronounced Moroccan cooking one of the great cuisines of the world. Essentially it is a combination of the desert nomads' diet of mutton, vegetables and dairy produce and refined and exotically-spiced specialities – the latter of Syrian origin and introduced by Moulay Idriss along with the Muslim religion.

But it has incorporated other influences over the centuries: southern European (olives, olive oil, fruit, tomatoes); black African; and most recently French, particularly apparent in the country's restaurants. The cooking is neither over-oily nor heavy and the seasonings are a blend of sweet and savoury. Almonds, honey and fruit combine with spicy meats; *pastilla* (*bisteeya*), the famous Moroccan pigeon pie, is dusted with a generous layer of icing-sugar.

Home cooking: Allegedly, the best Moroccan food is found in the home. Certainly, many "restaurants" are of the humble kind, serving charcoal-grilled chicken or *brochettes* (kebabs of marinated liver or lamb), spicy sausages known as *merguez*, and *kefta* (minced lamb shaped into small cakes and served with a pepper sauce).

There are, though, excellent restaurants reflecting the rich range of Moroccan cooking and in the classier places it is perfectly possible to order specialities not on the menu if the chef is given prior warning. Something such as *pastilla*, for example, consisting of wafer-thin layers of *warkha* pastry filled, lasagna-style, with a mixture of pigeon meat and almonds, is a complicated dish requiring a full day to prepare. Locals and visitors alike tend to order and eat this dish in one of the restaurants across the country which has perfected the recipe. (L'Anmbra in Fez is one such establishment.)

Couscous, on the other hand, a base of steamed grain covered with steamed chicken, mutton and vegetables (usually carrots and courgettes), is usually cooked in the home.

Traditionally, it is served at the end of the meal to ensure that all guests have eaten sufficient. A glossy sauce made from fried onions, crushed into the residue in which the chicken and meat were cooked, commonly accompanies it, and almonds and raisins may either be scattered over the couscous or added to the sauce.

Everyone makes this national dish a mite differently. But even in Morocco convenience methods have evolved and pre-cooked couscous is widely used.

The ubiquitous *tajine* is a basic beef or lamb stew (sometimes just vegetables) simmered for hours in an earthenware dish covered by a cone-shaped lid, into which almost everything can go. There are very refined variations: *barrogog bis basela*, a lamb stew with prunes; *safardjaliyya*, a beef stew with quince; *sikbadj*, a lamb stew with dates and apricots; and *tajine bel hout*, a fish *tajine* containing tomatoes, ginger, saffron, and sweet and hot red peppers. Apples and pears may be thrown in when in season and black olives are invariably added to the honey-flavoured sauce.

One of the rewards of walking in the Atlas

Preceding pages: fish is plentiful; all meat is hallal. Left, the chef at A Ma Bretagne, probably Morocco's best restaurant. Above, street vendor during the period of Ramadan.

is to order a *tajine* from a Berber café before setting off and to find it cooked on your return. Tourists often end up buying one of the glazed earthenware *tajine* dishes to try reproducing a *tajine* stew at home. In Morocco, though, *tajines* are usually cooked over the low, even heat of charcoal. When using a more direct heat such as gas or electric, a heat diffusing mat should be used. Also, just as one "seasons" a new frying-pan before using it, it is necessary to eliminate the flavour of earthenware from the *tajine* pot by doing the same.

The other popular everyday meat is chicken, *djej*. *Matisha Mesla* is an ancient Moroccan dish in which the chicken is cooked

menus of humble restaurants or being sold by itinerant food vendors).

M'choui, a whole sheep roasted on a spit and brought to the table for everyone to carve and dip into little dishes of cumin, is the ceremonial dish marking Aid el Kebir, the feast commemorating Abraham's sacrifice of a lamb instead of his son, held 70 days after Ramadan. Incidentally, Ramadan, when not even a drop of water should pass a Muslim's lips from sunrise until sundown, is still very much observed, though many modern Moroccans have come to regard it as a health programme.

Fish restaurants: Established during the occupations of the French and Spanish, these

in a sauce of tomatoes, honey, ginger and cinnamon; *djej bil loz* is chicken with spices and blanched almonds; and *djej mqualli* contains preserved lemons and green olives. The mashed livers of the chickens add body to the sauces.

Ramadan: As in most countries, special occasions in Morocco are celebrated by feasts and specially prepared foods. During Ramadan Moroccans always break their daily fast with *harira*, a thick soup of beans, lentils and lamb. Every café will have this soup available for those unable to reach their home by the appointed hour. Outside Ramadan you sometimes find *harira* on the

can be found along the Mediterranean coast to Ceuta and on the Atlantic coast from Tangier south. The most outstanding (with Michelin commendations) is A Ma Bretagne, near Casablanca – though, for simpler preparations, Sam's in Essaouira is hard to beat. Giant prawns caught off Agadir (where the country's fishing fleet is based), octopus, squid, boned and stuffed sardines (try those grilled at the open-air stalls on the corniche at Essaouira or outside the fishing harbour in Agadir), sea wolf, skate and sole in all its international guises are available at the most modest quayside restaurant. Worth trying anywhere more upmarket is *samak mahshi be roz*, of Syrian origin, which is any large white fish stuffed with rice, pine nuts and almonds and served with a tamarind sauce.

Food to go: The Moroccan pleasure in food is reflected in the amazing range of snacks sold by the great army of street vendors – particularly in Marrakesh, Fez, Tangier and Rabat,which attract farmers and travellers from the surrounding countryside. These range from cactus-fruit (said to settle upset stomachs) to freshly roasted chickpeas, and snails, flavoured with cumin and rough salt, ladled out of giant vats to homeward-bound office workers.

As in restaurants in Morocco, the chances of poisoning from takeaway food can usu-

ally be gauged. The busier the stall, the less likely it is. If you eschew all such food, you will undoubtedly miss out. A glass of freshly-squeezed orange juice from a stall on the Djemma el Fna in Marrakesh costs one-twentieth of the inferior carton variety served at La Mamounia Hotel.

One of the pleasures of motoring in Morocco is the variety of produce to be bought along the way. In the north, Rif women hold out covered plates of tangy white cheese; in the south during the autumn, boys proffer

<u>Left</u>, chicken and fennel tajine. <u>Above</u>, couscous, usually best eaten at home.

baskets of freshly harvested dates. In the Atlas, dependent on season, you will find almonds, walnuts, pine-buts and lychees; and on the Atlantic coast, honeydew melons costing just three or four dirhams each, and freshly caught fish.

A drop to drink: Alcohol is not used in cooking apart from in French restaurants. Morocco does, however, brew beer and produce wine. The beer, light and Continental-tasting, comes in four varieties: Stork (the lightest), Flag Speciale (a favourite beer in squat green bottles), Flag Pilsner (more difficult to find) and Extra 25 (which comes in short brown bottles).

Moroccan wine is beginning to find its way on to the shelves of Europe's super-markets, mostly in the form of red wines, since the whites and the rosés do not travel well. The best known vineyards are in the Fez and Meknes region, and the wines most frequently listed on wine-lists are white Oustalet, Valpierre and Spéciale Coquillage, all three light and delicious and best served well-chilled. A rosé, Sidi Bouhai, has a grey-ish hue and is a good summer wine, while Vieux Papes, Cabernet-President, Club des Baillis, and Clairet Méknès Vins are top-class table varieties.

The most common refreshment is, of course, mint tea prepared in bulbous, silver-coloured teapots and served in glasses. It is an infusion of mint leaves and either green or *nègre* (black) tea (a solicitous host will offer a choice). The mint is placed either in the glass or in the tea-pot. When the tea is poured, the pot is usually held high above the glass in order to "aerate" the liquid as it falls. Tea is served throughout the day and after any meal. Sometimes, instead of mint, it is laced with pinenuts or orange blossom.

Other drinks include milkshakes, made with seasonal fruits, and freshly squeezed fruit juices – grape, orange, black cherry or pomegranate, dependent on season. In the afternoon it is usual to adjourn to a café cum cake shop (they tend to operate as one unit) for tea and pastries. Almonds and honey are the most popular sweet combination; *cornes de gazelle*, almond-filled pastry crescents, are a national sensation. If you are in Morocco during Ramadan, try *shebakkia*, deep-fried knots of pastry dipped in honey and sprinkled with sesame seeds, traditionally served as a sweet follow-on to *harira*.

Moroccan architecture is dominated by Islam. But factors specific to the country – natural resources, European imperialism, climate and a tribal history – have all modified the Eastern stamp. Early Islamic influences had weakened by the time they reached the extreme west of North Africa, leaving many indigenous practices intact. And, as a staging-post on African, Saharan and Mediterranean trade routes, Morocco experienced a long and steady influx of various foreign styles.

High mountains separate desert conditions, in which unfired bricks and poor quality materials dictated a more rudimentary architecture, from damper, cooler coastal plains; they also support oak, pine and cedar forests – used lavishly in the internal ornamentation of larger houses and palaces. In the south, tribal warfare and the struggle of emerging dynasties have, without exception, determined defensive architecture: tall, crenellated *ksour* and kasbahs.

True believers: Nonetheless, the building of towns and villages presented an opportunity to express the ideals of the Islamic state. Islam touches every aspect of a Muslim's life, and architecture provides more than just a series of rules and customs laid down for religious buildings. Its emphasis on the community is reflected in the interlocked nature of housing. "Believer is to believer," said the Prophet, "as the mutually upholding sections of a building."

At the same time, Islam's asceticism is reflected in simplicity of form and respect for space. The Arabs of the seventh century, who had little architectural heritage, were never very far from the desert and its exceptional feel of expanse. Spaciousness and lack of distraction are suited to the observation of rituals and prayer.

The aesthetic role of buildings, important in the West, took second place to the practical function of defining a space, a purpose emphasised by dramatic gateways, enclosed courtyards and enormous defensive walls. A small gate in a blank wall will lead into a beautiful courtyard, possibly containing a gentle, trickling fountain, in which to rest or contemplate – within the communal whole an enclosed, personal oasis away from the heat and dust.

Because the Muslim religion forbids animate representation, the ornamentation of buildings reached a level of abstraction. While this rule was never totally observed and stylised plant and flower forms may often be identified, fine calligraphy is more usual.

Kufic script is highly stylised – to the extent that, practically in cipher, it can be difficult to read even for a classical Arabist.

Gold and silver were similarly frowned on, so less lavish materials were used. Stucco, worked into delicate lace-like patterns, arrived in the 13th century while mosaic (or *zellige*) of green, blue, black and red tiling became popular in the 1300s. Both were Eastern techniques perfected in Andalusia and imported to Morocco by the Muslims of Spain, under whom the decorative arts flourished. Similarly in the Andalusian fashion, elaborate iron-work, which lends itself so readily to abstract design, was employed for

Preceding pages: stucco, faïence and wood carving – the basics of Islamic decoration. **Left,** Medrassa el Attarine in Fez. **Above,** *ksar,* designed for defence.

the ubiquitous window and door grilles and for lanterns.

Building a religion: The mosque, the most important of religious buildings and the principal though not the only meeting place for prayer, formed a loose prototype for all Islamic architecture. Modelled on those of Cordoba and Kairouan of 8th-century Spain and Tunisia (at that time, the most important cities of Western Islam), which, in turn, were based on Damascene models, most Moroccan mosques are rather plain on the outside. A highly decorated entrance door and a minaret are the most notable external features, and the roof is usually of simple, often green (the colour of Islam), tile work.

and the hall for prayer situated alongside, divided into aisles segregating the sexes. A niche in the wall (*mihrab*) indicates the direction of Mecca; and to the right of the *mihrab* is a pulpit called the *minbar*, often of carved cedar wood intricately inlaid. It is from here that the *imam* reads the Koran.

Religious buildings open to non-Muslims are the *medersa*, the schools where theology and Muslim law were taught and which served as early universities. While often attached to mosques, they developed from domestic buildings – sometimes the houses of the principal teachers – and were first established in the 12th century. Once again, a central courtyard with a fountain, often

Early mosques did not include minarets; in fact, the earliest mosques were not even formally enclosed. Originally the faithful were called to prayer from nearby roof-tops. The square-shaped minaret of the Maghreb, unlike the circular minarets of the Middle East, corresponds to the bell-tower of a church (generally they are four times their width in height) and were copied from early Christian towers in Damascus.

The interior of the mosque, which, alas, is out of bounds to non-Muslims in Morocco, though not in many other Muslim countries, comprises a courtyard (*sahn*), with a fountain or basin for preliminary ritual washing,

cloistered on the ground floor, was flanked by a chapel for prayer, classrooms and library. The pupils' living quarters were situated above, on the first floor.

Many of the *medersa* were founded by sultans, in particular the learned Merinids in the 14th century. They are elaborately decorated with detailed carving, mosaic tile and glass work, Kufic script and stucco. The most outstanding are the Medrassa Bou Inania begun in 1350 in Fez and Medrassa ben Youssef built in 1565 in Marrakesh.

In defence: As recently as the late 1930s, it could be quite dangerous to travel in Morocco. The defences around many towns are immediately evocative of a warlord past. Within are all the necessary buildings for defence: vast stables, barracks, food stores, granaries, arsenals and water cisterns. What is remarkable about them is their size rather than their level of architecture but the design of the *bab*, or gateway, is often the exception to this rule. Generally built of stone blocks and crenellated, two towers flank a central bay in which the gate is set. Above, its arch might be deeply carved in coloured stones like the Oudaya gate in Rabat, the Bab Agenau in Marrakesh, or the imposing Bab Mansour in Meknes.

Every dynasty left its own stamp on the defences of the cities, often demolishing to the *ksour*, Morocco's most imposing architecture.

In effect, *ksour* are fortified villages, comprising a central square, granary, well, mosque and warren-type streets and housing, contained by high walls punctuated by watch-towers. Made of crude mud brick and rubble or split palm-trunk (a material known as *pisé*), they are permeable to water and can withstand only a very dry climate. Rain constantly undermines this form of architecture; the south is littered with abandoned and ruined *ksour* often only decades old.

Strictly speaking, the difference between the kasbahs and *ksour* is that the former house individual families while the latter

much of the work of its predecessors. The Almohads in Rabat in the 12th century and the Merinids in Fez and Chella in the 13th and 14th centuries were particularly industrious in this respect.

It wasn't only the towns and cities that were in need of fortification. Even the poor, flat-roofed, stone-built farms built on terraces in the Middle Atlas, homes of the Berber Cleuhs, were – and still are – well defended. In the south these farms give way

Left, the "Mauresque" architecture of Rabat. **Above**, highly stylised script, in accordance with the Koran.

enclose a whole community. That said, throughout the rest of Morocco the word kasbah refers to the defensive stronghold of a town. Most towns possess one. It is in the south, however, along the Dadès valley (the "Route of the Kasbahs") that they are most evident. Square and built of crude brick, they show few openings on the outside. Yet their simplicity is often offset by geometric, African decorations carved into the mud bricks. Close to the desert, it becomes clear that another world, that of the Sahara, is beginning.

The palaces: Unlikely though it may seem, such blank exteriors have contained some of Morocco's richest palaces. The sheer luxury, colour and decoration, and the quality of life within surpassed the comforts of Europe for many centuries. Once again, the central feature was the courtyard, around which were grouped suites of rooms in a symmetrical pattern. Service areas would often be built on particular sides, and these in turn might have their own central courtyard, as wealth and necessity dictated.

The most famous was El Badi, "the incomparable", in Marrakesh, built for magnificent receptions by Ahmed el Mansour in the 16th century. Its courtyard had five elaborate pools, lined with coloured tiling, whose waters irrigated a series of gardens. Its marble came from Italy and its furnishings from as

probably the finest palace in Morocco. Its courtyard is several acres in size and even contains a *medrassa* and a mosque. The decoration within these palaces required the skills of the top Moroccan artists and craftsmen, and while it is true that development and quality of style had degenerated into showy exuberance by the 18th century, there are plenty of examples of good work preserved.

Nowadays many former small palaces house museums and hotels (e.g. the Palais Jamai Hotel in Fez; the Dar el Makhzen museum in Tangier, occupied by the deposed Sultan Moulay Hafid as recently as the beginning of this century, and the mu-

far as China. Its fabulous belvederes, kiosks, pavilions, towers and galleries made it a legend in Europe.

While the original structure of a palace was usually symmetrical, radiating from the courtyard, later additions were often haphazardly planned. Nonetheless certain essential features had to be incorporated. There was always a judgment hall and a *mechouar*, an open space to hold large audiences and dominated by a balcony called an *iwan,* where the sultan could receive homage from his tribesmen. The *harem*, which was a restricted area, had to be entirely separate.

The Dar el Makhzen Palace in Fez is the

seum in the Oudaya Kasbah in Rabat) and as such provide an opportunity for visitors to view them at close hand. King Hassan II's palaces (there is at least one in every major town) are generally recent but traditional in style, enclosed by extensive gardens and strictly out of bounds. Some sense of their scale may be glimpsed from their perimeters or when approaching a city by air.

Historical perspective: Against any other architecture, that of Islam has remained comparatively static. After the fall of Rome, urban development in Morocco did not begin again until after the Arab conquest. The Idrissid dynasty of the 8th to 10th centuries was the first to resume building, establishing Fez as its capital.

During the Almoravide dynasty of the 11th and 12th centuries, when many Muslims were expelled from Spain, the brilliant civilisation of Andalusia took root in Morocco. It is thought Abou Bakr founded Marrakesh and his son, Ali ben Youssef, built enormous fortifications at Taza, a city which, on the eastern approach to Fez (known as the Taza Gap), was an important line of defence. Mosques were rebuilt, and domes, pillars and semi-circular arches, together with plaster sculpture, were introduced.

The Almohads of the 12th and 13th centuries were prolific builders. Additions were

made to Marrakesh, most notably the walls. The power of masonry was the symbol of the period. The mosques of Koutoubia in Marrakesh and Hassan in Rabat were commissioned at this time.

The Merinid dynasty of the 13th to 15th centuries was a period of increasingly sophisticated work rather than imposing building. The Merinids were responsible for most of the country's *medersa*.

Under the Saadians during the 16th and 17th centuries Morocco became susceptible

Left, public housing in Marrakesh. **Above**, traditional but not old houses in Tinerhir.

to foreign influences. The Portuguese took coastal towns and built fortifications at Asilah, Safi and El Jadida. Art and architecture then tended to repeat the styles of the past rather than innovate, but sheer scale was celebrated by Ahmed el Mansour, who embellished Marrakesh to a degree that impressed a decadent Europe.

It is the unflagging industry of the Alaouite Sultan Moulay Ismail of the 17th century that is often so evident today. He built and rebuilt constantly. Sixteen miles (25 km) of wall was built around Meknes, and he achieved popular public works through the forced labours of slaves and Christian captives. In keeping with his personality, scale and grandeur took precedence over aesthetic considerations.

Modern architecture: There was little further development in architecture until the French and Spanish protectorates, when European styles dominated the northern and coastal cities. Marshal Lyautey, the first French Resident General, decreed that the European development of towns, to house the great influx of European administrators, should be separate from the medinas so as to preserve the traditional civilisation. The new architecture, combining French civic pomposity and Moorish motifs, was known as "Mauresque". The 1920s even brought a smattering of Art Deco to Casablanca and Marrakesh.

Nowadays, the newest civic architecture reflects traditional Moroccan design instead of mimicking French architectural styles. Other than in Casablanca, modern development has resisted introducing high-rise buildings. Tradition is for low buildings which the minaret of the mosque may dominate. Rabat's "skyscraper" is the "Immeuble Saidia", the low office block at the end of Boulevard Mohammed V, facing the medina.

Blocks of flats, the most common form of inexpensive housing, rarely rise above seven floors, but it is the ambition of any well-off individual to have a house built rather than buy a property second-hand. This has introduced a non-traditional practice: mortgages and credit. The Koran forbids usury – which was why, historically, the Jews had the monopoly on money-lending – but modern pressures have dictated a modern compromise. Sadly, with their wealth of fussy external decoration, many of the villas built with these loans display little of the characteristic restraint of traditional domestic architecture in Morocco.

MAKING MUSIC

Brion Gysin thought hearing the music of Morocco was enough to make one become a Muslim. The Rolling Stones didn't quite go that far, but they did dress in *djellabahs* and twice teamed up with the Master Musicians of Jojouka: once for the album *The Pipes of Pan*, recorded by Stones guitarist Brian Jones in 1968, and on the second occasion to make the track "Continental Drift" for the 1989 album *Steel Wheels*. Keith Richards summed up the extraordinary sounds of the Joujouka pipes and drums like this: "It sounds a bit like modern jazz, like John Coltrane or Ornette Coleman, although it's really pagan trance music."

Whoops of joy: Wherever you go in Morocco, you are likely to be assailed by wonderful rhythms, whether it's the most common musical phenomenon, the amplified voice of the *muezzin* calling the faithful to prayer, or the tinny sound of Egyptian taped music emanating from the doorway of a shop. Possibly it will be beating drums and the whoops of women celebrating a wedding long into the night.

But what you should actively seek out – early evening is the best time – are impromptu sessions at music cafés (often identified by the musical instruments hanging on their walls). It is to these that local musicians will come to drink tea and then sing songs.

Chabbi, meaning popular, is the most common music played at these venues. Akin to the folk music tradition of Europe and North America, it started out as music performed by travelling entertainers, who would collect and compose songs along their way. Now, having received media attention, it has moved off the public squares and on to radio and television. Abdelwahhab Doukali and Hamid Zahir, two of the most popular singers of *chabbi*, began their careers, respectively, in Bab el Makina in Fez and Djemma el Fna in Marrakesh.

Inevitably, groups have begun to electrify traditional instruments (for example, the *buzouk*, a long-necked lute) and to add gui-

Preceding pages: musicians at a *moussem*. **Left,** the drum, an essential accompaniment to many occasions. **Above**, street music.

tars and keyboards, but at local level it is still confined to the *l'oud* (11-string fretless lute), *kamanche* (violin), banjo and assorted percussion. At the end of a song an instrumental section called *leseb*, twice the speed of the piece, induces shouting and dancing and syncopated clapping.

Classical roots: Interestingly, some of the complex traditional forms of Moroccan music – Andalus, now exemplified by the orchestras of Fez, Méknès and Tangier (towns which were most influenced by Moorish

Spain), and *milhun*, an ancient form of sung poetry – have been combined with *chabbi* to produce a mixture of sophisticated instrumentals and popular lyrics. In contemporary *rai* music, too, which originated in western Algeria (though, in the Maghreb, one must remember that borders are political rather than ethnographical), style and lyrics have come a long way from their Bedouin roots.

Rai's preoccupations tend to be sex, drugs and cars; and the instruments are now brass, accordions, electric guitars and synthesizers rather than flutes, violins and lutes. Naturally, lyrics such as "Hey, Mama, your daughter she wants me" or "Beer is Arab, whisky

Music 99

is European" have not endeared it to the establishment. Morocco's own *rai* stars include Chaba Zahouania (whose family insist that her cassette cover bares the photograph of a bikini-clad model rather than her) and Cheb Kader.

Rural rituals: Berber music, generally found in the country areas, is quite distinct from Arabic-influenced *chabbi* or rock-style *rai*. It includes ritual music, tied to the agricultural calendar or performed during exorcisms and purifications, and sung poetry called *tamdyazi* performed with just drums and flutes.

At one time it was common for towns and villages to be visited by professional musicians from the Atlas known as *imdyazn*, itinerant bands of four members, whose role was to bring news of world affairs in poem form. Using drums, double clarinet and *rebab* (a single-string flute), the musicians improvised as they went. This still happens, but now, outstripped by television, their function is to entertain rather than inform.

Outside of weddings, it is in the entertainment squares that one is also likely to witness the music of the *gnaoua*, whose wild drum rhythms induce states of trance. The *gnaoua* brotherhood has devotees all over Morocco but particularly in Marrakesh.

The *gnaoua* claim spiritual descent from Bilal, an Ethiopian who was the Prophet's first *muezzin*. Most of their ceremonies are held with the intention of placating spirits, good or evil, which have inhabited person or place. Undoubtedly, the origins of these rites are in sub-Saharan Africa and a black African influence is evident in the rhythms.

Music to take home: One thing immediately noticeable in any town is the abundance of tape stalls. Few copyright laws exist in Morocco. Unlike in the West where a performer is paid royalties, in Morocco, and most other African countries, an artist will be paid handsomely for the initial recording but little thereafter. Tapes are copied shamelessly and sold legally for about 15 dirhams each. Don't be surprised if a tape stops abruptly, in the middle of a track; they're all like that. Tapes are of standard length and if the recording artist hasn't finished by the time it has run its course, he or she is cut off in mid-flow.

<u>Right</u>, music festivals, the most celebrated of which is in Asilah.

SKIING

It may be thought that skiing – an invention of the late 19th century imported from Scandinavia and developed as a pastime in the Alps – could have bypassed the hothouse of the Atlas. In fact, experiments in Moroccan *piste* skiing originated in the 1930s – before the winter sports fanfares of Courchevel and Val d'Isère could be heard.

During World War II expatriate Frenchmen installed primitive ski-tows in clearings of the Anti Atlas cedar forest and so set up the first equipped nursery slopes in the country. In 1942–43 the protagonists mounted several ski sorties into the Great Atlas; the spearhead was led by the now legendary André Fougerolles. By 1952 an 80-page guide to *piste* skiing and cross-country expeditions on skis had been issued, covering many ambitious projects – then achieved perhaps only once.

High hopes: Climatically, snow precipitations may occur in Morocco down to 3,330 feet (1,000 metres). Snow that is likely to lie for more than two months raises the minimum level to 5,600–6,500 feet (1,700–2,000 metres). From an early date, *ski de haute montagne* was considered more rewarding than oscillating up and down short, sometimes artificially maintained, nursery slopes.

Multinational parties confirmed during the 1950s that the High Atlas was essentially a mountain skiing domain, and the puposebuilt resort of **Oukaimeden** was conceived and completed in a few years. The modest weekend practice grounds at **Mischliffen-Jbel Hebri** on the west rim of the Anti Atlas remained fairly basic.

Nothing much has changed at Mischliffen in 40 years. Skiers generally commute to the three lifts from agreeable amenities in Azrou and Ifrane, 10–12 miles (15–20 km) away. Equipment hire is a hit-or-miss affair. In a poor year the season is short – maybe only five weeks, though usually extending to eight with runs falling through a modest vertical interval of 330–660 feet (100–200 metres). Obviously, Mischliffen is not a package-tour destination. Skiers are invariably the resident hoi-polloi of Fez, Meknes and Rabat. Youngsters and school groups, with amateur instructors, are much in evidence.

To widen the horizon, bolder skiers persuaded the authorities to open up **Bou Iblane** in the Anti Atlas as a high altitude resort. A road was pushed beyond the Taffert forestry hut to a site at the foot of the mountain, where an initial ski-lift was built. However, the carpark here, about 85 miles (140 km) from Fez, often cannot be reached in late winter because the road is not kept open by snowploughs – a case, as so often in Morocco, of economic viability versus the small number of participants. Those attending sleep rough at the hut, for there is no accommodation or restaurant – or indeed any other services – at the "resort". *Dortoirs* (self-catering flats) are on the drawing-board.

Across the quite suitable north-facing slopes and hollows of the several Bou Iblane summits, from 10,200 feet (3,100 metres) downhill sweeps of 2,300 feet (700 metres) are possible. The main problem is that good snowfalls may not last long. With a deteriorating surface, the skiing soon becomes of poor quality and, in the absence of waymarks, eventually a hazardous slalom among boulders. So here, too, one must count the season as short.

Oukaimeden, 47 miles (75 km) from Marrakesh, ranks as the premier ski-station in the country. The road is normally swept clear of snow and the season lasts from mid-December until early April. Now 30 years old, this resort has had Alpine-type trappings grafted on to it.

The chair-lift to the top of Jbel Oukaimeden (3,273 metres), the highest cableway in Africa, may be closed by mid-March. Its operation is not justified for spring and summer visitors, who mostly congregate at Imlil. Five ski-tows supplement the main lift; accessible beginners' slopes use portable drags. The graded runs are rather limited unless one is prepared to use skins and make out of bounds circuits.

Accommodation is available in two hotels, four skier-chalets, various apartment blocks (including some for renting), and hired private chalets.

Left, Lone skier at Oukaimeden, one of Morocco's two main ski resorts.

There are general food shops for self-caterers; equipment hire; but no garage repair. A splendid French Alpine Club establishment, with low charges, vies with the best commercial chalets for standards of comfort, but the *après-ski* of noise, alcohol and "party games" lacks the sophistication of Alpine resorts.

Youth clubs and schools are encouraged by a government-sponsored national body (FRMSM) to assemble parties to train at Ouka for competitive downhill and cross-country skiing. Special firms now aspire to arrange ski journeys supported, below the snowline, by mules and porters.

In the **Toubkal massif**, British parties even here skis are removed by most parties 30 minutes from the top.

One for the professionals: The outstanding expedition ski ascent in the area is Tazaghärt – coincidentally offering the best winter gully climbs as well – but it is very serious stuff, helped along by the strong Berber backup available at Imlil.

The high level routes of summer become popular ski tours in winter, threading the high valleys and crossing passes to reach their ultimate destination. The rigours of these excursions undoubtedly demand a brand of enthusiasm usually confined to mountain skiing fanatics.

Ambitious plans are on the drawing-board

have excelled in formulating tactics for unique long-distance experiences on skis. *Ski-mulet* is a description that figured prominently in holiday brochures of the 1980s. As an explanation of the term, some indigenous cartoonists have depicted mules wearing the skis and sweat-soaked tourists in tow behind carrying bags marked "hay".

Spurious, misleading claims abound about ski climbs in the Toubkal massif. Most of the desirable peaks cannot be reached on skis; these must be shed some way below the summits and parties proceed on foot using climbing techniques as conditions dictate. Mount Toubkal itself is an exception, though

for turning the **Bou Guemez valley** in the Central High Atlas into a skiing paradise. Specifically, a consultative document has been produced detailing certain options. A fundamental disagreement between the promoters pivots on downhill infrastructure – lifts and tows, chalets and shops, or a chain of huts, to link up with other valleys, for touring.

Another scheme, favoured by ecologists and environmentalists, would have the district preserved altogether from pylons and cables, and allow only wealthy heli-skiers to be flown in from Beni-Mellal hotels and collected the same way. Clearly, the Berbers are totally opposed to this idea. Finding the funds to realise any of the grand designs published so far will hinder advancement, but Azurki and Izourar huts should soon be open for business.

A lot of skiers already make the rough journey to **Azurki** mountain 12,000 feet (3,677 metres). As long ago as 1950, this huge smooth-sided mass was pronounced potentially the finest skiing location in Morocco – coupled with its equally bulky neighbour Ouaoulzat. Skis have glided over every facet, spur and depression where trails of 1,000 metres can be plotted. Snow retention on mountains round the Bou Guemez is traditionally good and skiing in favourable

well-trained alpinist and is avalanche-prone in some prevailing conditions.

Close to Midelt, the gigantic **Ayyachi** will tax the fittest exponent. Doubtless a gratifying feat, incredibly it has half a dozen ascent-descent routes described in specialist publications, with a preciseness suggesting scores of ascents have been made. In fact, some of these are believed to have been helicopter-assisted. Air charter is a growing business in Marrakesh and Beni-Mellal and the demands of skiers have been making a significant contribution.

In the skiing season, daily forecasts of weather and ground conditions for Mischliffen and Ouka are available in towns and

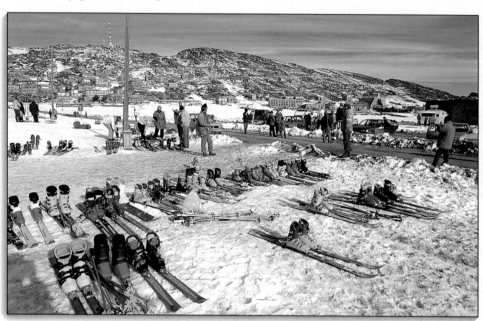

years continues until around mid-May.

Skiing further east enters the realms of wilderness exploits, in which the *ski-mulet* recourse might be essential to success and perhaps survival. The amount of pre-planning, organisation and local knowledge that is required will defeat many hopefuls.

Jebel Masker, near Tounfite, has been singled out as a solitary noble ski ascent objective. This has been accomplished many times, but it is strictly the province of the

cities all over Morocco. If based in Marrakesh or Meknes, one can go at short notice to either in a couple of hours.

Final word of advice: Wherever you ski in Morocco, it is necessary to be properly equipped. Personal, portable rescue beacons are absolutely essential. Small battery-operated radio transmitter/receiver devices of the type worn by cross-country and touring skiers in Europe cannot function in the Atlas mountains where rescue services are distant and in any case have no compatible electronic receiving equipment. Make certain you have adequate rescue and air repatriation insurance for skiing in the Atlas.

Left, falling down is part of the fun. **Above**, the resort of Oukaimeden, still to become a Moroccan Val d'Isère.

PLACES

Travel in Morocco has come a long way since the days when Europeans needed to disguise themselves in *djellabahs* and veils in order to penetrate anywhere beyond Tangier. Dusty old tomes on Morocco all contain photographs of their authors in native dress – though Wyndham Lewis seemed to think this had more to do with a desire to "dress up as Arabs" than any real fear of attack.

In fact Berbers, being naturally resourceful, have proved the very opposite of their famously violent image; they have welcomed tourism and at a local level, particularly in the Atlas, have been quick to profit from it, often undermining the government's broader attempts to capitalise on big spending by foreign visitors.

Some hotel development has spawned on the Rif coast, especially south of the Spanish enclave of Ceuta, but, amazingly for a country so close to Europe with sandy beaches and reliable sunshine, Morocco has largely escaped the type of intensive coastal development that mushroomed on the southern coasts of Spain, Turkey and Portugal. The Moroccan government, reputedly seeking a better class of holidaymaker, has earmarked the southern valleys, for many years the favoured territory of middle-class French holidaymakers, for upmarket tourist development, with well-hidden, traditionally designed luxury hotels proliferating yearly. Even Agadir, where Morocco strives to achieve the image of a "playground resort", is not without attractive qualities.

But, despite long blonde, blue-skied beaches, fortified Portuguese fishing ports, lush oases in pink desert plains, mountain ranges offering walking, climbing and winter skiing, the extraordinary attractions of Morocco are still the imperial cities of Fez, Meknes and Marrakesh. Founded in the Middle Ages and expanded by succeeding dynasties, they contain superb examples of early Islamic architecture. Even more remarkable, the trades and practices of their medinas still function much as they did in medieval times throughout North Africa and the Middle East.

Morocco's capital, Rabat, though with similar historic claims to the other imperial cities, seems European by comparison: the French-style cafés and "Mauresque" architecture on the verdant Boulevard Mohammed V reflect an urban style not confined to the down-town area. Here, more than anywhere, is a reminder that a large part of Morocco was governed by the French. If Rabat seems bourgeois, Azrou and Ifrane, south of Fez in the Middle Atlas, with their steep roofs and carved gables, would not be out of place in the Alps. Incredible, then, that just 200 or so miles (320 km) away, radiating from the foothills of the Atlas, lie the deserts and palm oases of the south – landscapes that helped win acclaim for David Lean's classic film *Lawrence of Arabia*.

Preceding pages: winter in the Dades Valley; darkness falls over Fez; the ferry from Rabat to Salé. **Left,** whitewashed streets of Chaouen, in the Rif.

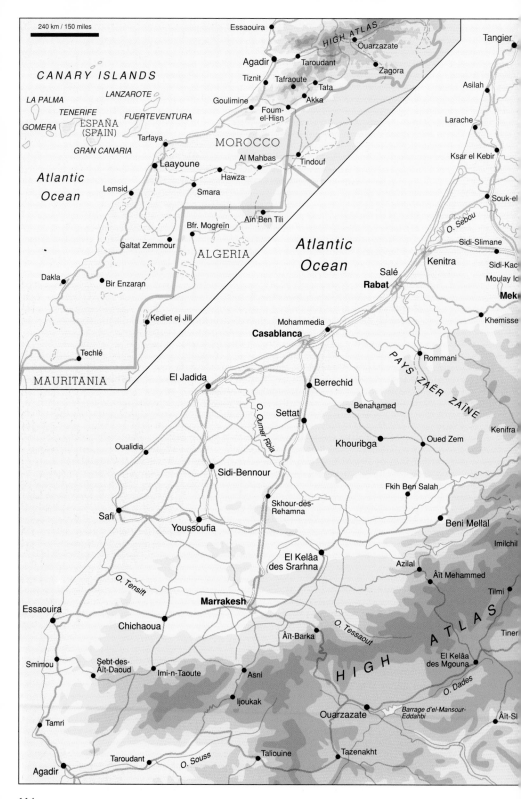

240 km / 150 miles

CANARY ISLANDS

LA PALMA
TENERIFE
GOMERA
ESPAÑA
(SPAIN)
GRAN CANARIA
LANZAROTE
FUERTEVENTURA

Atlantic
Ocean

Dakla
Bir Enzaran
Lemsid
Galtat Zemmour
Kediet ej Jill
Techlé

MAURITANIA

Tarfaya
Laayoune
Hawza
Smara
Bfr. Mogreïn
Aïn Ben Tili
ALGERIA

Essaouira
HIGH ATLAS
Agadir
Taroudant
Ouarzazate
Tiznit
Tafraoute
Zagora
Goulimine
Foum-
el-Hisn
Akka
Tata
MOROCCO
Al Mahbas
Tindouf

Tangier
Asilah
Larache
Ksar el Kebir
Souk-el
O. Sebou
Sidi-Slimane
Kenitra
Sidi-Kac
Moulay Io
Mek

Atlantic
Ocean

Salé
Rabat
Khemisse

Mohammedia
Casablanca

El Jadida
Berrechid
Settat
Benahamed
Khouribga
Oued Zem
Rommani
PAYS ZAËR ZAÏNE
Kenifra

Oualidia
Sidi-Bennour
O. Oumer Rbia
Skhour-des-
Rehamna
Fkih Ben Salah
Beni Mellal
Imilchil

Safi
Youssoufia
El Kelâa
des Srarhna
Azilal
Aït Mehammed
Tilmi

O. Tensift
Marrakesh
Essaouira
Chichaoua
Âït-Barka
O. Tessaout
HIGH ATLAS
Tiner
El Kelâa
des Mgouna
O. Dades

Smimou
Sebt-des-
Aït-Daoud
Imi-n-Taoute
Asni
Ijoukak
Ouarzazate
Barrage d'el-Mansour-
Eddahbi
Aït-Sl

Tamri
Taroudant
O. Souss
Taliouine
Tazenakht
Agadir

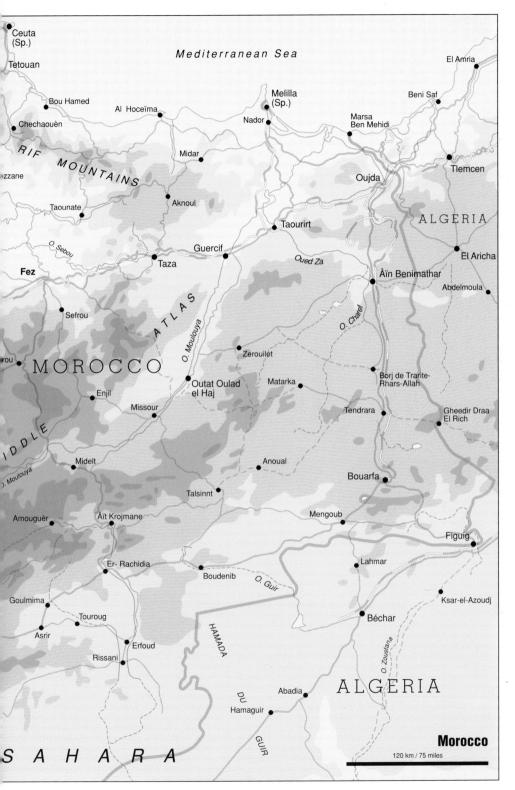

Ceuta
(Sp.)

Tetouan

Mediterranean Sea

El Amria

Bou Hamed

Al Hoceïma

Melilla
(Sp.)

Beni Saf

Chechaouèn

Nador

Marsa
Ben Mehidi

RIF MOUNTAINS

Midar

zzane

Oujda

Tlemcen

Taounate

Aknoul

Taourirt

ALGERIA

Guercif

Oued Za

El Aricha

Fez

Taza

Âïn Benimathar

Abdelmoula

ATLAS

Sefrou

O. Charef

O. Moulouya

rou

Zerouilet

MOROCCO

Outat Oulad
el Haj

Matarka

Borj de Trarite-
Rhars-Allah

Enjil

Missour

Tendrara

Gheedir Draa
El Rich

IDDLE

Anoual

Midelt

J. Moulouya

Bouarfa

Talsinnt

Amouguèr

Aït Krojmane

Mengoub

Figuig

Er- Rachidia

Lahmar

Boudenib

O. Guir

Ksar-el-Azoudj

Goulmima

Touroug

Béchar

O. Zousfana

Asrir

Erfoud

HAMADA

Rissani

DU

Abadia

ALGERIA

Hamaguir

GUIR

Morocco

S A H A R A

120 km / 75 miles

115

TANGIER

"That ragamuffin city" was Truman Capote's affectionate description of **Tangier** in 1949. It's a strange fact that the rich and famous, who could be up among the stars, never mind looking at them, often prefer the frisson of the gutter. In its heyday, Tangier was up there with Cannes on the international set's calendar. It was frequented by Tennesse Williams, Cecil Beaton, William Burroughs and Tallulah Bankhead. Brion Gysin, Paul Bowles and the Honourable David Herbert, younger son of the 16th Earl of Pembroke, made their homes in the town, and Barbara Hutton, fabulous hostess and Woolworth heiress, bought a house – Sidi Hosni – in the medina.

Tangier's tax-free status attracted world bankers and unscrupulous profiteers. In its squares, the Grand and Petit Soccos, whose very names reflect the town's hybrid character, anything could be found and purchased. It was truly an international zone.

Until, that is, six months after Morocco's independence in 1956, when Tangier's international status was revoked and the administrative infrastructure dismantled. It was typical that Tangier, a city of indulgence, should be granted these few months' grace. Nonetheless transition was a shock to a city whose prosperity was based purely on its free-port status. It underwent a sharp decline from which it only steadily recovered.

Vestiges of its former character survive. There are still retainers from the international era, including Paul Bowles, who have been joined by younger writers and artists. The famous bars it used to boast have nearly all closed, but there are others and Tangier remains a late-night city, much more so than Fez, Marrakesh or Rabat.

The homosexual mecca that it became in the 1950s still to some extent pertains. And around mid-afternoon Café de Paris in the Place de France continues to attract a sprinkling of genteel old men wearing white linen trousers and shaded spectacles.

Covetable asset: Tangier has excited a long history of foreign interest – hardly surprising, considering its strategic importance at the mouth of the Mediterranean. The Carthaginians established a trading port and gave it the name Tingis. Next came the Romans; followed by the Vandals, Byzantines and Visigoths (when Christianity gained a foothold). By 705 the Arabs had arrived.

Tangier prospered under the Berber dynasties until the 14th century, when internal order broke down and Morocco's north and northwest coast became infested with pirates. This prompted the Portuguese to intervene in North Africa, and, having already captured Ceuta, they eventually seized Tangier.

Mosques were destroyed and churches were built. But Berber resistance was persistent, and after two centuries, in 1661, the Portuguese finally passed Tangier to England as part of Catherine of Braganza's dowry on her marriage to Charles II.

England deemed Tangier a covetable asset. Even Samuel Pepys, who loathed

**Left**, all steps in the medina lead to the Kasbah. **Right**, Boulevard Pasteur. Tangier has expanded considerably since independence.

Tangier and described it as an "excrescence of the earth", reckoned it would be "the King's most important outpost in the world". But the British were unable to repel the constant Berber attacks and they withdrew in 1684, after deliberately destroying the principal improvements they had introduced.

From then on, Britain's prime objective in Tangier was to uphold the authority of the sultan and keep any single European power from colonising it. Britain had held Gibraltar since 1713 and it was vital to have a close, cooperative source of food and supplies for the tiny territory. Other powers were equally jealous of Tangier, and by the 19th century the town was overrun by diplomats.

Foreign control: Europe tightened its hold on the town by making various improvements: a lighthouse was built at Cap Spartel (by then the treacherous rocks, not pirates, were the main hazard along the Strait), and in 1872 a Sanitary Council was formed in response to outbreaks of plague. But European influence was also exerted in a less philan-

thropic way; special privileges granted to natives working in the legations and consulates included exemption from sultanic taxes and justice – advantages which Tangier's Jewish population found particularly valuable. Before long the consulates were selling "protection" for exorbitant sums of money.

By the signing of the Treaty of Fez in 1912, which established the French and Spanish protectorates, Tangier was already virtually an international zone. The Treaty of Algeciras put this on an official footing; and in 1923 another statute handed Tangier to the victors of World War I: France, Spain, Britain, Portugal, Sweden, Holland, Belgium and Italy. For the next 33 years Tangier was a centre for unregulated financial services, prostitution, smuggling and espionage.

Tangier today: Following independence, and the collapse of Tangier's spurious economy, the town was left to recover, somewhat neglected by the Moroccan government. Then closely huddled around its corniche, medina,

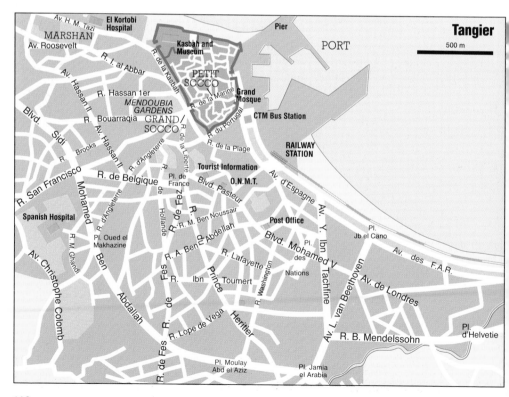

Boulevard Pasteur, Marshan and The Mountain (the latter two a couple of manicured hills populated by the villa-owning classes), it slowly expanded into a large town boasting suburbs and an industrial region to the south. Food and textile manufacturing apart, tourism is now its biggest industry.

Even in the 19th century, Europeans visited Tangier for its weather, and climate is supposed to be one of the town's enduring attractions. In the summer, it rarely becomes unbearable. It is warm well into October, even November, and in mid-winter, when it is often cold and wet (made worse by the complete absence of any heating in most houses, and some hotels), there are always some hours of sunshine during the day.

However, the *chergui*, an eastern wind, bearable in the town, seems always to be at its most violent on the beach. It guarantees a steady business for the long line of beach clubs, sometimes the only convenient respite.

Tangier's low cost of living and proximity to Europe accounts for its popularity as a package-tour destination – witness the rash of medium-priced hotels, nearby holiday complexes, and Club Mediterranée in Malabata over the bay. The town attracts many British (pleased to discover it is one of the few places in Morocco where English is widely spoken), some of whom are on day trips from the Costa del Sol and Gibraltar.

However, Tangier is primarily a summer resort for Moroccans. Any summer evening the streets between Boulevard Pasteur and the Grand Socco are solid with freshly-dressed families "*faisant le boulevard*". Many of them are visiting Fassis escaping the intense heat of summer in Fez.

Orientation: Boulevard Pasteur (also known as Avenue Pasteur) running up from Boulevard Mohammed V and the central post office, is Tangier's high street. To its right, on the ocean side, streets containing small hotels wind steeply down to the bay; behind it, away from the coast, are shops, restaurants, nightclubs and bars. The large banks and the **tourist office** (No 29) are on the

Boulevard, along with the well-stocked European bookshop **Librairie des Colonnes**, a lifeline to the expatriate writers living in Tangier.

The Boulevard, lined by the town's more upmarket cafés and *salons de thé*, runs down to a platform, complete with cannons, with a view over roofs and tree-tops to the harbour, and joins Rue du Mexique, the main shopping street, in the Place de France – an animated circus containing the famous Café de Paris. From here Rue de la Liberté curls past El Minzah Hotel and the Galerie Delacroix, while the Rue de Belgique leads to Rue d'Angleterre and the English church. Following either route you can find your way to the Grand Socco, a large sloping square overlooked by the coloured, tiled minaret of the Sidi Bouabid mosque, the first mosque to be built outside Tangier's old walls. Directly opposite the top of the square is the main, horseshoe-shaped gate into the medina.

Rue de la Liberté: The **El Minzah Hotel** is the best hotel in Tangier. It was originally the home of a wealthy American and later the Palmarium Casino, but its design reflects traditional Moorish architecture: a discreet entrance off the street precedes an elegant lobby leading to a tiled open courtyard overlooked by the hotel's upper storeys. An exit on the opposite side of the quadrangle leads to a terrace, small swimming-pool and gardens – a cool spot for afternoon tea.

The **Galerie Delacroix**, part of the **French Cultural Centre** directly opposite El Minzah, is a small gallery containing works by Eugène Delacroix, the French painter who toured North Africa in 1832, works by aspiring Moroccan artists and images of Morocco by foreign painters (entrance is free). The French Cultural Centre is extremely active (check noticeboard for forthcoming events), and the French Lycée, off Boulevard Pasteur, contains the **Salle Bastianelli**, a venue for good French theatre and international films. (Spanish culture is offered at Ramon Y Cajal, Lycée Polytecnico Espanol).

The old British consulate building, at

The Grand Socco.

120

52 Rue d'Angleterre (from Rue de la Liberté, cut up Rue Amérique du Sud), has been turned into the **Musée d'Art Contemporain de Tanger**, an attractive modern art gallery. Close by, is the **Anglican Church**, St Andrew's, built to serve the expatriates. It contains an exotic mix of styles. Islamic features – delicate stucco tracery, thin pencil pillars, Kufic script and keyhole arches – combine with English village-church trappings: pews and hassocks, organ and pulpit, copies of the Book of Common Prayer and, on the wall, the flower-arranging rota.

In the graveyard, the venerable Moustafa, the church's enthusiastic, and Muslim, caretaker, will point out Walter Harris's grave. Harris, famous correspondent for the London *Times* and devoted Arabist, wrote many revered tomes on the country, including the classic *Morocco That Was*. His tombstone reads: "He loved the Moorish people and was their friend". Other notable tombs include those of Caid Sir Harry McClean, an Englishman who was ap-

pointed to train the sultan's army in 1877, and Emily, Sherifa of Ouezzane, a 19th-century English governess who married the Sherif of Ouezzane. One of the latest of the colourful expatriates to be buried here is David Herbert (*see page 79*), who presided over the expatriate life of Tangier right up until his death in 1995.

Not far from the church, in Rue de Hollande, is the **Grand Hôtel Villa de France**, where Henri Matisse stayed and painted on two fruitful visits to Tangier in 1912 and 1913. Matisse came in pursuit of an "artistic paradise". Sadly, the dilapidated but still elegant hotel was closed in 1992 and its fate has yet to be decided. It is now in the hands of the Iraqi venture behind **Dawliz**, the entertainment complex just opposite the hotel (good cinema and restaurants, plus an attractive *salon de thé* decorated with Matisse prints and with the best view in Tangier from its terrace).

Downhill from the church is one of Tangier's main market areas. Small shops, not much larger than cupboards

Left, Café society on Boulevard Pasteur. **Right**, a street vendor in every doorway.

and selling everyday items such as *babouches*, the open-backed leather footwear (traditionally in yellow, white – for the mosque – or red), earthenware cooking pots and clothing, extend to the edge of the Grand Socco. Halfway along, through a gap flanked by Riffians crouched over bunches of mint or flat-leafed parsley and fattened hens, is one of Tangier's three food markets – spices, vegetables, cheeses, olives, and grisly butchers' stalls – fulfilling every touristic expectation of a Moroccan souk.

The **Grand Socco**, where Rue d'Angleterre and Rue de la Liberté converge, is a large irregular-shaped area, ringed by cafés, that used to be the main market square. It is still a gathering point, where women come to sell their bread. On the far side of the *socco* is the keyhole gate into the medina.

The medina: Rue es Siaghin, to the right as you pass through, leads to the Petit Socco; **Rue d'Italie**, a steep, flagged street with broad steps on either side, leads directly up to the **Kasbah**, passing on the way the old **British tel-**egraph office. During the international era all the European powers had their own communications systems, and it was through the telegraph and post offices that Moroccan nationalists gleaned news of what was happening in the French and Spanish zones. A turning into the medina off Rue d'Italie leads to the **Tomb of Ibn Battouta**, an erudite 14th-century Arab geographer and traveller born in Tangier. Pilgrims come to visit the tomb, which is dimly-lit and draped in a green cloth.

The other route, **Rue es Siaghin**, meaning silversmiths' street, cuts deep into the medina. It was to the right of here, in the *mellah*, that the Jews lived, the traditional dealers in silver. Some jewellers still trade, but most Jews have moved on. Also on the right is the long disused **Spanish mission**.

The **American Legation**, also off the beginning of **Rue es Siaghin**, in the Rue d'Amerique, is less easy to find (strike right just past No 77 on Rue es Siaghin), and consequently rarely visited by the droves of tourists heading for the Petit

The Sea Gate.

Socco (an easier approach is from Rue du Portugal, outside the medina's walls). Although the building has served the Americans since 1684, the sultan gave the Legation to the US in 1821. Morocco was the first country to recognise US sovereignty and this legation was the first American government property outside the United States.

Today the elaborately decorated 17th- and 18th-century interior is used for concerts and exhibitions. Its permanent collection contains some of the best paintings, lithographs and photographs in Morocco, including work by Eugène Delacroix and contemporary Moroccan painters such as R'bati and Hamri; one by Yves St Laurent; and various naive and impressionist works. Tours are conducted by a knowledgeable French woman (who also speaks English).

The **Petit Socco** at the end of Rue es Siaghin still retains some the low-life glamour that drew the likes of William Burroughs and Brion Gysin. It was here, on the terrace of the Café Central, that Burroughs gained inspiration for *The Naked Lunch*. The cafés here are very different from those on Boulevard Pasteur. Most are packed with men seemingly watching television, but, in fact, watching each other. Individuals constantly sidle in and out to whisper in an ear or beckon. This is where "business" is done. Sit inside one of the cafés for long enough and you are bound to be hustled to buy hashish and be told of "upstairs rooms".

From the Petit Socco, **Rue des Cheratins** and **Rue Ben Raisouli**, festooned with kaftans, handbags and toy camels, meander up towards the Kasbah, which used to comprise the sultanic palace (now a museum), administrative quarter and prison. Within its walls are some of the most sought-after properties in Tangier. Barbara Hutton had a house here (**Sidi Hosn**i, opposite the café with the psychedelic wall painting) and so did Richard Hughes, author of *A High Wind in Jamaica*. The palace itself was occupied as recently as 1912 by the abdicate Sultan Moulay Hafid, though by all accounts his stay was uncomfortable.

Tangier's bay, often prone to east winds.

Like most Moroccan museums, the **Palace Museum**, on the west side of the *mechouar* (courtyard), is a feast for the eyes – the original Arabesques and *zellige* providing a stylish context for the artefacts. But typically, too, it is short on relevant literature. Exhibits, arranged in rooms lining the sides of two courtyards, include carpets, ceramics from Fez and Meknes, costumes, musical instruments, household implements and jewellery. The kitchen quarters house an **archaeological museum** containing a mosaic from Volubilis.

North of the *mechouar*, the **Rue Riad Sultan** curls left round the ocean side of the Kasbah to pass a door leading to an upstairs café called **Le Détroit**. Music, sometimes traditional, often a Moroccan rendering of a Western hit, either tempts or repels. This used to be the most exclusive restaurant in Tangier, where owner and writer Brion Gysin entertained an elite circle of friends. Now custom is reduced to package groups in the afternoons; it affords exciting views, though, with a clear sight of **York House**, the machiolated residence of the English governors in the 17th century and now a private house belonging to the designer Yves Vidal.

A short walk further west along **Rue Assad ibn Farrat** and **Rue Mohammed Tazi**, or reached by taking a number 1 or number 11 bus, is the **Forbes Museum of Military Miniatures** in **Palais Mendoub**, the Tangier home of American billionaire, publisher and Arabist, the late Malcolm Forbes. It was here that Forbes held his much-publicised 70th birthday bash in 1989. The party cost $2 million and the entertainment included 600 drummers, acrobats and belly dancers and 300 Berber horsemen. Guests included Henry Kissinger, a Getty or two, and Elizabeth Taylor, who also honeymooned here with her eighth husband, Larry Fortensky.

The house is the large white villa smothered in bougainvillea. There is no admission charge and to visit is like entering a private home. Forbes's own tastes are still much in evidence. Exhibits – war memorabilia, depictions of a

The courtyard of the Palace Museum.

soldier's life, war posters and photographs, as well as huge models of famous battles, many relating to Moroccan history – are well worth seeing.

Turn left as you leave the Forbes Museum and left again after the hospital and you will discover **Hafa**, a terraced cliff-top café, peaceful and secluded, with views over the Straits and fragrant with the scent of hashish.

Life after dark: Perhaps more than any other Moroccan town or city, Tangier has the most concentrated nightlife and it certainly keeps the latest hours; many restaurants and clubs don't open until 9 p.m. and don't close until 4 a.m. It was once famous for its bars: in particular the Safari, Les Liaisons and The Parade, none of which remain.

A bar's success depended upon the personality of its owners and in the late 1940s and early 1950s Tangier attracted its fair share of charismatic hosts and hostesses. **Dean's bar**, at one time more a fashionable club than a bar, is still here in **Rue Amerique du Sud**, but the eponymous Dean, who began his career

The beaches to the east of Tangier are the best.

as the lover of a rich and titled English gentleman, has long gone and nobody who's anybody goes here any more.

The **Koutoubia Palace** and the **Morocco Palace**, also discothèques, offer kitsch Moroccan decor, belly-dancing and girls. For lowlife, **Churchill's** in **Rue Moutanabi** still attracts a certain *demi-monde*, but now the arty and the crafty tend to go to the smart, new establishments that have opened, such as **Passarella's** on the beach.

The **English Pub**, 4 Rue Sorolla (with a restrictive door policy), is popular, as are **The Wine Bar** in Rue Khalil Metran and the **Caid's Bar** in El Minzah Hotel. For inexpensive drinking in a convivial, if overridingly gay, atmosphere, try the **Tanger Inn** in El Muniria Hotel (writing retreat of William Burroughs), Rue Magellan. Also worth trying is **Petanca**, a Spanish bar, next door to the Tanger Inn (it charges a small admission but provides *tapas*).

There are also some excellent restaurants: **Restaurant Hammadi** at the foot of Rue d'Italie is the best known Moroc-

can restaurant in Tangier, but the one preferred by most *Tanjaouis* is the Italian **San Remo** on Rue Murillo. Expatriates frequent **The Marquis** on Rue Tolstoy, where prices match elegance; or, famous in the international era, **Guitta's** in Place de Kuwait, with its huge garden and garrulous hostess. **Coeur de Tanger** on Boulevard Pasteur and Osso Bucco, on Rue Moulay Abdellah, are other options.

The beach bars: Although rentals are renewed at the start of each season, the beach bars only occasionally change hands and each bar has developed its own character. Some are 100 percent gay (**Miami Beach** and **Macumbu**, for instance); the **Yacht Club** (belonging to the port Yacht Club) is private; **BBC Emma's Bar** is popular with Europeans, expatriate or not; the **Chellah Beach Bar** and the **Golden Beach** are expensive (they cater mainly to residents from the Chellah and Solazur hotels) and the **Costa del Norte** is notorious for its prostitutes and fights. Several cuts above all these is **Passerella's**, which opened in 1995 and includes a pool.

During the day they provide changing facilities, sunbeds and a place to buy refreshments (all for around 30 dirhams a day) and many of them are open until the early hours of the morning, with **Trés Caravelas** and **Sun Beach** the liveliest and Passerella's the most sophisticated.

Sea air: To the west of Tangier, **Cap Spartel** offers alternative beaches to Tangier's well-populated sands. The most interesting route there leaves Tangier on the S701 Mountain road, passing Tangier's most exclusive properties, including houses belonging to the Royal family and a residence of the King of Saudi Arabia. The Mountain itself is, as Joe Orton observed, "a replica of a Surrey backwater...twisty lanes, foxgloves, large pink rambling roses, tennis courts and gardens watered by sprinklers".

Just off the road at the bottom of the the Mountain is the **People's Dispensary for Sick Animals Rest Home**, in fact a pets' cemetery. The road then loops the headland, passing the Cap Spartel lighthouse, erected by foreign diplomats in the 1870s, and the **Caves of Hercules**, rock chambers inhabited in prehistoric times and in the international era used as a venue for parties, including one hosted by Cecil Beaton, who served sea-cooled champagne and hashish. En route, are several s coves (one of the best is the first one you come to as you turn the corner away from the *cap* itself.

A little further on, you pass the ancient Roman ruins of **Cotta**, dating from the second and third centuries, which include a small temple and a bath-house. A turning left before the road to Rabat leads back to Tangier via the town's prison and the Coca-Cola factory. Continuing down the coast, a magnificent beach stretches 30 miles (45 km) to the fortified town of Asilah (see *page 145).*

Alternatively, east of Tangier, there are **Cap Malabata** (also with a lighthouse), now an upper-middle class residential area, and, along the coast to the east, a string of good beaches, beginning with **Plage des Amiraux**, and then **Ksar es Seghir**, with its tiny jetty and good fish restaurant called Lachari. The quietest and most idyllic beach along this stretch is **Dalia**.

Left, inevitably many prefer the hotel pool. **Right**, a more artful display of flesh.

THE RIF

"A naked, steep, savage-looking wall" was how the German explorer Gerhald Rohlfs described Morocco's **Rif** in the middle of the 19th century. The reputation of its people, too, is for ferocity. Blood revenge used to be a serious cause of population depletion and possibly deforestation, since trees and property as well as life were destroyed in a feud. It was said that a male Riffian who had not taken a life before he was married was not yet considered a man.

The Rif mountains rise sharply from the Mediterranean, where a craggy coast is punctuated by sandy coves. East of Tangier their foothills begin close to **Tetouan**. Here, contrasting strongly with the low hills and gentle colours of the Tangier hinterland, the landscape is impressively rugged.

Soaring cedars: To the immediate east trees begin to cloak the limestone peaks and as you climb into the central section of the Rif, dominated by the often snow-capped **Mount Tidiguin** (on which, myth has it, the Ark rested), squat holm-oaks and cork oaks give way to soaring cedar forests and the kif plantations of Ketama.

The further east you travel, the redder the hue of the mountain range becomes, a change that strikes the traveller on the road to **Al Hoceima** where the terrain becomes denuded and barren. From Al Hoceima to **Oujda** on the Algerian border, south of a fertile coastal plain, the land is desolate, crossed by cracked riverbeds.

More inviting, on the Rif coast directly below the range, are some of the finest sands in Morocco, a fact which has led to an explosion of large hotels and imitation "Club Med"-style holiday villages, fed by the international airport of Tangier and by the increasing custom of well-off Moroccans from Fez and elsewhere who come to escape the summer heat inland.

But many of these resorts are half-empty and it is still possible to find unspoilt secluded sands between the pockets of development. Some of the best fish restaurants in Morocco are along this shore (Moroccan waters are among the best stocked in the world). The "resorts" include **Restinga M'diq, Cabo Negro** (which also has an impressive new golf course), **Martil** and **Amsa**.

For a spectacular view of the coastline and mountains, it is possible to fly by small plane from the old airport, established by the Spanish just outside **Tetouan** (toward Ceuta), to the tiny but modern airport in **Al Hoceima** for around 200 dirhams. Trips to **Gibraltar** by catamaran from the port in M'diq run several times a week.

The people: The area has for centuries been influenced by Spain, as an Andalusian style of architecture in the towns, a common fluency in Spanish and foods such as paella, tortilla and *tapas* all testify. Many of the Andalusian Muslims who fled Spain in the 15th and 16th centuries settled here; and from 1912 until 1956 the Rif, plus the short stretch of Atlantic coast to just north of

Larache but excluding the international zone of Tangier, formed the bulk of the zone governed by the Spanish – what, in fact, in the scramble for Moroccan territory, France had wisely left them.

Until this time, the Riffians had existed outside authority in what was then known as *bled es siba* (land of lawlessness), those parts of Morocco where the inhabitants refused to pay taxes to the sultan or accept his garrisons. (Strictly speaking, the term Riffian should be applied only to the tribes of the middle Rif around Ketama; the J'bala, Arabic rather than Berber-speaking tribes, inhabit the extreme western Rif close to Tetouan. But the general term Riffian is usually used to refer to the inhabitants of the whole of the mountainous area in the north.)

The Spanish found the Rif tribes to be a force to be reckoned with. The Rif Rebellion of 1926, led by Abd el Krim and finally quashed by the Spanish but not without help from France, was the precedent for nationalist demands in the rest of Morocco. And since independence the Riffians, disappointed by what has been accomplished for them, and still with some of the *bled es siba* attitude they have been famous for, have been irksome to the Moroccan government. In December 1958 a rebellion stirred near Al Hoceima, which the then Crown Prince Moulay Hassan was sent to quell.

Despite illegal kif plantations (*see page 134*), illegal smuggling of goods from the tax-free ports in the Spanish enclaves of Melilla and Ceuta, the creation of a new steel plant at Nador, and a developing tourist industry, the area remains very poor. Its inhabitants still complain of economic deprivation and neglect by central government.

Heading east: By Moroccan standards, the P38 from Tangier to Tetouan is a busy stretch of road. As part of the main thoroughfare from the densely populated northwest of Morocco to the Spanish enclave of Ceuta, it is used by people heading to buy the cheap electrical goods and garments smuggled out of Ceuta to Tetouan. Consequently it is lined by

Left, elaborately tiled Tetouan townhouse. **Right,** hunting – a popular sport.

Riffians intent on selling the motorists their produce too.

J'bala women dressed in typical pom-pom sombreros, red and white striped *ftouh* and what can only be described as bathtowels (often rigged into a papoose to contain a baby) hold covered dishes of crumbling white cheese (either salted or unsalted) or honey. Men tout amethysts and pottery, and small boys pinenuts, walnuts or whatever else can be harvested for sale.

The flying customs officers and police, who also populate the lay-bys and verges, are looking for motorists' less innocuous purchases, but it is on the other side of Tetouan and Chaouen, towards the kif-growing areas of Ketama, that the road-blocks and customs checks become irksome.

Tetouan, flanked on all sides by ragged limestone mountains whose lower reaches are forested, is a surprising sight worthy of its name – meaning in Berber "open your eyes". In autumn it is prone to rain and low cloud, and in the winter to snow. It isn't until you arrive that you appreciate the town's locations and realise how high the road has climbed.

Tetouan's past importance as the capital of the Spanish zone, where the Spanish High Commisioner lived, is immediately apparent in its civic architecture. Imposing balconies beneath tall windows and curlicued grille-work are reminiscent of those in Seville. **Place Hassan II** (where a new royal palace has been built on the site of the old Caliphate palace), with its sweep of old market buildings, looks distinctly Andalusian. But more interesting is some of the older domestic architecture. The large, old mansions at the lower end of the *mellah* at the foot of **Rue Luneta** are in a state of dilapidation but even so the intricate, enamelled tiling and fancy wrought-iron work decorating their exteriors demonstrate a difference between Spanish and Moroccan styles of building; on Moroccan houses adornment is all internal.

Tetouan was a busy trading centre even before the Spanish protectorate added to its importance. At the begin-

Tetouan's bus station: a Moroccan experience.

KIF GROWING IN THE RIF

The road from Chaouen to Ketama is one of impressive beauty. It switches back and forth through the rugged heights of the Rif. As it approaches Ketama, it is flanked by cedar and evergreen-oak woodlands and the landscape feels more like the Black Forest than Morocco.

None of the inhabitants of these parts, though, believe for one moment that visitors are there to appreciate the scenery. From out of swirling patches of low cloud and from behind rocky outcrops youths loom brandishing lumps of cannabis resin pulled from their *djellabahs*, or miming a rolling movement with their fingers (rolling a joint) and gesticulating at all cars to stop. The rule is, don't.

Foreign embassies warn against travelling along this route. Most Moroccans, too, are wary. Horror stories propagate as abundantly as the plant itself. Everybody knows somebody whose vehicle was halted by a fallen tree trunk, who was then hauled out and forced, some say at knifepoint, to buy hashish. The nightmare never ends there. A few miles up the road, the story goes, the innocent traveller is stopped by the police – who are in the drug hustlers' pay – and the hashish is discovered.

The cultivation, sale, use and transport of hashish (or kif as it is called before it is processed) is illegal. Nevertheless, it is smoked openly throughout Morocco, often in upstairs rooms above cafés and bars, and the plantations on the hill terraces around Ketama are clearly visible from the road: a dense, head-high crop with spear-shaped leaves.

The Koran, which prohibits alcohol, is ambivalent about kif. Wine is taboo because it is an intoxicant; kif, some say, was not banned by the Prophet precisely because it is not an intoxicant but a suppressant.

In Morocco, kif was grown for many years for local purposes, but it was in the 1960s that the expertise for turning it into a resin (hashish), a much stronger and more concentrated product easier to transport, was introduced, reputedly by the French. It was no coincidence that Morocco quickly became a draw on the hippie trail. Suddenly, the poor Riffian farmers, who until then eked out a subsistence living, had the means to become rich. Not rich by Western standards, of course – that was the privilege of the trafficker – but rich enough to afford new divans and a TV set.

The process for turning the kif seeds into hashish is simple: they are sieved, and then pushed through a muslin filter. The fine brown powder that emerges is pressed into bars. This is hashish resin. The more the powder is sifted, the smoother the end-product. Kif, on the other hand, is the cut and dried leaves of the plant. This is smoked in a long-stemmed kif pipe, or *sebsi*, containing a clay filter, and the effect is far milder.

These days it's the older generation who tend to use kif; the younger generation prefer the effects of hashish. Until recently, it was common for the wealthier households, desiring a convivial atmosphere, to lace the family tea with an expensive hashish preparation called *gaouza*. And *majoun*, jam with a kick, is traditionally home prepared (beware the cheap, street-touted variety).

The price of the resin quickly escalates the further one travels from Ketama, a town with more Mercedes cars than buildings. There, anyone stopping is assumed to be on "business". A few inches of resin in Ketama will cost as little as 10 dirhams. By the time it reaches Tangier the price will be six or seven times that.

The Rif is ideally situated for export purposes. The quiet fishing villages east of Tangier – such as Dalia and Oued Dalian – are fronts for more lucrative business than sardine-fishing. From these it is a short sea-crossing to Spain and Gibraltar, the latter a key base in the trans-Mediterranean drugs trade. The international airport of Tangier and the port of Casablanca are also within a few hours' drive.

In line with international pressure, the Moroccan government claims to be phasing out the cultivation of kif. This is partly why tourists caught dabbling in hashish smuggling are dealt with harshly: it is a way of demonstrating an intention to clamp down. In reality, the region is one neglected by the government, and the industry has become economically indispensable; the smuggling behind the café façades of Ketama continues unabated. ∎

ning of the 16th century, the Jews and Muslims who arrived here from Spain practised an old maritime profession, piracy. They made slaves of passengers and crews then extracted fabulous sums of ransom. Ships were attacked indiscriminately, but those of Spain particularly suffered, and Philip II closed down Tetouan's port on the river Martil. Later, under Moulay Ismail the town's economy prospered again.

Nowadays Tetouan strikes the visitor as a busy, bustling town, its energetic character stemming perhaps from its history as the focus of political resistance in the Rif. It was here, in 1954, that a rally of 30,000 tribesmen protested about the deposition of Sultan Mohammed V. In more recent years it has seen bread riots, demonstrations against the high prices of basic foodstuffs. Even the café life is not as totally idle as elsewhere. During the afternoon and early evening its numerous cafés resound to the slap of draughts being played.

Shopping is another cause of activity. Visiting Moroccans interested in buying cheap smuggled electrical goods and inexpensive clothing head for the **Souk Nador** in the west of the town, its entrance marked by a stall selling huge televison sets. (Like many other occupations in the Rif, this trade is illegal but tolerated by the state.)

The souks within the medina, entered through the **Bab el Rouah** on Place Hassan II, are more geared towards tourists – who are numerous, since Tetouan is a common first stop for those expelled by the Algeciras and Malaga ferries at Ceuta – but the **Souk el Houts** (literally "fish market") behind the Spanish Consulate is local in character.

Turning right at this souk leads to the **Bab Oqla** and an excellent **Museum of Moroccan Arts** containing examples of Riffian and J'bala traditonal crafts. In the **Place el Jala** there is an **archaeological museum** displaying Moroccan artefacts from the Roman and Phoenician periods.

Picturesque town: Chaouen, south of Tetouan, stacked into the hills, ranks among the world's prettiest higgledy-

Opposite, a kif plantation. Below, cloud lies low in autumn and winter.

piggledy, whitewashed, cobbled places. It has the sort of houses that look as though they have been sat upon: their walls bulge and the tiny windows look squashed. The town is startlingly clean; contours, worn smooth, are whitewashed or painted blue and the effect is not unlike that of a penguin pool at a zoo.

Women wear the white, rather than black, *haik* (unless they are in mourning when the reverse is true); in winter the town is visited by snow. Colour comes from the trellises of violet clematis, the red tiled roofs and the tiled lintels around the doors.

Chaouen was founded in 1471 by Moulay el ben Rashid as a base against Christians, though the kasbah was built in the 17th century by Moulay Ismail. The town was virtually closed to Christians until 1920 when the Spanish finally managed to conquer the town. When they did, they discovered a community of Jews, descended from the first refugee settlers, speaking 10th-century Castilian, a language extinct in Spain for over 400 years, and leather craftsmen working in tanned and decorated leather as their ancestors had done in 12th-century Cordoba.

The P28 leading to the town arrives just below the old walls. By climbing up through the market place you reach a brown gate called **Bab el Ain**, overhung by one of the town's typical wrought-iron lanterns. This leads to the main square. The cobbled **Plaza Uta el Hamman**, shaded by trees, strung with lights and lined by bowed cafés, is an excellent place to sit, appreciate the light and inhale the mountain air (not to be confused with the scent of kif drifting from the cafés' upper storeys).

It was here, until 1937, when the practice was outlawed by the Spanish, that boy homosexuals were auctioned. The Riffian tribes were staunchly anti-homosexual – Abd el Krim, leader of the Rif Rebellion, made homosexuality illegal – but the J'bala, Gomara and Sehhadja tribes, who populated this area in the western Rif, didn't share their aversion and homosexual relations between young men was common.

Left, a surfeit of white-wash. **Right**, Chaouen's steep and winding streets.

In glowing sandstone on the opposite side of the square, in vivid contrast to the tiled-roofed, sugar-cube housing, is the ruined **kasbah** with its quiet gardens. It can be visited for a few dirhams. To the right of this are the cells where Abd el Krim was eventually imprisoned in 1926.

By following the main throughfare to the back of the town, through the **Place du Makhzen** and its cluster of pottery and gemstone stalls, past the succession of tiny shops opening directly on to the steep, cobbled street, you reach the point under the mountains where a waterfall hits the river. Here women wash clothes and sheep's wool. A new car park and tourist facilities are about to do their worst, something the town has generally managed to avoid happening until now, despite having more than its quota of day-trippers from Tangier and the northern resorts.

The Berbers of this region are renowned for their reverence of *marabouts* and it is an area with many religious associations. Chaouen is considered a holy city, as is **Ouezzane**, reached along the P28 travelling southwest of Chaouen, on the boundary between the old *bled el makhzen* and the *bled es siba*. It was chosen by Moulay Abdullah, a descendant of Idriss II, to found the Taibia brotherhood in 1727.

The *zaouia*, or centre, prospered. Its *shereef*, who lived in a sanctuary separated from the town, was – and still is – considered one of the holiest men in the land. While the authority of the sultans didn't extend to the *bled es siba*, that of the shereef of Ouezzane did. Pilgrims from all over Morocco would come for his blessing and criminals sought immunity here.

The sanctuary, surrounded by gardens, was supposed to represent the Islamic paradise. In reality, it had at least one foot in hell. Wine, spirits and kif were sold along its approach and the shereefian family had its share of mortal troubles, caused by congenital insanity.

Sidi Mohammed, shereef in the middle of the 19th century, had a psychopath and a kif-addict among his sons. And

A _moussem_ in Ouezzane.

he, at the least, was eccentric. Admiring all things European, he decided to marry an English governess called Emily Keene. The marriage was not a success, foundering on Sidi Mohammed's drinking and womanising. Nevertheless the Englishwoman was calculating enough to extract a large payment from him which lasted the rest of her life.

The *zaouia*, with its distinctive octagonal minaret, attracts people today. The shereef of Ouezzane is still a person of moral influence consulted on matters of religious philosophy. Pilgrims are particularly visible in the spring when they arrive for the annual *moussem*.

In character, the town is rather like Chaouen, though more sprawling its white houses climbing up the mountain Bou Hellol. Again, there is a strong Andalusian flavour. The larger houses are faced by decorative tiling and fronted by wrought-iron balconies.

Switchback ride: Ouezzane, some would argue, does not really fall in the Rif at all. Below it stretches a fertile plain and the heavily-populated triangle of Souk el Arba, Rabat and Meknes. It formed part of the French zone during the protectorates and it was one of the places where French troops rallied in order to help Spain defeat the Rif Rebellion. The Rif proper continues along the P39 to Ketama.

This journey along the spine of the range passes through the most spectacular scenery in the region. Each switchback reveals a new panorama or unexpected scene, such as a whole village celebrating a wedding on an otherwise deserted mountainside, bride and bridegroom carried shoulder high. Driving is slow, but the road is wide, and outside of winter the route is safe enough.

Vegetation is a strange mixture of holm-oak, cork-oak pine, gorse and cactus. **Ketama** is heralded by cedar and kif plantations and a large number of Berbers, looking like Franciscan monks in hooded brown *djellabas*, attempting to persuade drivers to stop and buy chunks of hashish. The town has little to recommend it apart from its location, though the Tourist Office plugs

The hills above Chaouen.

its virtues as a boar-hunting and [doubtful] skiing centre.

East beyond Ketama, trees become fewer, and the red sandstone of the mountain a more violent colour. **Targuist**, the last stronghold of Abd el Krim and from where the Rifians' ammunition was distributed on muleback, is a gritty, workaday place situated on a small plain. Its streets are laid out in grid fashion. Perhaps for this reason it has the feel of a small North American steel town, though its importance is administrative rather than industrial.

Al Hoceima to the north, on the other hand, reached by taking the P39a from Ait Yussef ou Ali (birthplace of the Abd el Krim brothers), is a seaside resort popular with Moroccan tourists, though it's seen more exciting visitors in its time. It was at Al Hoceima that King Hassan, then crown prince, emulating Spanish tactics in the capture of Abd el Krim, landed with his troops in smuggling boats and a rented British-owned ferry, managing to surprise and defeat the small-scale Rif rebellion of 1959.

The town, on the west side of a large crescent-shaped bay, has a noticeably large number of small hotels. A much larger hotel complex, with the full-range of amenities, appears to take up most of the beach and gives the impression of owning it; in fact, it is perfectly possible for people not staying at the hotel to bathe here.

For a real bargain, and character, **Hotel Florido**, unmistakable in **Place du Rif**, offers a double room for around 60 dirhams. It is a round, tiered, 1930s building whose rooms have elegant, French-windows; the ground floor is a popular café, but the haze of tobacco-smoke and general animation make it feel more like a saloon. Hotel Florido would not be out of place in a spaghetti Western.

To the Border: From Al Hoceima to Nador, the landscape changes from the fertile Nekor River plain to virtual desert just south of the Spanish enclave of **Melilla**. **Nador**, below Melilla, is known particularly for its steel plant, an industrial scheme, promised in the wake of

Arcadian idyll.

independence, which took a long time to materialise. The government planned to develop what was then just a small village into a regional capital. Consequently many poor mountain Berbers descended on Nador, expecting economic prosperity.

It is also a university town which, along with Oujda, draws all students from the eastern Rif (in the west they go to Tetouan), but it can't be the most stimulating environment for the young. Along with Tetouan and Marrakesh (also a university town), Nador experienced bead riots in 1984.

Beyond this is a cultivated plain, watered by the **River Moulouya**. This river, whose Barrage Mohammed V has greatly aided irrigation, marked the boundary between the French and Spanish protectorates. Historically, it has helped form a barrier against Algeria. However, the Beni Merin tribe, from which sprang the Merenid dynasty, entered Morocco at this point by taking control of the river valley, then cutting a route through the Taza Gap. The leader of the tribe, Abou Yahya, captured Fez in 1248.

Borders in the Maghreb are determined by politics rather than cultural differences, and an Algerian influence is instantly felt in **Oujda**. The language is similar to Algerian Arabic and many women have adopted an Algerian style of dress (the veils of Algerian women are tiny, covering only the nose and mouth, not extending to the chin and neck as they do in Morocco – which seems surprising in view of Algeria's conservative reputation. The music of Oujda, too, is more in tune with Algeria. The type known as Andalusian, which forms the classical music of Northern Morocco – Tangier, Tetouan, Fez – evolved from that of Seville and Cordoba. The Andalusian music of Oujda and Algeria, on the other hand, has its origins in Granada and is more structured in style. Modern *rai* music, now fashionable in Europe as well as the Maghreb, developed in the brothels of the border towns of Oujda and Algeria's Oran.

The beaches are excellent.

Owing to its strategic importance, Oujda has always been fought over. Since its founding in 994, it has passed through many hands: the Almoravides, the Almohads, the Merinids, the Saadians, the Alaouites, not to mention the Turks whose empire didn't penetrate much further west than this. It was also the first town to be threatened by the French, who were hovering on the Algerian border long before their protectorate was agreed in 1912.

Apart from the hardcore rucksack contingent and French Jeep drivers planning to plough on to Algeria, comparatively few Western tourists venture as far as Oujda, for despite its turbulent history there is little to see. Most of the bustle is caused by visiting Algerians who holiday on the coast at **Saidia**, just to the north.

Sidi Yahya, however, four miles (six km) off a built-up suburban road southeast, is a popular excursion for Moroccans and Algerians. The body of Sidi Yahya, reputed to have been John the Baptist, is said to be buried here, and Jewish, Muslim and Christian pilgrims gather. It is a strange place, associated with hermits and steeped in religious rites. Usually it is packed with visitors.

Pieces of coloured cloth are hung in the trees; in the domed tombs animal sacrifices are made, and women seeking fertility wash in the streams. There is also a grotto called the **Ghar el Houriyat**, or Cave of Houris, the handmaidens of Paradise.

Since 1988, political tensions between Algeria and Morocco have fluctuated. After easing somewhat in the late 1980s (plans for a Union du Grand Maghreb were even muted), tensions resumed in the 1990s when fundamentalist violence gripped Algeria. The continuing stalemate in the Western Sahara (*see page 64*) exacerbates the difficult relations between the two countries. Travel across the border to the picturesque town of **Tlemcen** to see the Almoravide mosque, or to **Mansoura** for the Merenid ruins is out of the question while Algeria's civil war continues, particularly as Western tourists and expatriates have been targets for terrorist attacks.

Natural assets: The road from Nador to Oujda skirts the **Beni Snassen** mountains. If the Rif hasn't produced an aversion to any landscape much above sealevel, an agreeable detour might be to visit the richly cultivated **Zezgel gorges** via **Taforalt**, a small village with a Wednesday market, and the **Grotte du Chameau**, a cave which, as its name suggests, contains a stalactite shaped like a camel and is reputed to cure sterility.

Routes through the Rif: There are three main passages through the Rif. The **P26** from Ouezzane skirts the grander peaks, and for those wanting only an impression of the range, with less tricky mountain driving, this is the best route to Fez; it offers plenty of impressive scenery along the way.

An even more spectacular route, however, is the **S302** from **Ketama**. This is known as the **Route de l'Unité**, which was built along the old caravan passage to Fez by voluntary national effort after independence. Initiated by Mehdi ben Barka, a prominent figure in the nationalist left before his radical, verging on republican, views prompted his exile and later disappearance in Paris, it was intended to link the French and Spanish zones. Like "Operation Ploughing", a scheme to cultivate over 300,000 wasted acres (120,000 hectares), it was as much a public relations exercise as useful development of the country.

Nevertheless, begun in 1957 when the country was still enjoying the euphoria of freedom, this was the first road to be built from north to south in the Rif – the Spanish never having been very enterprising in the development of their zone. The other main throughfare through the mountains is the equally beautiful **S312** off the P39 at **Talamagait**. Both are punctuated by villages containing petrol stations.

The advantage of the latter route is that it leads to **Taza**, an important town strategically and the capital of Morocco at the beginning of the Almohad, Merenid and Alaouite dynasties – hence its impressive fortifications. It was through Taza that Moulay Idriss, founder of the first orthodox Muslim dynasty, came in the 8th century.

THE NORTHWEST COAST

The triangle of land delineated by the main roads connecting **Souk el Arba du Rharb**, **Fez** and **Rabat/Casablanca** is the most densely populated in Morocco. The P2 from Tangier, therefore, is one of the busiest stretches of highway. It links the rest of Morocco, and indeed Africa, to the point of closest contact with Europe.

Along here the migrant workers ferry. Roadside stalls, selling anything from melons to pottery, are many; and "meat-sandwich" cafés, all looking identical, their smoking braziers casting a veritable cloud over the road, abound – Moroccans being frequent stoppers and constant eaters on any journey.

The coast along this Atlantic stretch has been heavily influenced by Spain and Portugal. In the 15th and 16th centuries the Moroccan ports were regularly besieged, and one by one they fell to either Spanish or Portuguese forces. The area, along with Tangier, Ceuta, Tetouan and Rabat, also formed part of what was known in the 17th century as the Barbary Coast, plagued by corsairs, many of whom, contrary to popular belief, were not Muslim pirates at all, but European.

Asilah, lying 30 miles (46 km) south of Tangier, and **Larache** (54 miles/87 km distant) are most reminiscent of Portugal and Spain, having been colonised by both intermittently until 1691 and 1689 respectively. These early influences were compounded by the Treaty of Fez in 1912, when both towns fell under the Spanish protectorate. They contain large populations of Spanish origin and Spanish rather than French is the second language. Architecture and food also reflect a Spanish heritage.

Asilah, a favourite excursion from Tangier, is a model town. Citrus trees and good, informal fish restaurants, with outdoor tables sporting check tablecloths, line its streets, and its medina looks positively vacuumed, such is the conspicuously high level of hygiene. Like Essaouira, in the south, it draws artists and many of the white houses of its medina are enlivened by brightly-painted murals.

At the end of July an annual music festival attracts popular, classical, jazz and folk performers from all over the world, and any time of the year its cafés are good places to experience live Moroccan music – usually in the late afternoons.

Asilah's walls, punctuated by vantage points with views of the excellent beach and the harbour (where they are now building a marina), were originally built by the Portuguese. The **Palace**, where the music festival is held, is more recent. It was built in 1909 by **Shereef Ahmed el Raisuni**, a self-styled leader credited with considerable *baraka* by the J'bala tribesmen in the hills around Tangier. He achieved fame through a series of kidnappings, most notably of the London *Times* journalist Walter Harris, who, though imprisoned with a headless corpse, was forgiving enough to befriend his captor and later invite him to his villa in Tangier.

El Raisuni's relationship with the

Preceding pages: wall painting in Asilah. Left, villa-fringed Atlantic coast near Rabat. Right, fishermen inspect their catch.

Spanish protectors was more equivocal, and out of fear rather than admiration they made him governor of the region. Revelling in his new-found grandeur, he established his palace in Asilah. The peasants who were forced to build it called the palace "the House of Tears", alluding to the hardship of their labours. Being a man of spirit, however, Raisuni was not content to languish in splendour and was soon in revolt again. He fought the Spanish sporadically for a further eight years. An Englishwoman called Rosita Forbes visited Raisuni in 1924 and recorded his biography, a classic work on Morocco.

Larache, on the mouth of the Oued Loukos, is more Spanish than Portuguese in character. **Stork's Castle**, the fortification overlooking the bay, was built by its 17th-century Spanish masters. The **Place de la Liberation** (previously Plaza de España), the main circus, was built during the time of the protectorate, when Larache served as the chief port for the Spanish zone. Hotels, bars and restaurants – many serving excellent fish – all reflect the Spanish influence, though the blue and white paintwork is badly peeling and the stucco embellishments a little knocked about. Larache's decayed elegance combines with a laid-back charm.

The best view of the town is from its beach on the far side of the **Oued Loukos**, approached by a circuitous route following the turning off to Lixus, a kilometre or so to the north of the town, or after crossing the estuary by boat. From here, there is a pretty view of the town: a foreground of moored fishing vessels is backed by the walls of Stork's Castle and the medina rising in a higgledy-piggledy crown.

The Roman town of **Lixus**, its remains scattered over a hill on the right-hand side of the road which leads to the beach, was actually founded by the Phoenicians in about 1100BC. It is one of several claimants to the site of the mythical Garden of Hesperides containing the golden apples sought by Hercules in his penultimate labour. Apart from some megalithic stones, built into

Moonrise over the ramparts of Asilah.

the acropolis and oriented towards the sun, few remains pre-date the Roman period. At the top of the hill there are foundations of temples, a theatre and amphitheatre, ramparts and houses and, near the bottom, the remains of salt and *garum* (anchovy paste) factories.

Further south, the road passes the now functionary **Ksar el Kebir**, once an important power base coveted by the Spanish and Portuguese in Larache and Asilah, but which the British playwright Joe Orton more recently described as the "Leicester of Morocco". Beyond, outside Arbaoua, is the old **protectorate border** – the former checkpoint gathering weeds. During the French and Spanish protectorates, passports had to be shown in order to pass this point. After independence, Mohammed V made an ceremonial visit to the spot to declare the point closed.

Beyond is the turning to **Ouezzane** (a rewarding detour: see the chapter on the Rif, *page 137*); and the road to the resort and holy village of **Moulay Bousselham** across a large lagoon. A *moussem* is held in the village every summer, when pilgrims visit a cave, apparently – though hard to credit – to suck a sacred stalactite.

Back on the P2, the surrounding hills begin to level into a rich, well populated agricultural plain whose focus is the market town of **Souk el Arba du Rharb** (*rharb* meaning west). Its industrial centre is **Kenitra**, a large town founded by the French in 1913.

Kenitra is not particularly diverting, but the **Kasbah de Mehdiya** seven miles (11 km) to its south on the mouth of the Oued Sebou is impressive. The Spanish who captured the point in 1614 built the fortress upon a prototype conceived by Louis XIV's military engineer. Moulay Ismail, however, with his usual vigour, drove the Spanish out and established his own man there, the Caid Ali er Rif, the governor responsible for the Moroccan gateway and palace.

From Kenitra, Morocco's one and only motorway (toll: very low) begins. Leading south to Casablance, it will eventually also extend north to Tangier.

Donkey and trap: common transport in the west.

RABAT

Rabat was founded in the 10th century near the ruins of the Phoenician and later Roman port of Sala Colonia in the mouth of the River Bou Regreg. This first *ribat* (Islamic military community), later became the capital of the great 12th-century Almohad conqueror Yacoub el Mansour, who ruled from Tunisia to northern Spain. Ribat el Fath, the Fortress of Victory, was the assembly point for his armies, which bivouacked in the shelter of its 3-mile (5-km) long massive walls.

With the death of Yacoub el Mansour, Rabat lost much of its importance and was not to become the capital again until the French occupation in 1912. By then the town of Rabat – the present medina – was one of five separate entities: the medina itself; the adjoining Kasbah of the Oudayas; the *mechouar* or palace complex situated some distance away; beyond this the ruins of Chella; and finally, across the Bou Regreg from the Oudaya, the old town of Salé.

The centre of the modern town was then grazing land between the medina and the *mechouar*, still partly enclosed by the ruins of the Almohad walls. Horsemen galloped across this plain in the traditional fantasia to pay homage to the sultan on his infrequent visits to his Rabat palace.

Now all is engulfed in the Rabat-Salé agglomeration of over 1 million inhabitants, due to reach one and a half million by the end of the century. Modern **Rabat** is staid, heavily policed and respectable, with its poor areas conveniently well out of sight or camouflaged by "walls of shame". Casablancais may call it provincial, but by Moroccan standards Rabat is a tolerant and (unlike Salé) a Westernised city. The *ville nouvelle* or New Town built during the French Protectorate has filled the space between the medina and the Almohad walls and spilt over into other *quartiers*.

Despite the overflow, seen from the outside, these ochre walls still seem to encircle the town. From the great gate of **Bab Rouah**, finest of the five city gates and now an art gallery, they run down past lawns and orange-trees to **Bab el Hed** at the corner of the medina, where the **Marché Central** stands. It was at Bab el Hed that the last pre-protectorate sultan exhibited the heads of defeated rebels. Now for most of the year, swifts and martins flock there at dusk, nesting in the regular holes in the masonry (designed to support the crossbeams of small mobile platforms for repairwork to the walls).

On the other side of the town another well-preserved section of Almohad wall encloses the palace area and, beyond the palace, Chella overlooks the valley.

Principal sights: Following the road round above the valley, one comes to the principal Almohad site in Rabat, and the city's invariable symbol, the **Hassan Tower**, magnificently situated on the crest of a hill commanding both Salé and Rabat. This is the unfinished minaret of the great Hassan Mosque, constructed by Yacoub el Mansour in the

last five years of his reign after his victory over the kings of Castile and Leon at Alarcos .

At his death in 1199 work seems to have ceased, but the main structure of the mosque was well advanced. The design was monumental. Twenty-one east-to-west aisles in the prayer-hall, with space for 40,000 worshippers (double the capacity of the Kairouyine in Fez) made it the largest mosque in the west and the second in all Islam. El Mansour, it is said, wanted his whole army to pray together here.

The shell of the mosque was destroyed at the same time as the city of Lisbon in the earthquake of 1755. Many of the 400 columns have now been re-erected upon a foundation of modern flagstones. Parts of the mosque's outer wall survive, and a large sunken water-tank near the tower, which was to have fed the fountains in the ablutions court, has been converted into a monument to the victims of the independence struggle. But the site of the mosque is now no more than a great white open space

between the modern mausoleum of Mohammed V on one side and the Hassan Tower on the other.

The tower, designed by the same architect as the Giralda in Seville and the Koutoubia in Marrakesh, rises to only 165 feet (50 metres) – the height of the Koutoubia – out of its projected 265 feet (81 metres). Within the tower's 8-foot-thick walls is an internal ramp up which mules carried building materials and which (intermittent restoration permitting, of course) is usually open to visitors. The climb itself and the spendid view from the top are convincing proof of the real height of the truncated structure despite its stocky look.

With its 172 sq. feet (16-sq.-metre) cross-section, as against the Koutoubia's 39 feet (12 metres), the Hassan Tower would, if completed with its upper ranges of tilework and its lantern, have appeared more slender than either of its sister towers. But the harmonies of its decorative carving (different on each face at the lower level, the same on three faces at the upper), the magnificence of

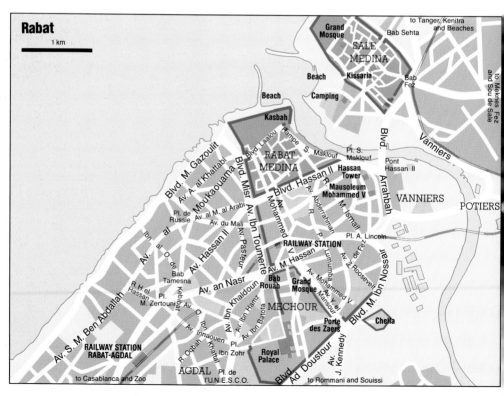

the site and the rich ochre of its stone (though sadly discoloured in places by over-zealous restoration) make it one of the most memorable pieces of architecture in Morocco.

It is, however, towards the latterday kitsch of **Mohammed V's Mausoleum**, on the other side of the rows of columns, that the busloads of visitors inevitably direct their attention. The main building, housing the tombs of the late King and of his youngest son, is flanked by a sunken mosque beyond which is the structure of another mausoleum, as yet unoccupied. All are the costly but uninspired products of architectural and decorative styles that haven't changed in 400 years.

But the mausoleum is redeemed by the genuine popular piety of its many Moroccan visitors. To the traditional religious veneration paid to a sultan is added respect for a notable hero of the independence movement and an affectionate memory of the first king in Moroccan history to have ruled in an unselfish manner.

Mausoleum of King Mohammed V.

From the Hassan Tower, roads lead down to the rather seedy **riverside** where fishing boats dock and a large fleet of rowing-boats ferry passengers across to Salé for a few dirhams. In earlier times lighters discharged cargo from ships moored outside the river mouth at these wharves. And it is from here, looking towards the sea, that the **Kasbah of the Oudayas** can be best seen.

Built by Yacoub el Mansour on the site of the original *ribat*, in former times the fortress of the Oudaya, itself a small town, also contained the sultan's residence in Rabat.

In the 17th century, the period of the corsair state known as the Republic of Bou Regreg, the Kasbah's inhabitants lived by piracy. Their captives used to be sold in the **Old Wool Market**, a triangular space now surrounded by souvenir shops, facing the Oudaya entrance on the medina side of the road.

Moulay Ismail, whose reign spanned and paralleled that of Louis XIV (*see page 46*), put an end to the vicious little republic, took over the corsair business

154

himself and constructed a new palace within the Kasbah, which is now the Museum of Moroccan Arts. He also installed in the Kasbah the warlike Oudaya tribe whom he charged with the tasks of subjugating the equally fractious Zaer tribe south of Rabat and keeping the corsairs in line.

Approaching the main entrance, the **Oudaya Gate**, you may want to purchase half an hour's peace and quiet by engaging one of the many freelance guides (although the kasbah is not as bewildering as in other towns). Thus protected, you can begin to take in the façade of this superb Almohad gate, with its extraordinary superposition of arch around arch, working outwards from the basic keyhole profile of the entrance to the massive square block of the whole gate. Contemplated at length, the façade begins to shimmer and dance with the tension between inward and outward pressures around the arch and the interplay of the different geometrical motifs.

Pass through the angled entrance in the side tower and you find yourself next to the interior face of the gate and in the main street of the Kasbah. Halfway along this street on the left is the **Oudaya Mosque**, rebuilt in the 18th century by the renegade English architect Ahmed el Ingles.

Any turning to the right off the main street followed downhill will bring you to the **Café Maure** on the ramparts overlooking the river, which connects with the Andalusian gardens and the **Museum of Moroccan Arts**. The latter not only contains a fine display of jewellery, costumes and carpets, but is of interest in itself as a handsomely decorated royal residence, with elegant reception rooms opening on to a central courtyard. Café Maure, with its cool breezes and shady rush-covered benches, is a delightful place to adjourn for sticky Moroccan pastries and a glass of mint tea.

The Oudaya Kasbah stands at the northwest corner of Rabat **medina**, the four sides of which run first along the river, then past the cemetery on the coast, down the Almohad walls running from the lighthouse in to Bab el Hed, and finally along the Andalusian walls on Avenue Hassan II. When in the 17th century the last wave of Muslim refugees were expelled from Spain, many of them settled in Salé and Rabat. They found the latter in ruins and almost deserted and the area within the old Almohad defences far too large for their needs. So they put up the Andalusian walls to contain the part they settled, and this – the present medina – they rebuilt in the architectural style of their Spanish homeland.

When, in 1912, the French made Rabat the protectorate capital, Marshal Lyautey, in a pattern later followed in all the old towns of Morocco, forbade the development of the medina by European builders and ordered the creation of a new town outside its walls. The initial consequence of this policy was urban segregation, which was much criticised by Moroccans, but in the long run it has preserved the traditional Moroccan towns better than any others in North Africa.

Carpetbaggers: One enters the medina a little downhill from the Oudaya Gate by the Rue des Consuls, the only street in which foreign consuls could formerly set up shop, and today largely but not exclusively a tourist shopping street. The first section is occupied by carpet, rug and wool merchants. Popular types of carpet include the Ribati, with gaudy reds and blues in geometrical patterns, and the generally smaller Taznacht with their softer-hued vegetable dyes and cruder patterns often including animal and plant motifs (never as strictly taboo in the Maghreb as elsewhere in the Muslim world).

Most of the big carpets are now produced by sweated labour in carpet factories, but private carpet-makers sell in the souk held in this street every Thursday morning.

If buying a carpet, bargain for yourself. For a given size and type and quality of carpet (knots per square cm), test the price in a shop first, but don't buy there. Ask the dealer's price and, when pressed for *your* price, name a figure a

Preceding pages: the dead face towards Mecca. **Below,** to the Andalusian gardens in the Kasbah of the Oudayas.

bit over half his. Always remain courteous and friendly, and be sure to admire the carpets.

The price the first dealer stops at is the price to try and beat in the next shop. If speaking French to him, asides to a companion in English (which the carpet-seller will understand) can be a useful tactic. But remember that what for you is a game is the dealer's livelihood, so be sure to mean what you say.

Lots of leather: Halfway up the Rue des Consuls, side by side on the left, are two old *fondouks* (inns for travelling merchants and their pack animals) which now house leather workers. A few yards further up on the left a more modern *fondouk* has become a cloth-sellers' *kissaria* (shopping arcade), arranged round a small garden. The street continues with leather and clothes shops until you come to a small crossroads.

Ahead and on the left is the former Jewish quarter, or *mellah*, while to the right the road leads through a covered market (mainly jewellers – closed on Fridays – and shoeshops) and past the medina's **Grand Mosque**. On the corner of the sidestreet beside the mosque is a 14th-century Merinid fountain, a survival of pre-Andalusian Rabat which has been incorporated into the facade of a bookshop.

The covered market leads straight on into the **Rue Souika**, the medina's main shopping street, which emerges at the **Marché Central**. While the Rabat medina is too Westernised to have preserved the strict street-by-street trade groupings, there is still a tendency for sellers of roast sheep's heads and cows' feet to cluster in one stretch and those of lingerie, spices, ironmongery or cassettes in others.

The area behind the Marché Central is veined with *derbs* – those narrow cul-de-sacs between windowless walls leading off the main thoroughfares. Within the *derb* massive iron-studded doors open, through the traditional blind entrance-way with a right-angle bend, into the courtyards of private houses. These old-style, inward-turned houses were described by Leonara Peets in 1932 as

"lidless clay boxes in which the Moroccan man hides his women and his home life… a rectangular well of two storeys, with all the windows directed onto the internal patio." It was on the roof terraces of such houses that the womenfolk, who otherwise never went out except to visit the baths, were allowed to emerge in the late afternoon, when men were banished from the rooftops.

Behind the Marché Central, to the left as one faces the medina, there is a small **flea-market** in which interesting oddments are sometimes found.

Government Property: The Marché Central faces the **Boulevard Mohammed V**, which runs through the centre of the New Town shopping area before broadening out into a rather elegant palm-lined promenade, scene of the evening walkabout, past the modern **Parliament building** and straight on up to the 18th-century **Grand Mosque** (effectively the cathedral mosque) of Rabat at the top of the hill.

Do not, like many tourists, take the school entrance next to the mosque for

that of the **Palace**, which is actually 200 yards further to the right, halfway between the mosque and Bab Rouah. Visitors are allowed to walk or drive through the archway into the *mechouar* (palace area, containing **Dar El Makhzen** – the House of Government).

Here one enters a town within a town, containing the modern palace, the Prime Minister's office and the Ministry of Religious Affairs. The resident population of 2,000 includes extended branches of the Alaouite ruling family (others are distributed among the palaces in other towns) as well as retainers serving and retired, a guards regiment and cavalry. The complex also contains a mosque, at which the King, when in Rabat, leads the midday Friday prayer on feast days. These occasions are accompanied by a great deal of ceremony, including impressive processions both to and from the mosque.

Burial of the dead: The central road through the *mechouar* brings you out through the Almohad walls on the far side, just 10 minutes' walk from the **Chella Necropolis** (towards the left). The walled area of Chella, stretching down the hillside almost to the level of the valley, was for 1,500 years the site of the port – Phoenician, Roman, Berber and finally Arab – of Sala, until, in the 13th century, its inhabitants took themselves and the name of their town across the estuary.

But Rabat remained the assembly point for armies bound for the Spanish wars, and the first three Merinid sultans in the 13th and 14th centuries used Chella as a burial place for their dynasty. (The other Merinid necropolis is outside the walls of Fez, their main capital.)

You pass through an unusual gate (more ornamental than defensive – Muslim graves contain no treasure) with stalactite corbels surmounting the gate towers like hands upraised in Muslim-style prayer. This gateway, whose style is positively sprightly after the massiveness of the Almohad gates, must once have blazed with colour from its now lost tilework.

Inside, paths lead down through half-wild gardens and scented trees (notably

A favourite nesting spot for storks.

the huge white trumpets of the halluci-nogenic *dattura* or belladonna tree) to the cluster of domed saints' tombs to one side of the ruined Merinid mosque and *zaouia*, and over on the left, the excavations of the Romano-Berber town. These remains of **Sala Colonia** – or what was left of it after the Merinids had quarried it for their own buildings – can be viewed from the outside only, but visitors can walk all over the ruins of the mosque and the royal tombs behind the mosque.

This is, incidentally, the only mosque in Morocco apart from Moulay Ismail's tomb in Meknes that non-Muslims are allowed to enter (following the ban imposed by Marshal Lyautey). One feels here, even more so than elsewhere in Morocco, the haunted charm of ruins which are not sterilised and minutely patched but intertwined with fig-trees, overgrown with flowers and grazed by sheep – much as travellers discovered Italy in the 17th century. Tomorrow's loss is today's gain.

The doorway into the mosque leads first into what was the ablutions court, and then into the prayer-hall, behind the rear wall of which were the burial chambers. Ahead and to the right is the **tomb of Abou el Hassan**, known as the Black Sultan, with part of a richly decorated wall still standing behind it. His wife, the former Christian slave Shems Ed Duna (Morning Sun), whose saintliness is commemorated in local legend, is buried to the far left (the sexes being segregated in death as in life). This mosque was built by Abou el Hassan's grandfather, Abou Youssef Yacoub, the "King of the *djinns*", who is believed to have buried his gold nearby and set the djinns to guard it.

To the left of the mosque stand the ruins of the Black Sultan's *zaouia*, a place of religious retreat and study. Small cubicles surround a courtyard with a central pool, beyond which a small prayer-hall culminates in a *mihrab* (niche pointing towards Mecca) encircled untypically by a narrow passageway, now blocked with thorn branches and rubble. Legend has it that walking seven

The ruins and wild gardens of Chella.

times around this *mihrab* is as good as a pilgrimage to Mecca – perhaps the reason why it is now blocked up.

At the other end of the central court, down some steps beside the minaret, are the old latrines with accommodation for eight (remarkably generous provision, surely, for the occupants of only 16 study cells). The inmates would, of course, have slept in dormitories above the cublicles. The minarets of both *zaouia* and mosque, as well as some of the plane-trees and saints' shrines, are hosts to that bringer of good luck, the stork's nest.

Emerging again from the mosque on the side opposite the Roman remains, you find the ground slopes down to the ruins of a *hammam* (steam bath), in which a sunken pool now houses a colony of three and four-foot eels. Fed with hardboiled eggs on sale from helpful children, these sacred creatures confer fertility upon women and aches and pains upon those who doubt their power or seek to harm them. They are supposedly ruled over by a giant eel with long hair and golden rings, and draw their magic from the saintly Shems, as does the small spring rising in the gardens below the ruins.

Archaeological remains: Those disappointed by the ruins of Sala Colonia should console themselves with a visit to the **Archaeological Museum** – by no means the least of Rabat's splendours. A five-minute walk from the Grand Mosque, in a sidestreet next to Radio Télévision Marocaine, this collection is notable for the superb bronzes recovered from the excavations at Volubilis, the Romano-Berber capital of Mauritania Tingitana.

When Rome ordered the evacuation of Volubilis in the 3rd century, the citizens, expecting to return shortly, quickly buried their works of art outside the city, where they were to remain undisturbed for 17 centuries. These pieces are kept apart in the separate **Salle des Bronzes** (tip required).

In addition to many charming small Graeco-Roman statuettes, there are three or four pieces of such grandeur that one wonders at most visitors' neglect of this museum: the Guard-Dog (centrepiece of a fountain); the ivy-crowned Youth (the Ephebus, copied from Praxiteles); the Rider; and above all the busts presumed to be those of Cato the Younger and the young King Juba II of Mauritania Tingitana. The Head of Cato, not unlike Sir John Gielgud in its austere and fastidious attitude, is entirely convincing as the enemy of Octavius Caesar who killed himself for a principle.

The Head of Juba, however, is the *pièce de résistance* of the collection – the product of *"pays berbère, occupant romain, esthétique grecque"*.

Undoubtedly a Berber youth, it could easily have been a sculpture of their king. The short *retroussé* upper-lip is characteristic and seen all over Morocco. It is the Chaplinesque appearance (all moustache and front teeth) seen hunched over the wheel in all Rabat taxis as they edge their way through the traffic, cautious and scrupulous, and unlike any other taxis in the country.

The historical Juba, a famous scholar of his time, was a protégé of the Emperor Augustus, and married Cleopatra Silene, the daughter of Anthony and Cleopatra. He reigned for 45 years. Their son Ptolemy, summoned to Caligula's games at Lyons, was murdered by the mad emperor, allegedly for wearing a more brilliant purple toga than Caligula himself. (Apart from animals for the amphitheatres, indigo dye derived from a shellfish and wheat were ancient Morocco's main exports.)

From Roman Games to modern: King Hassan is a keen golfer and the Robert Trent Jones designed **Royal Dar-es-Salam Golf Club**, on the outskirts of Rabat off the Rommani road, comprises two excellent 18-hole courses and a 9-hole course with an international reputation. The Hassan II Trophy takes place in November and the Moroccan Open, part of the Volvo PGA is held in January. Visitors have access to the club as temporary members.

Capital restaurants: Eating out in Rabat is no problem, even if the choice is a little limited for a capital city. A traditional Moroccan restaurant off the Place Piètry in the New Town, **L'Oasis** serves moderately priced formal meals in a traditional setting. An excellent and very cheap Lebanese restaurant in an arcade opposite the Hôtel Terminus by the station serves good meat and vegetarian dishes (but no alcohol).

Perhaps more typical of local tastes in eating out are the Spanish-style fish restaurants. The cheapest and most Moroccan of these is **Le Mont Doré** in l'Océan (the quarter next to the medina). Other possibilities include the beach restaurant on the lighthouse side of the Oudaya and the **Miramar** on the beach at El Harhoura, on the coast road just south of Rabat.

There are also good Chinese restaurants – for example, **La Pagoda** behind the railway station, and **Le Dragon d'Or**, slightly out of town, next to Supermarché Souissi. Good pizzerias include **La Mamma** behind the Hôtel Balima in the town centre and the **Sorrento** in the Place de Bourgogne. There is a pancake restaurant called **Le Crépescule** near the curiously appealing Maghrebin-Gothic cathedral in the town centre, and French cooking is to be had in all the main hotels.

Twin city: Crossing the main Hassan II bridge over the **River Bou Regreg** (Father of Reflection) brings one directly to the centre of Rabat's twin city. It is hard to believe that **Salé** and Rabat are nowadays part of a single conglomeration. Crossing the river is a journey in time and certainly in moral space. For Salé, despite its prodigious current growth, remains strictly Muslim (a dry town), culturally resistant and (theoretically) maintains an anti-European tradition going back to the last wave of Andalusian refugees from the Spanish Inquisition and the tradition of the corsairs, who were active well into the 19th century. But the *Slawis'* courtesy today compares well with most, and foreigners have no hassles here.

The town of Salé has been so called since 1260 when, following the sack of the former town on this site by Alfonso X of Castile and the enslavement of most of its inhabitants, the population of Chella (Sala) crossed the river to settle

Rabat's beach.

here and rebuild the town. For the next six centuries Salé's economic importance was greater than that of Rabat.

From the 13th to the 16th century it was Morocco's principal trading port and when, after the last wave of Andalusian resettlement in the early 17th century, Rabat and Salé formed the short-lived corsair state of Bou Regreg, Salé was predominant. The hero of Daniel Defoe's story *Robinson Crusoe* was captured and sold into slavery by the Sallee Rovers.

From the Salé end of the Hassan II Bridge, the first town gate you see is the unusually tall **Bab Mrisa** (Port Gate), built by the Merinid sultans to admit sea-going boats by means of a now-vanished canal to a dock within the town walls. Following the outer walls up to the left brings one to a crossroads (Bab el Haja) in front of the Town Hall. Turn right here and take the left-hand side of the square ahead of you.

Straight ahead and bearing left, you enter the main trading streets of the **medina**. Here craftsmen and shop-keepers flock together by trades, grouped guild-like in their own narrow streets. This is very much a traditional Moroccan town, visited by few tourists and entirely free of hustlers.

The long straight road up to the left (Rue de la Grande Mosquée) takes you to the area of merchants' mansions and religious centres (*zaouias*) around the Grand Mosque. Behind the mosque to the right is the **Medrassa el Hassan** – a lovely little Merinid religious college, just as finely wrought and well preserved as the great Bou Inania *medersa* in Fez and Méknès, but much smaller. There is the same ubiquity of decoration – first *zellige* (faïence mosaic), then incised stucco, and finally carved cedar-wood. Visitors are admitted to the dormitories in the upper storey and even to the roof, with its view across the river to Rabat.

Beyond the Grand Mosque on the seaward side lies the shrine of **Sidi Abdallah ben Hassan**, a 16th-century saint revered by the corsairs. His cult survives in an annual procession on the eve of Mouloud (the Prophet's birthday); men in period costume carry large lanterns, intricately made of coloured wax, from Bab Mrisa up to the saint's shrine, where they dance and sing.

Away from the town, there is a thriving cooperative of **potteries**, on the Salé side of the river, beside the airport road out of Rabat. Salé pottery is marked by delicate economical designs in white and pastel shades, often including the Roman *fibula*, or brooch fastener – a traditional motif in Berber decoration. Unfortunately this faïence work chips easily, unlike the hotter-fired Fez stoneware with its characteristic scrollwork and resonant blues and whites.

Six miles (10 km) north of Salé on the Kenitra road, recognisable by the coloured sun-hats for sale on racks outside an arched metal gate, are the **Jardins Exotiques**, a botanical adventureland with liana bridges and winding jungle paths. Designed by a French conservationist to illustrate a variety of ecosystems, the gardens are rather run down, but the obstacle course is still fun.

Four miles (six km) further north there

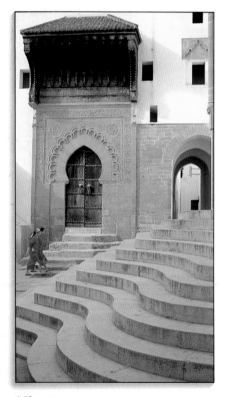

To the Grand Mosque.

is a turning off to the five-star Hôtel Firdaous and the attractive sandy beaches of the *Plage des Nations* (where the sea is dangerous).

Rabat to Casablanca: Many of the Atlantic beaches are subject to currents which make swimming dangerous. But a number of small sandy bays between Rabat and Casablanca are both attractive and safe. Six miles (10 km) south of Rabat on the coast road brings you to **Temara Plage**, with a series of beaches – Contrebandiers, Sables d'Or (Sidi el Abed) and Sehb ed Dahab. Around Sables d'Or there are several restaurants and discos, also sports facilities, while Sehb ed Dahab boasts a new marina. In summer, however, these beaches are appallingly crowded.

Temara Ville, a couple of kilometres inland, has Morocco's only zoo, a well-maintained collection (originally the King's own) in extensive grounds.

A little further south, where the coast road crosses the small Oued Ykem river (by the Ain Atiq motorway exit), two campsites and two restaurants cater for

visitors to the attractive **Plage Rose-Marie**. The Hôtel Le Kasbah hires out horses which you can ride along the beach, has a good pool and, in summer, a nightclub. If camping in summer, be warned: in the holiday season Moroccan campsites are often chock-a-block with semi-permanent tent cities, and camp life is far from restful.

At **Skhirate**, 19 miles (30 km) south of Rabat, the King's seaside palace – scene of a bloody attempted coup in 1971 – is flanked by excellent beaches.

Forty-four miles (70 km) after Rabat and 19 miles (30 km) before Casa lies the long thin coastal strip of **Mohammedia** – a town with a split personality: on the Casa side, an oil port, industry and poor districts; on the Rabat side (described as East Mohammedia), a playground for rich Casablancais, with hotels, nice beaches and sports facilities that include an 18-hole golf-course, a marina, water sports, riding (Hôtel Samir), a casino and a racecourse. It's a relaxed sort of place and has two excellent Spanish-style fish restaurants.

Bricks and pots, Salé.

CASABLANCA

To most English speakers, the name of **Casablanca** evokes good living, romance and adventure in a tropical setting. This was the Sin City image that the 1943 Bogart film conveyed to cinema-goers in the drab war years. It has long been associated with brothels. More recently, it gained notoriety as a centre for sex-change operations.

But nothing could be further from the prosaic reality of Morocco's economic capital. For many fun-seeking Gulf Arabs (known to Moroccans as "penguins"), Casablanca may have replaced Beirut, but it is still a city that shuts down before 10pm, and from which Moroccans and foreigners escape when they want to enjoy themselves. It is also a city of extensive poor areas and sealed off *bidonvilles* which have been the scene of murderous bread riots twice in the last decade. The first *bidonvilles* sprung up as long ago as the 19th century; they mushroomed in the Post-War years; and still little has been done to address their problem.

Industrial powerhouse: The original Berber town of Anfa was destroyed by the 1755 Lisbon earthquake. Rebuilt as Dar el Beida (the White House, or Casa Blanca), its population by the turn of the century had barely reached 20,000 – not a tenth of that of Fez at the time. Since then, however, it has risen to be the main port and industrial powerhouse of Morocco, with a population variously estimated from the official figure of nearly three million up to an unofficial five million. This makes it Africa's second city after Cairo.

At the centre of Casablanca are two large squares, the Place des Nations Unies and the Place Mohammed V. From the latter, a road runs down to the port entrance and Casa-Port railway station. This road marks the eastern edge of Casablanca's small and rather dull **old medina**, at the lower end of which, facing the sea, stands the 18th-century fort, the **Borj Sidi Mohammed ben Abdullah**, built to resist Portuguese raids. The only reason for visiting the medina is to go shopping in Derb Omar, in which, the Casablancais boast, "you can buy anything" – its only resemblance to Harrods.

On the other side of the Place Mohammed V there is a modern pedestrians-only **shopping precinct**, between the Place d'Aknoul and the Boulevard de Paris.

Architectural attractions: Around the **Place des Nations Unies**, on the other side of the Place Mohammed V from the medina, stand four monumental public buildings from the protectorate period – very much the sort of thing that Moroccan visitors to the city come to see: the **Grande Poste**; the **Wilaya** (Prefecture), with its clock tower, the **Palais de Justice** with elaborately tiled courtyards; and the **Banque d'Etat**. The first three are in the neo-Mauresque style cooked up by French architects in the 1920s and 1930s. Other examples of the exuberant exploitation of exotic themes by European architects, combined with local craftsmanship, are seen in particular

Preceding pages: Casablanca, Morocco's high-rise city. **Left,** the Royal Mansour Hotel. **Right,** Casablancan elegance.

along the **Boulevard Mohammed V** and in the surrounding streets, where carved façades abound, often with decorative tiles or *zellige* mosaics, ornate entrance-ways and some striking Art Deco grillework on staircases and balconies. Local government officials have broached the idea of establishing an Art Deco historic district.

A 10-minute drive from the centre takes you to the **new medina**, alias **Quartier Habbous**, a French orientalist folly built in the 1930s. This charming but spurious complex, in which a range of Hispano-Mauresque styles are represented, is now a shopping district (not primarily for tourists) specialising in Arabic bookshops and utilitarian objects of a traditional nature. It's a Disneyland medina, fun to walk around and agreeably hassle-free. Worth visiting here is the famous **Patisserie Bennis** in the Rue Fkih El Gabbas.

Along the corniche: From the entrance to the port, the **Corniche** leads westwards along the shore to the fashionable beach clubs (admission DH 50 and up-wards) and restaurants of **Ain Diab**, a rich residential area of Saudi palaces, bikini-clad girls and veiled domestics, and the **Marabout of Sidi Abderahmen**, a picturesque cluster of white tombs rising on a rocky outcrop just offshore. At low tide pilgrims wade through the waves to reach it.

On the way is the **Hassan II Mosque**, the gift of a grateful nation to its sovereign on the occasion of his 60th birthday in 1989 (it was inaugurated in 1993). This costly building, complete with library, museum, steam baths, Koranic school and conference facilities and built on the sea-bed with water on three sides, and was designed by French architect Michel Pinseau and financed by universal voluntary subscriptions. Its position complies nicely with a Koranic saying: "Allah has His throne on the water."

The cost, in all more than £357 million), was met by various means. Special officials collected contributions from every home in the land, and some employers deducted a percentage from their workers' wages. The King's high-

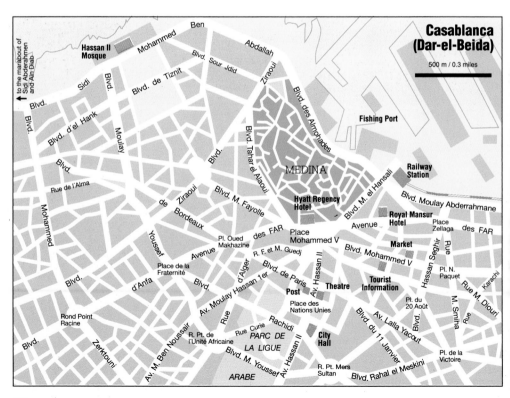

est officials are said to have fallen over themselves to be generous.

The prayer-hall, with an electrically-operated sun-roof over the central court, has space for 20,000 worshippers while another 80,000 can pray on the surrounding esplanade. The marble minaret is 82 ft (25 metres) square and 575 ft (175 metres) high, which makes it the tallest religious building in the world, beating the Great Pyramid of Cheops by 98 ft (30 metres) and St Peter's by 131 ft (40 metres). It took 35,000 workers 50 million man-hours to complete.

A 20-mile-long visible laser beam, *Star Wars*-style, points, like a giant finger, from the top of the minaret towards Mecca. Visible for hundreds of miles out to sea, this is the largest mosque outside Medina and Mecca and the westernmost monument of Islam.

Where to eat: The gourmet is well served in Casablanca. Moroccan-style restaurants include the pleasant and reasonably priced **Ouarzazate** (Rue Mohamed El Qorri, off Boulevard Mohammed V), the **Bahj** (Rue Colbert, also off Mohammed V), or the more up-market **Al Mounia** (Rue du Prince Moulay Abdallah, off the Boulevard de Paris) and the **Sijilmassa** (Rue de Biarritz – an extension of the Corniche at Ain Diab). For the latter establishments, arm yourself with a copious supply of 10-dirham notes to tuck into the girdle of the *shikha*, or bellydancer, when she comes and wiggles at your table.

Good fish restaurants are plentiful around the Corniche, but for atmosphere and quality at modest prices go to the **Restaurant du Port de Pêche** (through the port entrance, immediately left and straight on to the first restaurant you come to). Vietnamese and even Japanese and Korean restaurants are to be found at Ain Diab and among the eating places clustered around the left-bankish Rond-Point de Mers Sultan, five minutes' walk from the Place des Nations Unies. Finally, for lovers of up-market French cooking, the **A Ma Bretagne** in Ain Diab (along from the Marabout of Sidi Abderahmen) is reputedly the best restaurant in Morocco.

Hassan II Mosque.

SOUTH OF CASABLANCA

The Atlantic coastal strip south of Casablanca is served by two roads: the busier (and therefore not necessarily faster) **P8**, and the **S121**, the more scenic coast route (without the attendant poor surface the description usually implies). The scenery, though, is not as obviously dramatic as elsewhere in the country.

To the west vast stretches of Atlantic breakers are intermittently hidden by sand dunes, still lagoons or long lines of wind-breaking sugar canes sheltering tomato plantations. To the east is a still and stony plain populated by grazing sheep and scattered farm buildings.

Occasionally the melancholy character of the region is relieved when the road sweeps within feet of an unexpected and inviting sandy cove. Mules *and* carts (complete with number plates) suggest a more affluent peasantry than that of the south. Even the occasional horse is spotted.

Fifty miles (80 km) south of Casablanca at the mouth of the **River Oum Er Rbia** (Mother of Spring) the main road passes the little town of **Azemmour**. The view of the town from across the river is one of the most memorable in this country of set-piece, almost contrived, painterly views. The white of the square buildings stacked up behind the walls is set off in this case by the astonishing colours of the river – reds or greens depending on whether it has rained in the hills or not.

From within, the town is unspectacular but pleasant. One can walk round the Portuguese ramparts and reflect on the extraordinary energy of that small country in the 14th and 15th centuries, when at one time or another it held most of Morocco's Atlantic ports.

The annual *moussem* in Azemmour commemorates a Jewish holy man, but the Jewish population, like most Moroccan Jews, fled to Israel in 1967 fearing reprisals for the Six-Day War. The *mellah* is now in ruins, but the rather plain little synagogue is opened up for determined sightseers.

Sixty-three miles (100 km) south of Casablanca is the seaside resort of **El Jadida**, a refuge in summer for *Marrakshis* fleeing the suffocating heat of the *chergui*, the east wind. Its miles of sandy beaches (often obscured by mysterious hot fogs), its carefree atmosphere and the interesting old **Portuguese Town** make it a pleasant stopping place, though usually it is crowded in summer.

The Portuguese held the town, which they called Mazagan, for 250 years and built the fortified and moated medina adjoining the harbour. The most remarkable Portuguese relic is the underground cistern, pillared and vaulted like a church crypt, and astonishingly lovely with oblique shafts of sunlight reflected in the shallow water. Orson Welles filmed part of his *Othello* here. Round the corner the old church, now restored, stands in a quiet square in the centre of the Portuguese Town. The minaret of the nearby mosque was once, as you can see, the Portuguese lighthouse.

Fifty-six miles (90 km) further south,

past a series of coastal salt-marshes, you come to the charming little bay of **Oualidia**, famous for its oyster-beds. There are two hotels with good seafood restaurants, two campsites, a 17th-century kasbah and a royal villa. Though also crowded in summer, especially at weekends the atmosphere is pleasant and the swimming excellent.

Safi: Ninety-four miles (150 km) south of El Jadida is an important phosphate and fishing port with a thriving and very smelly chemical industry south of the town. Its two main monuments were left behind by the Portuguese, who occupied Safi briefly in the early 16th century. The **Dar el Bahr** (Château de la Mer), on the shore below the medina, is well preserved. The different origins of the cannon on its ramparts reflect the European competition for commercial influence after the Portuguese were driven out. In the 17th century Safi was Morocco's chief port.

Up on the hill behind the medina, another Portuguese stronghold, the **Kechla**, was beautified and added to by a spendthrift son of Moulay Ismail, who, inheriting the extravagant tastes but not the industry of his father, squandered the money the Sultan intended for military purposes on high living.

Incongruously, in the middle of the medina, the Portuguese **St Catherine's Chapel**, once part of a now-vanished cathedral, bears the arms of King Manuel I and is an attractive blend of Gothic and Renaissance elements.

On the hillside to the north of the medina are the Safi **potteries**, which turn out brightly coloured earthenware plates and vases with distinctively bold geometrical patterns. Naturally, these are sold at the numerous roadside stalls along this stretch of coast. They make great buys – if you can get one home.

The road up to the clifftop north of the town brings you to the village of **Sidi Bouzid** with its *zaouia*, good restaurant and magnificent view of town and port. One can watch the long procession of sardine boats returning to port from their night's fishing and sample the deliciously spiced sardines that are the local speciality.

THE IMPERIAL CITIES

Before the Arabs arrived in Morocco in the 7th century, communities were organised into small but numerous Berber settlements and a few trading ports. Not since the Roman era had anything much resembling towns existed. But the Arabs – an urban people whose religion emphasised the communal benefits of the city, exemplified in the holy city of Medina – were quick to build centralised communities, where trade could develop, Islam flourish, and from which they could govern the rest of the country effectively. Moulay Idriss I, the father of the first Arab dynasty in Morocco, established the city of Moulay Idriss close to the Roman city of Volubilis, and then, in AD 789, founded Fez, which was to become the political capital of the whole of the Western Maghreb and southern Spain.

The pre-eminence of Fez wasn't challenged until the Almoravides developed Marrakesh in the 11th century, after which the two cities vied for supremacy. The Almohads raised the status of Rabat but Fez and Marrakesh were still pre-eminent. Until European encroachment and the eventual shift of power to Rabat, only the Alaouite sultan Moulay Ismail departed from this pattern. He ruled a strong and prosperous Morocco from Meknes (40 miles/60 km west of Fez), whose relatively limited architecture presented him with more opportunities to express his large personality.

When Rabat became the French capital in 1912, Fez continued to be the intellectual and cultural hub of Morocco. Even today, Fassis are proud of this heritage. Fez contains an abundance of impressive architecture, but the old city, Fez el Bali, is more than fine buildings. It is a medieval city in motion. Marrakesh has its architectural sights – the Koutoubia, the palaces, the Saadian tombs, the Ben Youssef Medersa – but its most enduring attraction is the Djemma el Fna, the market-cum-circus which evolves each afternoon outside the medina and expires late in the night. The purists may complain that the buildings around the square are now modern and dull in character (following a fire at the beginning of the 1960s) but it is still an evocative reminder that Morocco is in Africa.

Fez and Marrakesh are both surrounded by lush countryside, a reason for escaping the cities' summer heat, which even in Fez can be ferocious. From Marrakesh it is easy to travel into the Atlas mountains or west to Essaouira on the coast. Fez, Meknes, Moulay Idriss and Volubilis are close to the fertile lowlands south of the Rif and the lakes and cedar forests surrounding Azrou and Ifrane. Just a few miles from Fez there are the hot springs and cool sources of Sidi Harazem – where the ubiquitous table water is bottled.

Preceding pages: relics of an imperial past; Fez from the old wall near Bab Guissa. **Left,** a fantasia rider.

FEZ

High up by the fort that dominates the two cities of Old Fez, students in their *djellabahs* sit in the evening sun surrounded by Coca-Cola cans and test each other for their university exams. Below them in the valley lies their past: the old medina, with its domes and minarets, embraced by high walls behind which hooded figures move swiftly down narrow streets, trains of heavily-laden donkeys with baskets full of rubble pass through the crowds, and beggars crouch by the gates of the mosques.

Two miles (3 km) to the right, up on the plain that is bitterly cold in the winter but full of summer breezes, stretch the boulevards and squares which could belong to any of a hundred old French colonial towns. The Tricoleur flies above only the French Embassy now, but for all the world this could be France, with its cafés, cinemas and villas.

For the students, this land of bougainvillea and comparative Western plenty holds the promise of the future. The medina – the hotly debated, anachronistic, wholly impractical, decaying yet treasured, lauded and always loved medina – represents everything that made Morocco.

For the casual visitor, Fez is mysterious, exotic and, for all the warmth of the people, a hidden place. Once the poets praised it for the beauty of its mosques, the quality of its water and the palms that lined the banks of the sweet river flowing through its centre.

But where rulers once fought for it and craftsmen gave their lives to adorn it, today politicians and historians fight to preserve this chipped and battered jewel of North Africa. In places the river now runs fetid and the palaces are falling down, but the world watches to see if it, along with Venice, can survive the ravages of an industrial world.

Motorbike escort: There's no need to look for Fez. If you arrive by car, you'll be flanked at the first traffic-lights by motor-biked guides offering to lead you into the city. It will cost you a few dirhams. The route to the New Town, where the majority of hotels are, or to Old Fez (Fez el Bali and Fez Jdid) is clearly marked, but it's a question of keeping your nerve. The boys will drop back quickly if you look as though you know what you want and where you're going. All Moroccans watch carefully the movements of newcomers; after a few days the hustle-patter will die down.

If you are staying in the **New Town** (most hotels are here), it is easy to find your way around. Built by the French after World War I on a simple grid system, it doesn't have the charm of Rabat (or even Casablanca), where the French incorporated their design into the Moroccan structure. The streets here are plain and wide. Lots of cafés, restaurants, banks and shops but not much atmosphere and not even a very exciting nightlife. (Old Fez has much more to offer after dark.)

Marshall Lyautey declared Fez el Bali and Fez Jdid, which make up the medina, a historic monument and slapped a preservation order on it. New Fez was built

some two miles away as the industrial and colonial centre. The administrative buildings are here and, ironically, so is the centre overseeing the preservation of Old Fez. Transport between the new and the old town, though it is quite possible to walk, is frequent and easily available (buses and taxis leave from the main squares).

An overview: The best way to get your bearings and a feeling of the size and complexity of the **Old City** is to take the route **Tour de Fes**. It circumvents the city walls, taking you first to the west of the palace and up to the **Merinid tombs** on the hillside.

There is some mystery attached to the tombs, mausoleums of the last Merinid sultans; it is not known exactly who is there. Described in the chronicles as beautiful white marble with vividly coloured epitaphs, they are now a crumbling ruin, more a landmark than of any particular architectural interest. If the King is in residence, the tombs are guarded and you cannot clamber among them, but you are still allowed on the hillside.

The view is sensational. Once you are in the Old City, there is seldom an opportunity to see the overall structure and dimensions of the mosques and *medersa* to such advantage. From here you can appreciate the structure of the town and the scale of its finer buildings. The view is best at dawn and dusk; then the light is magical.

At the foot of the hillside **Fez el Bali** stretches out on both sides of the river. The quarter on the west bank dates from about 925 when over 2,000 Arab families from Kairouan in Tunisia came as refugees to Fez. The Andalous quarter on the east bank had been established 100 years earlier, when 8,000 Arab families settled here, expelled from Andalusia by the Christians. With them came skills and learning which were to make Fez an outstanding centre of culture and craftsmanship.

As Arab rule in Spain drew to its end, further influxes of refugees from Cordoba, Seville and Granada arrived. They introduced the mosques, stucco, mosaics and other decorative arts and a vari-

Selling candles outside the *zaouia* of Moulay Idriss II.

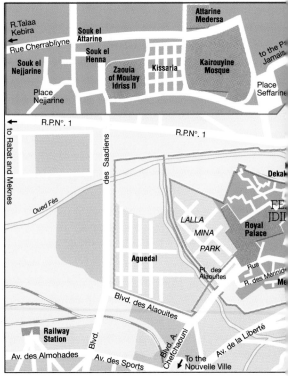

ety of trades that are still central to the medina's economic survival.

The strategic division between the two quarters was used by warring factions through the centuries until Youssef ben Tashfine of the Almoravide dynasty took control in the 11th century. Although Marrakesh was his capital, he did great things for Fez. He began by demolishing the wall dividing the two quarters and building a bridge across the river; this helped, but even today you are aware of the distinction between the two.

His greatest contribution was the re-routing of the river. Engineers were instructed to create an elaborate system of channels and by the late 11th century every mosque, *medrassa*, *fondouk*, street fountain and public bath, as well as most of the richer households, had water. The system included a successful method of flushing the drains.

Mosques were built in each quarter and, seen from above, the quarters appear to form a kind of amphitheatre around the Kairouyine Mosque (Fez's most important building), the green tiles marking out its total area.

To the right of the Kairouyine as you look down on Fez, a thin minaret marks the other great religious monument of Fez, the Zaouia of Moulay Idriss II. The Andalous Mosque, a similar focal point, is on the east bank.

To the right of the two minarets you can see the vast area of royal palace and grounds, with Fez Jdid (Fez the New) beside it. Built by the Merinids in the 13th century, Fez Jdid primarily provided a superior royal residence for the sultan and those connected with the palace, the administration and the army. The *mellah* is at the east end. With the emphasis on grandeur and open space, Fez Jdid contrasts with Fez el Bali.

The two parts of the Old City are linked by the **Avenue des Français**, which borders the peaceful and attractive **Boujeloud Gardens** on one side. The walls between the two were joined at the end of the 19th century and some of the buildings around this area date from that time.

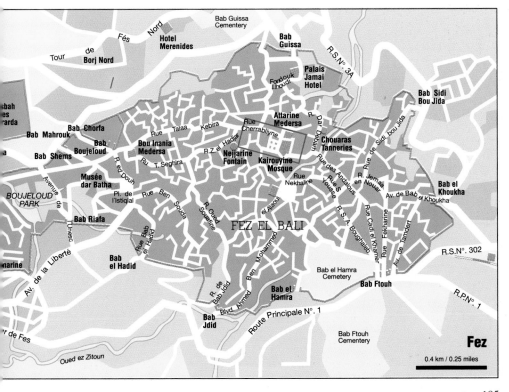

This is probably the clearest view you will get of the layout of the city. Once down in the medina there are no vistas and it's only by design that you can get a glimpse of a minaret or a roof top. Most of the *medersa* have good views from their roofs, if you are able to reach them. The carpet emporiums frequently use their roof-top views as bait to entice tourists.

Behind the Merinid tombs is the five-star **Hotel Merenids**, an ugly but brilliantly positioned hotel, not surprisingly a matter of contention when planned. The hotel suffered extensive fire damage when it was attacked during riots in 1991, but has since been restored. The **Borj Nord**, a fortress dating from Saadian times is just below the hotel and houses a collection of arms, in particular a large number of muskets. Its opening times are erratic, so unless you are particularly interested in weaponry it is probably not worth a visit. However, if you are up here, and it is open, why not? Again there are superb views.

On the opposite hillside the **Borj Sud** stands sentinel amid olive trees and grave stones; there are plans to build additional housing around this area. Many of the hillsides surrounding Fez are dotted with white stones – the cemeteries have to be outside the medina as there is no room for graves inside the city. The Tour de Fes takes you on from the tombs and the Borj Nord past the Bab Guissa to the Borj Sud and then sweeps back towards the New Town, leaving Fez Jdid on its right.

Fez is the medina: Within the city walls everything and nothing is revealed. At street level in the non-souk areas plain walls are continuous and blank except for dark doorways. Each of these opens into a darkened passage which in turn opens into the centre of a house, its beauty invisible to passers-by. Its centre is the courtyard, often paved or tiled in mosaics, with walls and pillars supporting a gallery in carved stucco or wood; the courtyard is open to the sky and all the rooms look on to it.

The houses are part of the city but at the same time closed off from it. Unless

Among the Merenid tombs.

you're lucky enough to be invited to join a Moroccan family meal, the nearest you'll get to seeing the design is from the old houses that have been converted into carpet co-operatives, or in snatched glances through briefly-opening doors.

Getting around the medina is a challenge. It is a good idea to get a guide at the beginning. He can take you to all the main sights, which can serve as landmarks on your own excursions later. Fix a price to begin with. This is important, although at the end he will disarmingly suggest you pay what you think he's worth. Don't get drawn into that – your evaluation and his may radically differ and things can then get complicated and even unpleasant.

There are fixed rates for official guides, so work on that basis, adding extra for qualifications, language skills, etc. You can arrange an official guide through your hotel, an unofficial guide will find you. Students are many and in some cases are much more interesting company than a bored official guide.

Another warning: The close relationship between the people and their city means that everybody knows somebody with something to sell – and a sale helps the community. Part of your tour will inevitably include a visit to a carpet emporium or co-operative. If you have no desire to buy and are short of time, try and make this clear to your guide at the outset, although he won't believe you. If you *do* find yourself being sucked into the sales patter, retreat politely as soon as you can; the longer you're there the more difficult it becomes.

If you are guideless and taking your chance alone in the medina, remember that any young lad will guide you out (for a few dirhams) should you get lost. Contrary to some first impressions, Fez is not a frightening city.

A tour: One of the main entrances to the medina is through the **Bab Boujeloud** to the east of the palace area. Cars are not allowed in the medina but parking is easy around the gates. Expect to pay a small sum for a "*gardien* of the car", who will appear as you draw up.

The distinctive green-tiled roofs of the Kairouyine Mosque.

THE FUTURE OF THE MEDINA

All Arab cities with some history have their medina. The Prophet Mohammed founded the first Islamic community in a city named Medina, which was second in importance to Mecca, and it quickly became the prototype for all other towns in the Arab world.

To a follower of the Islamic faith the pursuit of this ideal of the just and ordered city was (and in theory still is) obligatory. It is believed that on the Day of Judgment men and women will be assessed not only on their own merits but also on their performance in society. The design of the medinas, therefore, reflected communal values. Each quarter contributed to the benefit of the whole.

Even during the French and Spanish protectorates, the integrity of the medinas was respected. Marshal Lyautey, the first French Resident General, decreed that new developments to serve the influx of European administrators should be set apart from the medinas in order to preserve the old towns' way of life.

In the long run, such good intentions have created their own problems. Though many of the medinas are intact and in some cases still function much as they did in medieval times, they have generally lost their administrative and political importance to the new towns. After independence the

richer and most influential families in Fez often moved to the more modern quarters vacated by the Europeans, leaving the medina to the powerless and populous poor.

Fez embodies all the problems facing medinas in the modern world. For centuries it was the political and cultural capital of Morocco. In fact, it is still seen as the home of intellectual values in the country. But its 1,000-year-old medina relies upon the interdependence of industries and social structures for its continuing efficiency and survival and this is gravely threatened. Contrary to some visitors' impressions, it doesn't exist as a museum for tourists, and its souks do not stock merely the tourist trinkets; the Fassis rely on their industries, and their leather goods, silverware and cedarwork are sold throughout the country – to Moroccans.

Over 20,000 people live and work in Fez's medina and it's clear to anyone wandering through the packed souks that tourists are irrelevant to most of the inhabitants.

Old methods are still used by the dyers, tanners and the brass and silver craftsmen. There isn't room in the city to introduce new technology, open new factories and streamline production, even if they were wanted. So far only potteries have been moved out of the centre of Fez to hillsides close by, where new technology could be introduced. But such progress is beset by problems: break a part of the vast structure of the medina and it all might crumble.

Overcrowding is the main cause of Fez's ills. Over the past 50 years people have been moving into the town from the countryside to find work and fulfil dreams of prosperity. This has put Fez under severe strain. Certain public infrastructures, such as water supplies and 13th-century sewage systems, are at breaking point. There is no new housing available and shanty towns have spawned on the hillside near Fez. The different quarters of the city, once so well defined, are gradually losing their individual functions.

Sadly, demographic, social and economic constraints have had detrimental effects on the city's architecture. Fez's ancient mosques, medersa, palaces, fondouks and houses – only a fraction of which the tourist sees – are crumbling. Toxic waste is being poured into the rivers and sewers; the small but numerous machines that are used by the craftsmen produce damaging vibrations.

In 1980 UNESCO launched an appeal and introduced an ambitious programme of works. Today, their plans make both optimistic and tragic reading. The task is enormous and would seem impossible, but work has started. The objective is to keep the medina as a working structure – reinforcing its foundations both physically and administratively. But it is difficult not to be pessimistic when the office dealing with restoration works has moved to the new town where services are more efficient.

To survive, the medina has to take account of progress. The task of "up-dating" may be impossible, but the most urgent objective is to lighten the pressure within the city walls and allow the medina to breathe. ∎

Buses or cabs can be taken from **Place Baghadi** just by the gate.

As dusk falls this area is thronging with people. A dusty flea-market stretches out across the waste ground just outside the city walls, with frequent buses passing and turning.

The Bab Boujeloud, built in 1913, is one of the most recent *babs* but traditionally tiled and decorated: blue and gold outside, green and gold inside. Inside the gate the square splits into the two main streets, **Talaa Kebira** (or Grand Tala), the upper one on the left, and the less interesting **Talaa Sghira**, running parallel below it on the right.

Just off the square, on the upper reaches of Talaa Kebira, is one of the most remarkable sights in Fez, the **Bou Inania Medrassa**, an exuberant example of a Merinid monument. M*edersa* used to play an important role in Morocco. Essentially urban, these buildings were used as lodging houses for students who were strangers to the town; the idea was that the isolation would help them concentrate on their religious studies. *Medersa* were supported by endowments from the sultans and revenue from local inhabitants. For convenience, they were built close to the mosque where the students went for their lessons.

Similar in structure to mosques and private houses, they are all based around a central courtyard and highly decorated with mosaic, *zellige* (elaborate tiling) and stucco. Students often spent more than 10 years at university, so places to live were at a premium.

Sultan Abou Inan commissioned the Bou Inania, built between 1350 and 1357, and the cost is legendary. The story goes that he threw the accounts into the river when it was finished – beauty, he said, being unaccountable. It was a surprise to his contemporaries that he built one at all. His impious reputation, including the evidence of 325 sons in 10 years, perhaps spurred him to atone.

Abou Inan set out to make a rival to the Kairouyine Mosque and the Medrassa did become one of the most

From raw material to finished goods.

important religious buildings in the city. However, he failed to achieve his greatest desire to have the call to prayer transferred here from the Kairouyine, but the Bou Inania was granted the status of Grand Mosque, unheard of for a *medrassa* in Morocco, and Friday prayers are still heard here (the only time when the *medrassa* is closed).

It follows the usual layout, but the quality and intricacy of the decoration are outstanding. The courtyard facade is decorated with carved stucco, above which the majestic cedarwood arches support a frieze and corbelled porch. The interior shows us some of the finest examples of cedarwood carving, stucco work, Kufic script writing and *zellige* work. It is Morocco's only building in religious use that can be entered by non-Muslims. Even then, they have access to only the courtyard, where you see the faithful carrying out their pre-prayer ablutions in the fountain watered by the Oued Fez.

Opposite the Bou Inania is a remarkable **water-clock**. Thirteen wooden blocks balancing 13 brass bowls (only seven original bowls remain) protrude beneath 13 windows. Sultan Abou Inan erected it opposite the Medrassa to ring out the hour of prayer, hoping its originality would bring further fame to the Medrassa.

Its 14th-century mechanics have defeated modern horologists and the clock has been silent for five centuries. The legend goes that a curse was put on the clock when a pregnant Jewess passing below was so alarmed by its chime that she miscarried her child.

In 1990, following the discovery of documents detailing the working of the clock, a programme of restoration was embarked upon. However, the work is proving more complex than expeced and the clock has yet to emerge from its cocoon of scaffolding.

The Talaa Kebira leads eventually to the Kairouyine Mosque and the Zaouia of Moulay Idriss, but along the way are plenty of interesting souks. Smells and sounds are enthralling. If you walked through blindfold, despite a lack of air **The corner grocer.**

and draughts, the pungent aromas of mint, spices, wood and leather would act as guides.

There is a feeling of perpetual motion. Craftsmen, sometimes four to a tiny stall, work intently on their tasks, looking out occasionally. Tourists are tolerated here and only in the shops geared to the traditional trades is any attempt made to interest and sell. Everyone is occupied and engrossed in their own particular task.

The younger generation show more interest and call out to passing groups, while the smaller children follow persistently just by the elbow, repeating "Madam, Monsieur....Madam, Monsieur...", to be swept aside by the guides or fade out of necessity in the path of an on-coming mule.

The contemplative life.

The overall impression of the medina is chaotic but its structure is quite rigid. Each quarter has its own mosque, *medrassa*, *foundouk*, Koranic school, water fountain, *hammam*, and bakery. Everyone in the quarter brings their own dough to be baked in the central ovens (marks of identification help avoid confusion). Daily prayers are taken in the mosque of the quarter, the Grand mosques being used on Fridays, when people flock from all areas for this special prayer day.

Daily life continues. Shouts of "*Balek! Balek!*" ("Watch out" or "Get out of the way") precede the long-suffering tread of the mules carrying huge, often precariously balanced, burdens, forcing the flowing crowd to pin themselves against the walls. If Westerners weren't so obvious by their dress, they would certainly still be identified by their sudden movements interrupting the otherwise smooth flow of the *Fassi* crowd.

The *Fassis* are so familiar with sounds that they duck and weave past obstructions, keeping on the move, but there is the occasional impossible load that brings even the Fassi to a standstill. It perhaps isn't surprising that these tend to be mechanical trucks going about the restoration programme rather than the malleable beasts of burden.

The crowds continue down Talaa

Kebira, whose roof, covered in rushes, lets in shafts of light. Uneven illumination creates some beautiful images. Brilliant colours of spices become patterns in shade and sun. Bundles and bundles of mint smell fresh and strong. Heaps of dried grass by the side of stalls are sold to Berber women for cleaning teeth. A type of Moroccan floss?

Walking down the street, you come across large buildings now mainly used as warehouses by traders in the souk; these are the *fondouks*, another integral part of the medina, created at about the same time as the *medersa,* as hotels for traders and doubling up as stables. There were over 200 *fondouks* in Fez el Bali; many survive and it is remarkable to see such highly decorated buildings now being used as warehouses. They have the familiar structure of a courtyard with galleried sleeping area. In particular, look out, on the left-hand side of the street and through a vine covered arch, for an old fondouk occupied by the butter and honey market (announced by the strong smell of *smen* – the aged butter used in the best *cous-cous*).

Nearing the end of Talaa Kebira, you might get a whiff of the strong smell from the **leatherworkers' fondouk**, which stores the drying skins from the slaughterhouse before they're sent to the dyers. Close by where the road becomes Rue ech Cherabliyin, the leatherworkers have their stalls.

Babouches, the famous leather slippers worn in various forms by most Moroccan men, are sold here. The most common colours are yellow and white (the former for everyday use and the latter for visits to the mosque, especially on Fridays), but in Fez you can also buy grey ones, which are considered unusual and therefore envied.

The street bends down towards the Grand Kairouyine Mosque. This area is the commercial and formal centre of the medina. Islam strongly approves of trade. Straight ahead, the **Souk el Attarine** (the perfume and spice-sellers' souk) and the **Kissaria** comprise what is considered the most sophisticated part of the medina. The Kissaria is famous for its embroidery stalls, silks and brocades, as well as stalls for imported goods. The fire that wiped out the Kissaria in 1954 leaves it rather characterless in structure with modern roofing, but you are quickly distracted by the dazzling display of goods.

Off the Kissaria, at the end of Souk el Attarine, is the **Attarine Medrassa**, another Merinid structure, designed to serve the Kairouyine Mosque. It was built by Sultan Abou Said between 1322 and 1325. Its roof (if necessary, tip for access) offers a bird's-eye view into the courtyard of the Kairouyine Mosque.

Below **Souk el Attarine** is the *horm*, a sacred area around the **Shrine of Moulay Idriss II**, the effective founder of Fez. A wooden bar at donkey-neck height denotes the area. Until the French protectorate this barred not only mules and donkeys but also Jews and Christians. It also marked a refuge for Muslims, who could not be arrested in this area. Today it is a popular spot for beggars hoping to tap pilgrims on their way to devotions. Rows of stalls sell candles of all sizes and colours, incense,

No way out but up.

and many other religious and devotional materials, mainly bought by women to lay before the great Idriss's tomb.

The tomb was built by the Idrissids in the 9th century but was allowed to fall into decay by ensuing dynasties until it was rebuilt in the 13th century by the Merinids. The Wattasids rediscovered the tomb and from this period it became the revered shrine it is now. A glimpse through the doorway reveals a colourful and mystical sight – the smell of incense and the flickering lights of candles surround prostrate figures.

The street follows the wall of the *zaouia*, and through another very richly decorated doorway you can see the room of prayer. This contains innumerable chandeliers and, around the tomb, a rather surprising collection of clocks, considered an upmarket offering in the 19th century.

Follow your nose to the **Souk Nejjarine** (carpenters' souk) filled with the intoxicating smell of cedarwood. Here craftsmen crouch over finely carved tables, bedheads, chairs and every

kind of wooden creation. Most Moroccan furniture seen in hotels and private houses is wooden and made with meticulous care in the medinas. Also note the large octagonal wooden trays used for carrying brides or newly circumcised boys.

Place Nejjarine, alongside the souk, is one of the oldest in Fez, and the *fondouk* at the corner of the square dates from the late 17th century. It is currently being restored. The **Nejjarine Fountain**, the focal point of the square, is an outstanding example of *zellige* decoration and stands almost like a shrine to water. From here, in regaining Souk el Attarine, you pass the entrance to the **henna souk,** where an inexhaustible supply of hand and face dyes (especially henna, camomile and antimony) are packed into the stalls. Women stand about testing the dyes and experimenting with elaborate patterns on their hands.

All roads in the medina lead to the **Kairouyine Mosque**, or so the saying goes. Rivalled in size only by King Hassan's new mosque in Casablanca, it

A photographer displays his art.

can accommodate 20,000 people, only a fifth of the number that live and work in the medina. It was founded in 859 by a woman from Kairouyine (in modern-day Tunisia) in memory of her father; each ruler added to it and changed it.

The Merinids' alterations in the 13th century cast it in its present mould. Green tiled roofs cover 16 naves, and the tiled courtyards have two end pavilions and a beautiful 16th-century fountain reminiscent of the Court of Lions of the Alhambra Palace in Granada. It is jealously guarded from the eyes of non-Muslims but you can snatch glimpses of the interior from the doorways.

The sanctuary interior is austerely simple with horseshoe arches over plain columns. It was the first university in the Western world and its reputation attracted over 8,000 students in the 14th century. Considered one of the great seats of learning, it even boasts a pope as one of its past students.

The **Kairouyine Library**, on one side of the mosque, is also thought to have been built in the 9th century. Closed to the public, it contains one of the most renowned collections of Islamic literature in the world.

Below the library is **Place Seffarine** (the area of metalworkers), an enchanting square shaded by trees. Huge cauldrons are stacked in every available space, donkeys are loaded up, work is in progress – all accompanied by a cacophany of hammering. Cauldrons and giant trays are specially made for feast days and weddings.

The same skills were used on the redecoration of the great doors to the King's palace (visible across Place des Alaouites as you approach Fez Jdid from the New Town). Place Seffarine is one of the prettiest squares in the medina, and if you can gain access to the **Seffarine Medrassa** close by, the roof offers a view of the overall scene.

The **dyers' quarter** constitutes a narrow unevenly cobbled street close by the Place Seffarine. Cauldrons of dye stand at the doorways and all around skeins of freshly dipped silk and wool drip their bright colours into the gutters. These join in streams hurtling towards the river. The men stand around with stained feet and hands, the narrowness of the street giving them little room to manoeuvre amid the constant pressure of people. Tourists dodge the coloured water determined to wage war on their espadrilles.

The **tanneries**, also near the river offer a yet more extreme experience. The area has hardly changed since medieval times. The position of stone vats, one against the other, make shifting the skins in and out of the different dyes an athletic achievement. Scantily-clad men crouch and balance over vats dipping the hides; roofs around are thick with drying skins. Natural colours are still used: yellow (saffron), red (poppy), blue (indigo) and black (antimony).

The tanneries are run as a co-operative, with each foreman responsible for his own workforce and tools. Jobs are practically hereditary. This primitive but skilled trade, carried out mostly in intense heat and restricted surroundings, is the most haunting in Fez. The strong smell of animal skins, dye mixed

Left and **right**, the tanneries: Moroccan leather has a worldwide reputation

with cow urine (for preservation), and human sweat, is at times nauseating, but you get used to it.

Tourists are trooped through the walkways and helped up small uneven steps to vantage points for photographs. Terrible bottlenecks of mint-sniffing visitors move hesitantly along the walls and roof tops.

The Andalous quarter: From here you can cross the bridge to the **Andalous quarter**. The **Andalous Mosque** was founded shortly after the Kairouyine was founded in the ninth century and embellished by the Almohads at the beginning of the 13th century. It is the main sanctuary on the east bank and has some beautiful carved cedarwork, but viewing is difficult. Of the two *medersa* in this quarter, the **Es Sahrij**, early 14th-century, is worth seeing. Its *zellige* decorations are some of the oldest in the country and there is plenty of fine wood carving.

This quarter is less intense, both in its structure and number of inhabitants. Walking up the hill towards the **Bab**

Ftouh, which marks the eastern limits of the medina, you pass the potters quarter. Fez pottery, with its distinctive blue design, is sold all over Morocco and its craftsmen are much admired.

By retracing your steps past the Kairouyine and walking up the hill westwards, you emerge beside the **Palais Jamai Hotel** beside the Bab Guissa. It was built by Si Mohammed ben Arib el Jamai at end of the 19th century and is a finer example of the architect's work than the palace of the same name built in Meknes and now housing the Musuem of Morrocan Arts.

Now an extremely comfortable, expensive hotel, its position on the edge of the medina, enclosed in a walled garden of palm trees and roses lulled by the sound of water and birdsong, is probably the best in Fez. The sound of the 5am call to prayer – *"Allah Akbar"* – echoing across the medina from the Kairouyine Mosque, joined by a chorus of *muezzins* from neighbouring mosques, is in itself a good reason to stay within earshot of the medina – it is a voice of Morocco and should be heard at least once during your stay.

A short taxi ride from Bab Guissa and you're back at Bab Boujeloud.

A look at Fez Jdid: Despite its name, **Fez Jdid** (New Fez) was planned by the Merinids during the 13th century to incorporate an impressive royal palace and gardens (entry to both now prohibited) and as the administrative centre of Fez. The role of this part of the city diminished when the governmental function was moved to Rabat by the French. At about this time it became known as the red-light district of Fez and now remains a slightly melancholy area with the almost deserted *mellah* (Jewish quarter) tacked on to the south-eastern corner.

The **Grand Mosque** presides over the north end of Fez Jdid, with the **Grand Rue de Fez Jdid** the main artery linking this part of town with the *mellah*. The main street, lined with souks selling vegetables, textiles and household items, is not of any particular interest and offers none of the cohesion and mystery of Fez el Bali.

Outside the Attarine Madressa.

The **mellah** was originally sited by the Bab Guissa. When Fez Jdid was built the Jews were ordered to move to their new quarter near the sultan's palace. Many Jews who had interests in the medina preferred to become Muslims and thus stay in Fez el Bali. Those who did move were promised protection in consideration of supplementary taxes.

This ghetto was given the name *mellah*, which means "salt" in Arabic, because it was the Jews' task to drain and salt the heads of decapitated rebels before they were impaled on the gates of the town. The Jews' position has always been ambiguous and, although ostensibly under the sultan's protection, their lives before the protectorates were severely limited. No Jew was allowed to wear shoes or ride outside the *mellah* and further restrictions were placed on their travel elsewhere.

Very few Jewish families remain; most left for France, with a few setting up home in Casablanca. What remains are their tall, very un-Arab buildings retaining a certain dignity even in their fast-decaying form. There is a sad rather run-down souk mainly of clothes and household item, tapes, T-shirts and other cheap, generally low-quality Western goods.

One of the oddities of this area – and quite difficult to find among the twisting, abandoned streets – is the **Hebrew cemetery**. Rows of pristine white gravestones very close together cluster on the slope of the hill stretching down towards the river.

The area between Fez Jdid and Fez el Bali, joined in the late 19th century by Moulay el Hassan, contains the **Dar Batha Palace**. Formerly part of the link between the two, with gates at both ends, it now houses the excellent **Museum of Moroccan Arts**. Definitely worth a visit (except on Tuesdays, when it is closed), it has a fascinating collection of artefacts, carpets, mosaics, pottery and jewellery. It also offers many interesting examples of stucco work and carving – useful to see (because they give a good idea of developments in techniques) before embarking on the tour of *medersa* and moxsques.

The *mellah* in Fez el Jedid.

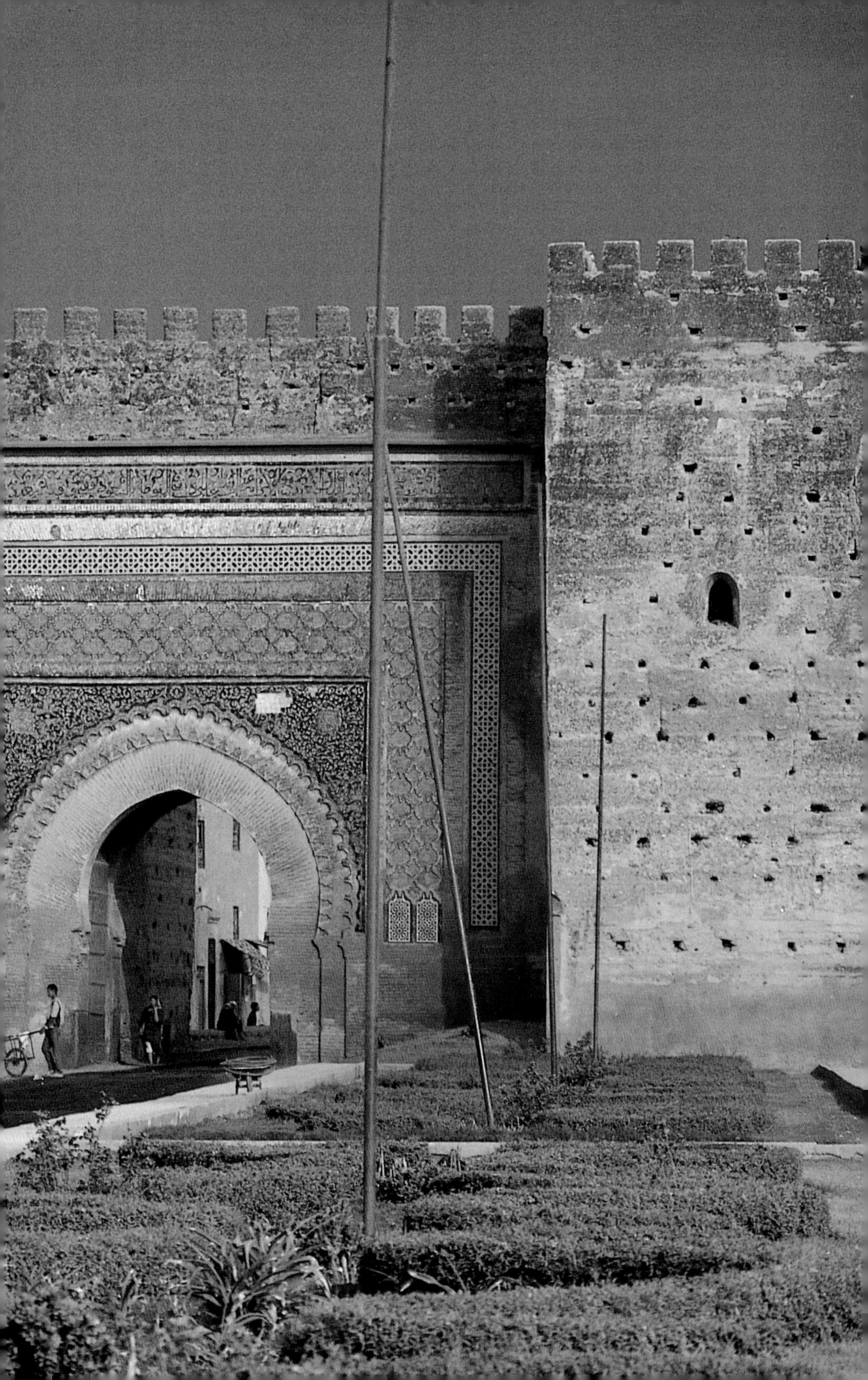

MEKNES

As a celebratory gift to mark the beginning of his long rule in the mid-17th century, Moulay Ismail displayed 700 heads on the walls of Fez, thus setting the tone of what turned out to be a reign of terror.

Infamous Ismail: Moulay Ismail's love of blood is legendary. The British diplomat John Windus, who visited Ismail's palace in 1725 and recorded his impressions in *A Journey to Mequinez*, observed how "about eight or nine [in the morning] his trembling court assemble, which consists of his great officers, and alacaydes, blacks, whites, tawnies and his favourite Jews, all barefooted; and there is bowing and whispering to this and the other eunuch, to know if the Emperor has been abroad (for if he keeps within doors there is no seeing him unless sent for), if he is in a good humour, which is well known by his very looks and motions and sometimes by the colour of the habit he wears, yellow being observed to be his killing colour; from all of which they calculate whether they may hope to live twenty-four hours longer."

Moulay Ismail was an effective sultan. He ruled Morocco from his capital, Meknes, for 55 years, more or less as a united country. During that period Morocco became a noteworthy country in Europe and the sultan considered Louis XIV, his contemporary in France, a close friend.

Meknes has been called the "Versailles of Morocco" and there is evidence that Ismail saw himself as a Moroccan Louis XIV, albeit superior to the French monarch, to whom he suggested the Muslim faith and offered himself as husband to one of the French princesses. Both these suggestions were politely turned down. The two grandfather clocks on display inside Moulay Ismail's mausoleum are reputed to be gifts which the French king sent to mollify the disappointed sultan.

Although surrounded by fertile land and a good choice in terms of trade connections, Meknes was not very easy to defend. Before Moulay Ismail took control it had experienced a turbulent history. Founded in the 10th century by a Berber tribe known as Meknassass, it passed through the hands of the 11th-century Almoravides and the 12th-century Almohads to the Merinids and then the Saadis.

Before becoming sultan, Moulay Ismail had been the governor of Meknes on behalf of his father, the Alaouite Sultan er Rashid, whom he succeeded in 1672. His excesses, both as governor and sultan, were notorious. Statistics vary wildly but it was said that his harem comprised 500 women. Of the many hundreds of children he fathered he had the girls strangled at birth and was not averse to slicing off the limbs of erring sons.

His vision of power, amounting to mania, has left Meknes a graveyard of huge palaces and buildings. The 16 miles (25 km) of walls built around the city were only part of his grand plan. He gathered together an army of 30,000

Sudanese soldiers – a "peace-keeping" force – who roamed the country, keeping the tribes in check.

Back in Meknes, more than 25,000 unfortunate captives were brought in to execute his vision of grand palaces, walls and fortresses. At night they were herded into dark, subterranean chambers dug for their habitation. Describing Moulay Ismail's brutal teatment of his slaves, Scott O'Connor, in *Vision of Morocco*, adds: "When the slaves died they were used as building material and immured in the rising walls, their blood mixed with the cement that still holds them together in its grip."

There are plenty more blood-curdling stories. Meknes has suffered from a history of such grim blood-letting. Its medina and imperial city now present rather a tragic sight, "Miles upon miles of cemented walls run their mournful course about the city" is how it was described early in the 20th century.

Within these walls lie the remains of a dream of some 30 royal palaces, 20 gates, mosques, barracks, and ornamental gardens. It is magnificent and lunatic in its scale of conception, and Moulay Ismail has to be admired for his single-mindedness. He built Meknes into one of the four great imperial cities and it remained capital until his death in 1727 when his heir removed to Marrakesh. The son destroyed a number of buildings as a parting shot and from then the city declined.

A tour of the town: The French built the **New Town** on the opposite side of the **Oued Boufekrane**, which runs through the valley between the city's two halfs. It remains a prosperous provincial town. Local industry and excellent farm land account for its wealth. Vineyards cover nearby hills.

There is little of interest in the new part of town – a few hotels offer uninspiring accommodation. One five-star hotel, the Hotel Transatlantique to the west of town, provides views across the river to the medina and has a good restaurant. Fairly lively by day, Meknes, new and old, has died by about 10pm.

The main part of a visit to Meknes should be dedicated to **old Meknes** and the **imperial city** on the west bank of the river. All roads lead to **Place el Hedim** (the sinisterly named Place of Destruction). Now a huge square graced by shooting fountains, it used to be part of the medina but was razed to the ground by Moulay Ismail to create an approach to the main entrance of his palace via Bab Mansour.

The square is almost too large to be lively. Stalls cling to the east side and benches line the west. A fairly constant stream of people cross from the medina to Bab Mansour and round towards the new town; buses forever disgorge their bulging loads into the square, though it no longer serves as the bus terminus (which is now outside Bab Khemis). Briefly the square fills, then just as quickly it empties.

The area is dominated by the **Bab Mansour**, commissioned by Moulay Ismail himself but finished during his son's reign, in 1732. Brilliantly decorated in green and white ceramic tiling, it is flanked by two square bastions supported in part by marble columns

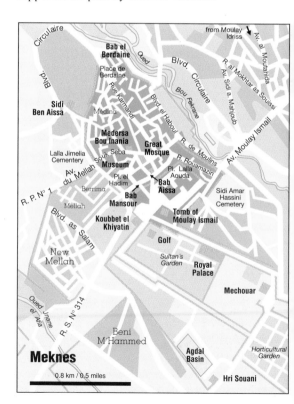

taken from Volubilis. Though remarkable for its size and symmetry, like much of Ismail's grand vision it proves overpowering and heavy.

A tour of the Imperial city should start from here. Although a guide – picked up in Place el Hadim or around Bab Mansour – can be useful, the layout of the city is easy to grasp and it is possible to manage without one.

Proceeding through Bab Mansour, you come to **Place Lalla Aouda**, a popular gathering place for womenfolk in the late afternoon. Close by (walk to the right as you come from Bab Mansour), is a simple domed pavilion, the **Koubbet el Khiyatin**, thought to have been used for receiving visiting ambassadors and for bargaining over the ransoms demanded for Christian victims of Barbary Coast piracy, in which Moulay Ismail had a controlling interest. Adjacent to the pavilion is a stairway leading into subterranean chambers used to house either grain or slaves – again, nobody is certain. The chambers, blocked off by the French, who also added the sky-

lights, once extended 7 km (4 miles) each way.

The gardens stretching out behind the walls have been turned into a **royal golf course**. Following the road round, through another gate, you come upon one of Meknes's main sights, the **Tomb of Moulay Ismail**. Restored by Mohammed V, it is the only shrine in Morocco apart from the mausoleum of Mohammed V in Rabat and the shrine of Sidi Yahiya near Oujda that can be visited by non-Muslims. Only the courtyards are open, but you can peek through the door of the sanctuary to see the tomb. The fine tile panels are in excellent condition; simple geometric patterns contribute to the splendour. The walls and courtyard are highly patterned and the stucco work is striking.

Moulay Ismail's reputation for violence and cruelty does not seem to have diminished the reverence paid to him. It is perhaps odd that such a keen blood-letting ruler should have a shrine of such magnificence, and one that still attracts Muslims from all over Morocco. The

Left, Ismail's granaries: ready for a siege. **Right**, the water seller, familiar in all imperial cities.

people believe that his tomb has *baraka* (magical powers) which will rub off on believers. A doorway off the mausoleum opens on to a private cemetery (no entry) for those wishing to be buried alongside this famous ruler.

From the tomb it is possible to walk along a corridor-like road to the Heri el Souani (follow the signs). Massive walls, riddled with nesting birds, rise on both sides of the thoroughfare. Most of the palaces behind them are crumbling ruins, but a few have been restored for military or educational purposes; you can catch glimpses of these through breaches in the walls.

The **Dar el Kebira**, Moulay Ismail's main palace complex, was destroyed by his son and remains a sad ruin. **The Dar el Makhzen**, one of the last palaces completed at the end of the 18th century, has been restored and is used by the present royal family as an occasional residence.

One of the most remarkable sights within the Imperial city is the **Heri as Souani** – high vaulted chambers now overgrown at their bases – which were used as store-rooms and granaries. The chambers are immense. Moulay Ismail was always ready for a siege. For a good overview of the complex, climb the stairs to the café on the remaining part of the roof. Olive trees provide shade.

The **Aguedal Basin**, round the corner from the Heri el Souani, covers 10 acres (4 hectares) but, as with all the sights within the Imperial city, its abandoned grandeur creates a mournful and gloomy atmosphere. Moulay Ismail's vision was mighty but the spaces he created were never filled – the scale was too huge.

The **Royal stables**, further along the route in the quarter of Heri el Mansour, are the best example of Moulay Ismail's excess. They were built for more than 12,000 horses, each with its own groom and slave. The grain was stored below in the granaries, at a temperature kept constant by the thick walls. Ismail also constructed a canal providing fresh water for the horses without them having to move from their stalls.

The imperial complex stretches for

Sixteen miles of wall surround the city

almost 3 miles (5 km) and the crumbling remains still given an indication of the extent of decoration that once existed; tiles and *zelliges* are visible on pieces of partially overgrown wall. The place now belongs to goats.

The medina: Returning to the Bab Mansour, enter the **medina** at the west end of the Place el Hedim. **The Museum of Moroccan Arts** housed in the Dar Jamai is discreetly positioned at the corner of the square beside the entrance to the medina. It is worth a visit to see the fine examples of Berber rugs, especially if you are intending to visit any carpet shops. It also has an interesting collection of local artefacts and pottery.

The building itself was built by the architect who designed the Palais Jamai hotel in Fez at the end of the 19th century, though it is on a less grand scale. Some of the upper rooms are decorated and furnished to give an idea of domestic life in the 19th century. Like all the other grand palaces, it has a wonderful garden filled with flowering shrubs and birdsong.

For the best view of the layout of the area, go up to the roof of the **Medrassa Bou Inania**. From here, you can see the green tiled minarets of the mosques of each quarter and the roof of the Grand Mosque. This Medrassa was started by Sultan Abou Hassan but finished by Sultan Abou Inan (1350–58). It is similar to other Merinid *medersa* with a central fountain in a tiled courtyard, student quarters on two levels and a prayer hall on one side. As usual, every inch of wall is painstakingly covered in abstract patterns and stylised script, creating a mesmerising intensity designed to reflect and reiterate the greatness and oneness of God.

The main street, covered by a corrugated iron roof, contains most of the usual stalls and is an animated, bustling thoroughfare. The **carpenters' souk** is permeated by the sweet smell of cedar and thuya wood. If you find yourself in the souk as darkness falls, the light can be deceptive and it's very easy to get hopelessly lost. You can be pursuing a shaft of light, thinking it will draw you to the outside, only to find yourself beside an illuminated stall with another street stretching in front of you.

If you continue through the carpenters' souk, you eventually emerge at the west end where the artisans' markets are in full swing. It is quite a scruffy area but has some interesting co-operative workshops – basket-makers, saddlers, etc. Fruit and food stalls are found spasmodically placed both in this area and in the souk.

The Aissawa Brotherhood: Out of the medina, beside the **Bab el Berdain**, is a huge cemetery containing the shrine of **Sidi ben Aissa**, built in the 18th century (it is not open to non-Muslims). A Sufi cult, the Aissawa brotherhood was founded in the 15th century and spread all over North Africa. Sidi Ben Aissa was supposed to confer magical powers on his followers – apparently they could eat anything, however grim, without the slightest ill-effects.

On the eve of Mouloud, the date of their annual *moussem*, over 50,000 devotees would gather and in a state of induced trance devour live animals and pierce their tongues and cheeks. Their rituals were similar to those of the Hammaacha of Moulay Idriss, whose *moussem* is so vividly described in Paul Bowles's *The Spider's House*. The government has outlawed the most extreme practices of these cults, but their annual *moussems* still take place.

The new and old *mellahs* to the west of the medina and Place el Hedim have markets and souks of their own. It is a busy but very run-down area, with buildings built into the crumbling walls of the old houses. It is one of the poorest parts of town.

Whether because of the bloody actions of Moulay Ismail, reputed to have slaughtered over 36,000 with his own hands, or the combination of grandeur and decay, Meknes has a strange atmosphere. The emptiness of the vast crumbling edifices in contrast to the intensity of the slightly shabby medina reinforce the feeling. Meknes lacks the cohesive feel of Fez; its inhabitants have none of the proud confidence in their city that the Fassis show. Maybe Meknes simply lived with fear for too long.

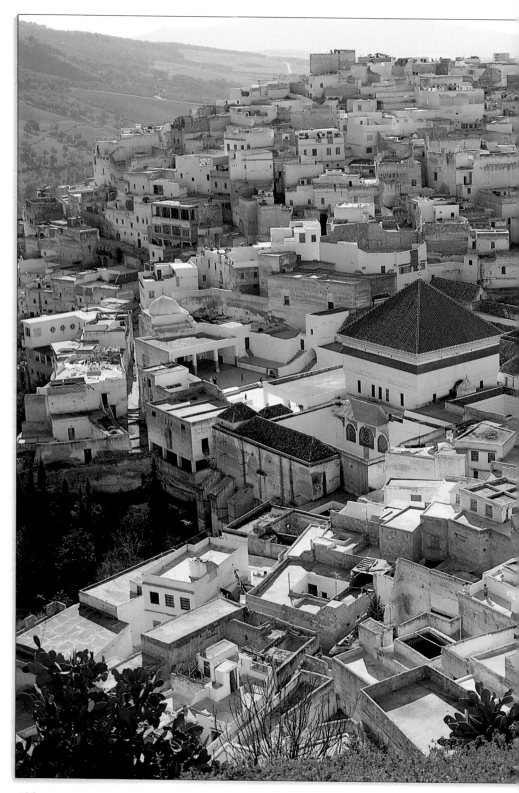

MOULAY IDRISS

You are visiting a town; but it is essentially a shrine to Moulay Idriss I, whose tomb rests here.

It is hard to imagine when you first catch sight of the cluster of white houses on the hillside that this is where the sects of Hamaacha and Dghoughia, trance-induced, performed grim and violent rituals during the annual *moussem*. Slicing into their heads with hatchets and heading cannon balls were only two of their more popular antics. The more extreme activities of the sects have been outlawed by the government, but it is rumoured that they continue in places unobserved.

The *moussem* is held after the harvest, usually beginning on the last Thursday in August. It lasts for several weeks and is considered the most important religious festival in Morocco. Pilgrims unable to make the journey to Mecca can settle for Moulay Idriss, rated as second in sacredness to Mecca in Morocco, though the revered courtesy title of "*el Hadj*" is bestowed only on those who reach Mecca.

Originally a purely religious festival, it has come to include fantasias, singing, dancing and markets. The hillsides are covered with tents, and prayer, feasting and general rejoicing continue throughout the festival. Tourists are tolerated but it is a purely Muslim festival and it's probably sensible to visit during the daytime rather than at night.

The origins of the town: At the end of the 8th century, Moulay Idriss el Akhbar (the elder) arrived in the village of Zerhoun. The great-grandson of the Prophet Mohammed, he fled to Morocco to escape persecution and death. He stopped first at Volubilis, later building his town nearby, and set about his task of converting the Berbers to the Islamic faith. He was well received by the mountain people, who recognised him as their leader. He became the founder of the first Arab dynasty in Morocco. A year later he began the founding of Fez – a labour completed by Idriss II.

News of his popularity and success reached his enemies in the east and an emissary was sent to poison him in 791. His dynasty lived on through his son, born two months after his death.

The town: Moulay Idriss is set in the spur of the hills just east of Volubilis. As you approach from Meknes, the town looks a compact, predominantly white whole, but it is really two villages. The Khiber and the Tasga quarters join together around the mosque and shrine.

Arriving by car, you can park either in a small area close to the main square, or to the north of the centre. It is not a tourist attraction and, although a peaceful and simple place, there is much poverty. The streets are clean, a few children play on ice-blue doorsteps, and women, invariably veiled, move silently about their chores.

Moulay Idriss exists seemingly oblivious of the 20th century, although Meknes is only 16 miles (25 km) away. There are few concessions to Western visitors. The souks – insofar as they exist at all – sell basic wares and are in the Khiber quarter, spreading rather thinly back up the hill from the *zaouia*. The best views of the town are from the terrace **Sidi Abdallah el Hajjam**, above the Khiber quarter. The thin empty streets make up a complicated network and it's easy to climb into a dead end. There are, however, plenty of boys happy to lead you to the terrace for a few dirhams. A rather reticent biscuit and postcard seller sometimes appears on the mud terrace, but there is no pressure to buy.

From here the structure of the town is clear. White and grey cubes fall down below you to where the quarters merge beside the tomb and *zaouia* of Moulay Idriss. The green-tiled roofs and arched courtyards of the mosque and shrine are clearly visible.

The mausoleum was rebuilt by Moulay Ismail, who destroyed the first structure at the end of the 18th century in order to create a more beautiful one. This was later embellished by the Sultan Moulay Abderrahmen. The minaret, somewhat paradoxically in this almost

Preceding pages: Moulay Idriss. Below left, a Heath Robinson-type construction near the city gate. Below right, the annual *moussem*.

timeless town, was rebuilt in the 1930s. Its striking cylindrical shape is unique to Morocco.

You can get a reasonable look at half of it from one of the streets close by. The green ceramic tiles are decorated with stylised printing from the Koran. Non-Muslims are forbidden entry to the tomb and shrine. The *horm* (sanctuary area) is clearly delineated by a low wooden bar placed across the entry to repel Christians and any beasts of burden bent on gaining access.

The main square – more of a rectangle – opens out from the holy area. It is the busiest part of the town, especially around the beautiful tiled fountain. Opposite the entrance is a group of make-shift stalls selling nougat and nuts in abundance. Nougat, giant poles of it, like furled umbrellas in every imaginable colour, is a speciality of the town, as it is in any place of pilgrimage in the Arab world.

Quite a wide road with a smattering of stalls leads down to the city gate where people wait for lifts. Transport is either by bus, communal taxi or pick-up trucks, which stop and are filled in an instant by those bound for Meknes, Fez or Sidi Kacem.

Before you go: Worth looking out for on the left as you walk down to the main city gate is an extraordinary house. A Heath Robinson-type construction, a mish-mash of materials – TVs, motorbike parts, bits of cloth and metal – rising three storeys, it is almost the only building acknowledging the modern world in Moulay Idriss. It's remarkable in its incongruity.

Although hundreds of tourist buses visit Volubilis, only one kilometre away, there are very few to be seen in Moulay Idriss. At one time Christians were forbidden in the town, and until recently not permitted to stay overnight. Nobody is unfriendly, but you may feel you are invading their privacy. Bear this possibility in mind if you can because it is a unique place and, with the new luxury hotel above Volubilis (a good place to stay nonetheless), its days of peace may be numbered.

Ceremonial serving dishes are prepared for the *moussem*.

VOLUBILIS

Volubilis makes a worthwhile excursion from Fez or Meknes, especially when combined with Moulay Idriss. From Fez, a round trip combining Moulay Idriss, Volubilis and Meknes can be done in a day: it is 94 miles (150 km) in total. However, if you want to stay the night and enjoy the rural peace of the spot, the Volubilis Inn, a new luxury hotel with swimming pool, overlooks the site at a respectful distance (*see Travel Tips, page 304*).

Approaching **Volubilis** from Meknes, you slowly climb the hillside until, rounding a corner, you see Volubilis stretched out on the ledge of a triangular plateau 127 feet (390 metres) high. Bypassing the turn to Moulay Idriss (clustered between two hillsides to the northeast), take a left fork. The sand-coloured buildings around the entrance to Volubilis will be visible. A car-park and a couple of souvenir shacks welcome visitors. Just beside the entrance is a well-positioned shady café looking across to the site.

Important discoveries: There is a small, **open-air museum** in the garden as you enter through the southeast gate. Many pieces of inscribed stone and other fragments lie haphazardly around. The archaeologically important finds have been removed to the archaeological museum in Rabat.

Following a well-worn path through olive groves and across the small **Fertassa river**, clamber leftwards up the opposite hill to the start of the site. The sense of peace is immediate, unless you're unlucky enough to arrive with a batch of coaches. Best times are early morning before they arrive, or evening when the buses have left. The most important remains are clearly labelled and the arrows describe a roughly clockwise tour.

Traces of a Neolithic settlement have been found here, and also those of an important Berber village, thought to have been the capital of the Berber kingdom of Mauritania. Caligula was responsible for taking over this kingdom and from AD 45 Volubilis was subject to direct Roman rule, making it the Empire's most remote base.

During this time, oil production and copper were the city's main assets. The profusion of oil presses on the site confirms this – one or two to a house. Most of the buildings date from the beginning of the 3rd century, when the number of inhabitants was probably around 20,000. By the end of the 3rd century the Romans had gone.

After this, change was very gradual; Volubilis maintained its Latinised structure and when the Arabs arrived in the 7th century the mixed population of Berbers, Jews and Syrians still spoke Latin. The culture and teachings of Islam took over and by 786, when Moulay Idriss I arrived, most of the inhabitants were already converted. He chose to build a new city (Moulay Idriss) nearby, and Volubilis began to decline. Much later, in the 18th century, Moulay Ismail desecrated Volubilis by removing the

marble to adorn his palaces in Meknes.

The Lisbon earthquake in 1755 damaged the city and it fell into ruin. It was rediscovered by two diplomats on a tour of the area at the end of the 19th century, though it is hard to believe it could have been ignored for so long considering the splendid Triumphal Arch, the only edifice to remain standing after the earthquake, keeping sentinel over the site. Excavations were begun during the French protectorate in 1915 and continue today, funded by the Moroccan government.

Volubilis is small and easy to cover. Some of the main buildings have been half restored or reconstructed. The most remarkable finds include bronze statues (now in Rabat) and the amazingly well-preserved **mosaics**, many of which remain *in situ*. For purposes of identification, the houses are named after the subject of the mosaic they contain.

All the houses follow the same basic structure: each had its public and private rooms. The mosaics usually decorated the public rooms and internal courtyards; the baths and kitchens being the private areas of the house. The first house you come to on the clockwise tour of the site is the **House of Orpheus**, the largest house in its quarter. It has three mosaics: a circular mosaic of Orpheus (God of music) charming the animals with his lyre, remarkable for its detail and colours; another of nine dolphins, believed by the Romans to bring good luck; and a third portraying Amphitrite in a chariot drawn by a seahorse.

From here, cut up to the new square building containing a reconstructed olive press, one of several that have been found on the site.

Wandering up the wide paved street, you pass the remains of the **public baths** restored by Gallienus in the 3rd century. Bathing was given high priority by the Romans and public baths provided a meeting place to chat, gossip, do business, exercise, eat and drink. Grand houses had their own elaborate heating systems providing hot water and steam for baths and heat.

From here, the street leads to the Fo-

The Triumphal arch.

rum (public square), Capitol and Basilica, an impressive collection of administrative buildings which comprised the centre of the city.

The **Capitol** is a small rectangular building of classic type; originally the central area would have contained a temple fronted by four columns and been surrounded by porticoes. The terrace, reached by a flight of 13 steps, and several Corinthian columns have been reconstructed. Inscription dates it 217 and dedicates the temple to the cult of Capitoline, Jove and Minerva.

The **Basilica** is a larger building beside the Capitol. It isn't easy to see its structure now but it would have been divided into five aisles (note the stumpy columns) with an apse at both ends. It doubled as the law courts and commercial exchange.

The **Forum,** which completes the administrative centre, is an open space which was used for public and political meetings (a glorified Speakers' Corner). It is of modest proportions and nothing remains of the statues of digni-

taries that would have adorned the surrounding buildings.

Between the Forum and the unmistakable Triumphal Arch is the **Acrobat's House**, containing two well preserved mosaics. The main one depicts an acrobat riding his mount back-to-front and holding up his prize. Another house nearby contained the famous Bronze Dog in the archaeological museum in Rabat.

The **Triumphal Arch** is the centrepoint of Volubilis. It was an impressive, if non-functional, ceremonial monument. Contemporary to the Capitol, it was built by Marcus Aurelius Sebastenus in honour of Caracalla and his mother Julia Domna. It is supported on marble columns and decorated only on the east side. Records and the inscription suggest it was surmounted by a huge bronze chariot and horses. It was built to celebrate the power of the Emperor Caracalla and remains a remarkable edifice.

The main paved street, **Decumanus Maximus**, stretches up to the **Tangier**

One of the well-preserved mosaics.

Gate (the only gate out of a total of eight which remains standing). The street is lined with what must have been the finest houses in town. Their frontages were rented to shopkeepers, who sold their wares from shaded porticoes on either side. The layout is not unlike a Moroccan street today.

Behind, in a number of ruined houses, are more splendid mosaics. The **House of Ephebus** boasts the Bacchus mosaic, depicting the god of wine in a chariot pulled by panthers. A bronze head of Ephebus was found in this house but has been despatched to Rabat. The **House of Columns**, recognisable by the remains of columns guarding the entrance to the courtyard, has an ornamental basin surrounded by brilliant red geraniums. The **Knight's House**, next to this, is in a poor state except for the stunning mosaic of Dionysus discovering the sleeping Ariadne, one of the loveliest sights of Volubilis.

Most of the larger houses off Decumanus Maximus contain several well-preserved mosaics; but in particular don't miss the **House of Venus** (marked by a single cypress tree) and the **House of Nereids**, a couple of streets in. The former must have been the home of an important dignitary, for here the bronze heads of Cato and Juba II were found (now in the museum in Rabat). Mosaics depict mythological scenes, including the abduction of Hylas by Nymphs and one of the bathing Diana being surprised by Acteon.

The well-worn path curls round behind the Basilica and Forum, bringing you back to the entrance, where you can adjourn for a mint tea in the café.

The position, atmosphere and mosaics of Volubilis combine to make the site an essential stop. The excavations and reconstructions are extensive enough to give an idea of life in the third century and later. Geckos running up and down the crumbling walls, darting into invisible holes, occasional whiffs of highly-scented flowers, the clear air and the silence on the plateau all enhance the magic.

Right, the Capitol.

MARRAKESH

Marrakesh is probably the most exotic city in Morocco, for it is the meeting place of cultures and continents. It was the first capital of a united Morocco (back in the 11th century) and is where tribesmen from the so-called Bled El Siba ("land of lawlessness") meet the Bled El Makhzen ("land of government"). Situated at the geographical centre of the country, it is the first great city north of the Sahara.

A vibrant centre of trade, with a population of about half a million, Marrakesh is expanding rapidly, with satellite suburbs under constant construction. Its modern economy, outside tourism, includes textile and light manufacturing industries. Hermès has a factory here, as do various other knitwear and clothing companies. Designers export metal furniture, painted wood and jewellery made to order, and Marrakesh craftsmen are discovering a lucrative foreign market for their well-made goods.

In recent years, especially since the building of the new Palais de Congrès on Avenue de France, the city has become a popular venue for international conferences. Good facilities, plentiful hotels and interesting possibilities for R & R attract everyone from opticians' organisations to heads of state. It was in the Palais de Congrès that the 1994 GATT (General Agreement on Tariffs and Trade) was signed, and almost every week Marrakesh hosts an international conference of some sort. Land Rover launched its 1993 range of vehicles here, flying in 2,000 sales reps for the occasion. The city's central location, varied scenery and low wages also make it a favourite location for commercials and fashion shoots.

Gateway to the south: In winter, Marrakesh is dominated by the towering Atlas. The snowcapped peaks loom over the city in the clear winter air, an unbroken wall filling the entire southern hori-

Preceding pages: wandering in the souks; Left, on the Djemma el Fna.

zon. In summer, the city roasts under a desert sun, which can push temperatures up to 50°C (34°F) in the shade. But winter or summer, the city has a perpetual party atmosphere. The *Marrakshi* accent is rough, crude, full of a barely controlled sensuality.

Marrakesh is split into at least two distinct cities, the walled medina and Gueliz. Of most interest to visitors is the **medina**, with its winding markets and historical monuments enclosed within pink walls of sunbaked mud. The medina can be further divided into quarters, with the most obvious partition falling between north and south of the central square, the Djemma el Fna. North of the square are twisting alleys and densely packed souks, each specialising in a particular trade. Behind and either side of the souks are residential quarters that offer little to the passing tourist, except for the odd eccentrically placed restaurant or mosque.

South of the square is the *mellah*, kasbah and royal palace, and the greatest concentration of historical monuments. Three main arteries serve this quarter: Avenue El Mouahidine/Avenue Houmman el Ftourak running from Avenue Mohammed V (Marrakesh's main street) past the Koutoubia mosque and *mellah* market and ending at the busy junction next to the Place des Ferblantiers (an easily recognisable square that acts as a useful reference point in navigating the area), and rues Riad Zitoune el Kedim and el Jdid (old and new), direct routes from the Djemma el Fna to Place des Ferblantiers.

While the medina holds most of the city's sights, its range of accommodation, restaurants and bars is decidedly lacking. For middle to upper range hotels (3-star and above), visitors are forced to look in **Gueliz**, the new part of town outside the walls. The French built the basis of this modern city. It is dominated by the broad Avenue Mohammed V, the main artery linking the modern city with the old Arab medina. Running north from the medina, beginning at the Koutoubia Mosque (where a busy junction leads off right to Club Med and the Djemma el Fna), this cuts through the

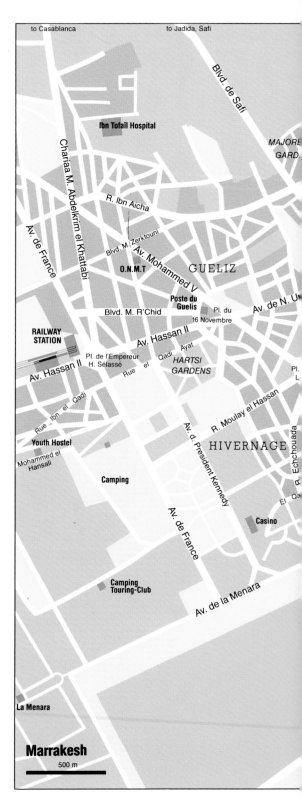

Av. el Jadida

to Fez Meknes

Route Principale N°. 24

Oued Issil

Route des Remparts

Sidi Bel Abbes Mosque

Derb Kaa el Mechra

Bab el Khemis

R. Assouel

R. de Bab Khemis

Zaouia Sidi Ben Slimane

R. de Bab Tarhzout

Antaki Hospital

R. Boutouil

R. el Gza

Bab Doukkala

Bab Debbarh

Kouba Almoravid

Medrassa ben Youssef

R. de Bab Debbarh

Tanneries

Bab Doukkala Mosque

Rue de Bab Doukkala

R. Fatima Zohra

MEDINA

R. Issebbryne

Bab Larissa

R. Azbezt

Bab Ailen

Town Hall

Echrob ou Choul Fountain

Pl. R. Kedima

R. de Bab Ailen

Av. Mohammed V

R. S. el Yamani

Rue Mouassine

R. S. Smarine

SOUKS

R. Dabachi

R. Bab Ahmad

R. A. el Abbes Sebti

Triq el Koutoubia

R.S. Mimoun

Djemma el Fna

Bank of Morocco

Medina Post Office

R. Riad Z. el Kedim

R. Riad Z. el Jdid

Koutoubia

R. el Mouahidine

R. Oqba Ben Nafaa

Av. H. el Fetouaki

La Bahia

Av. H. el Fetouaki

Pl. des Ferblantiers

R. Berrima

Badi Palace

Bab er Rob

Saadian Tombs

Royal Palace

Bab Ahmar

R. de Bab Ahmar

Route N°. 501

Route N°. 513

R. de Bab Irhli

AGDAL GARDENS

walls at the Bab Nkob and ends on the far side of Gueliz at a busy roundabout marking the start of the Casablanca road. Most of the western-style bars, restaurants and hotels lie on or in side streets off this main drag.

The historic sights: The tallest feature on the medina skyline is the **Koutoubia** (the mosque of the booksellers). Built by Sultan Abel Mouman at the beginning of Almohad rule, it is the city's most important landmark and serves as a useful point against which to the relate other sites in the city.

A mosque was originally built here by Morocco's first great dynasty, the Almoravides, fanatical religious nomads who exploded out of the Western Sahara in 1060 AD. Austere veiled warriors, much like the Tuareg, they built a walled kasbah alongside the mosque, which eventually became the capital of an empire that not only united all of modern Morocco, but also most of Spain and much of Algeria. Under the leadership of Youssef ben Tashfin, Marrakesh became a cosmopolitan centre of culture and learning with Andalusian-style mosques and palaces.

Little of the original city remains today, except the **Dar el Hajar** (House of Stone), the Almoravide stone fortress, which can still be traced in an excavation alongside the Koutoubia mosque. The legacy of the Almoravides remains most tangibly in the city's walls and system of underground irrigation channels that fed the new city and its fabulous gardens.

The original mosque was destroyed by the Almoravides' successors, the Almohads, who descended from Tinmal in the High Atlas and captured the city in 1147. The Almohads soon built their own Koutoubia mosque, but evidence suggests this may have been wrongly aligned to Mecca, for a second mosque was completed in 1158 as an extension of the first, presumably to correct the original alignment of the prayer hall.

Excavations undertaken in 1948 have revealed the foundations of columns which would have supported the roof of the first Almohad mosque, and it is still

Far left, the Koutoubia; **left**, zellige work.

possible to see, on the northern wall, the bricked up arches that connected the two buildings. The same excavations also revealed evidence of a machine to raise and lower a screen (a *maqsurah*) to separate the ruler from the general populace. This would have been a sensible precaution, as many a Muslim leader has been assassinated on his way to or from prayer.

The present-day mosque, like nearly all mosques in Morocco, is closed to non-Muslims but a spectacular *minbar* from the Koutoubia mosque can be seen in the El Badi museum. Inscriptions on the *minbar* (a moveable staircase from which a mosque's *imam* delivers his Friday sermon and leads prayers) show that it was made in Cordoba for the Koutoubia mosque but was most likely commissioned by the Sultan Ibn Tashfin, in around 1120, for the original Almoravide mosque.

The workmanship involved in the marquetry decoration of the staircase – no two of the 1,000 panels are exactly the same – shows something of the fabulous splendour of Marrakesh during the 12th century.

It is the minaret that is today the pride of the mosque. The mosque tower served as the model for the Tour Hassan in Rabat and the Giralda in Seville, later buildings of the Almohads. The minaret is nearly 70 metres (230ft) high, and follows the Almohad proportions of 1:5, with the tower five times as high as it is wide. It is a proportion found in nearly all Almohad mosques.

The exterior of the tower is decorated with carved stone tracery, each side displaying different patterns. The rough stone of the tower would once have been covered with plaster and decorated. Remnants of lines of enamel tiles could be seen at the top of the main tower until quite recently.

Alongside the tower, the excavated ruins of the original Koutoubia are in the process of being restored. The gardens, which cover the remains of the Almoravide kasbah, have been railed off and much clearing of rubbish and pruning back of weeds is in progress.

Carrying home the vegetables.

There is every prospect that in the near future the Koutoubia will form the central attraction of an elegant archaeological park and garden.

Due south of the Koutoubia, and most easily approached from Bab Agnaou, is the 12th-century **Kasbah mosque** (look out for its minaret). This mosque is the second Almohad monument in Marrakesh although practically nothing of what you see today dates from the original construction. Rebuilt for the first time about 30 years after the Koutoubia, but before Rabat's Tour Hassan, it is built from brick rather than stone and is decorated with tiles that have benefited from much restoration.

Next door to the mosque are the **Saadian Tombs** (signposted Tombeaux Saadiens), built by Ahmed el Mansour, the second Saadian sultan, on the site of an older cemetery which was reserved for descendents of the Prophet. The Saadians emerged from Tamgroute in the Draa Valley during the 16th century, when Morocco was in turmoil after the collapse of the Merenids. On a wave of religious fervour and nationalist sentiment, they swept through the country, capturing Marrakesh in 1524. When the religious leaders of Fez rebuffed their claims of Sheriffian descent (from the Prophet), they made Marrakesh their capital instead of Fez.

Abdullah el Ghalib succeeded to the Saadian throne after the murder of his rivals. A strong leader, he made a considerable impact on Marrakesh, rebuilding the original Ben Youssef *medrassa* (founded by a Merenid Sultan in the 14th century) and the kasbah, building the Mouassin mosque and founding the *mellah*. His successor, and half brother Ahmed el Dehbi (also called el Mansour, the victorious) built El Badi palace and the Saadian Tombs.

After the collapse of the Saadian dynasty, the tombs were bricked up by Moulay Ismail in the late 17th century, and only rediscovered by a French aerial survey of the medina. At one time entrance to the tombs was either via El Badi palace or through the Kasbah mosque; today visitors follow a narrow

Pedling religion on the Djemma el Fna.

passage alongside the outside wall of the mosque's prayer hall.

The mausoleum is built in the late Andalusian tradition and postdates the Alhambra by two centuries. It is one of the top historical sights of Marrakesh, containing the tombs of Mohammed ech Cheikh and Ahmed el Mansour, as well as numerous other members of the Saadian royal families. To appreciate the beauty and peace of the cemetery, it is best to visit in the early morning, before 10am.

El Badi Palace (near the Place des Ferblantiers) is an elegant ruin between the *mellah* and the imperial city. The open ruins of the Badi are the stage for Marrakesh's celebrated folklore festival in June. Built by Ahmed el Mansour in the 16th century, it was once a palace of outstanding beauty covered in white Italian marble. Little remains except an enormous open courtyard housing a rectangular pool and traces of the underground water system that once irrigated its gardens. The palace took 25 years to complete and, at the hands of Moulay

Ismail less than a century later, only 12 years to destroy.

Past the Place des Ferblantiers, in the Mellah, is **El Bahia Palace** built in the 19th century by grand vizers to the Alaouite sultans. Depending on your own tastes, the palace is either an impressive display of the period's post-Alhambra decoration or a degeneration of Andalusian art which borders on *kitsch*. Either way, its series of gardens, courtyards and cool reception halls are impressive if only for their scale and opulence. During the French Protectorate it served as the Governor's residence. Today, the palace is officially part of the Royal Palace and parts of it, including most of the upstairs rooms, are used for lodging guests.

Hidden riads: Contemporary with the palace are many grand merchants' houses, some of which have been converted into restaurants or small, exclusive hotels with Mamounia-style prices. On the Rue Riad Zitoune El Kedim, between the Djemaa el Fna and the Place Des Ferblantiers, is a *riad*

signposted in English and advertising itself as a tea house. This is run by Fakitah, an indomitable matriach who specialises in arranging weddings and women-only henna parties with sumptuous food and dancers. She will also occasionally lay on soirées for parties of tourists, if contacted in advance.

Off the Rue Riad Zitoun el Jedid is a narrow alley that passes Bert Flint's beautiful house, **Dar Tizkiwin**, which is both a private museum (visits are limited to half and hour) and residence. It contains a superb collection of Berber textiles and pottery (his jewellery collection is housed in his Agadir museum). Beyond Dar Tizkiwin, at a small fountain, a street leads to **Dar Si Said** (the Museum of Moroccan Art), a mix of artefacts of varying interest in a particularly impressive *riad*.

Evening assembly: The **Djemaa el Fna** is the heart of street life in Marrakesh, a huge square-cum-open space between the souk and Koutoubia mosque that is a magnet for foreign and Moroccan tourists alike, who are drawn to its jugglers, snake charmers, orange juice sellers and *fakirs*. Here teeth are pulled and fortunes told. Though activity is round the clock, it is at night – from around 5pm – that the Djemma is at its most intoxicating. Night vendors set up stalls selling a huge variety of food at unreliable prices. It is possible to eat anything from goats' heads to snails, *merguez*, *tajines* and *couscous*. Best value is the *harira* soup at just 1 dirham a bowl. The atmosphere is medieval, lamps glow amidst swirling clouds of smoke, pick pockets and con men dart through the crowds while dazed-looking foreign visitors clutch their bags and gawp. A less intimate way of enjoying the spectacle is from a terrace of one of the many ringside cafés, with the Café de France and Café Argana (which offers a backdrop view of the snow covered Atlas in winter) the favourites.

Boys beware of "poor Berber" girls bearing gifts of cheap jewellery. They are certainly after your money, and some will suggest that you sample the delights behind their exotic veils. If you do

Crowds soon gather.

226

fall into temptation you will certainly come out poorer, if not wiser, than you expected.

The Souks: Flowing northwards away from the Djemaa el Fna are the souks of the medina, a warren of shadowy tunnel-like streets punctuated by pools of electric light from tightly packed boutiques. The air is filled with whispers of "Come in, *bienvenue*, just for the pleasure *des yieux*". Stout matrons swathed in veils chaperone fashionably dressed daughters. Shouts of "*balek*" clear a path for overladen handcarts, bicycles and mopeds.

On one's first visit, the souk can feel overwhelmingly aggressive as would-be guides appear and disappear at your side offering their services. It is a more difficult place to feel at ease in than Fez, despite actually being much smaller. It may be wise to take a guide with you the first time here.

Though the souk appears to be a disorganised jumble of shops selling a head-spinning array of goods, the maze of twisting streets is really a network of specialist markets. Each separate souk has its own name, although there is little point in trying to remember all but a few of these as you will never see any signposts. What the experts call "rebound navigation", relating everything to a few easily recognisable landmarks, is the best way of finding your way around. Of most interest are the areas that have kept their medieval character and are still highly specialised.

Access is usually via two streets that lead off the square. The **Souk Semarine** is hidden by a few alleys selling olives, dried fruits, cheap shoes and ladies underwear. Its entrance proper is through a prominent arch additionally identified by a regular hawker of a bird-imitating whistle. Hear its high pitched warbling and you cannot be far away. The entrance is a busy junction. Straight ahead, through the key-hole arch is the broad paved and covered Semarine, its shops dominated by up-market cloth vendors and a couple of huge tourist emporiums. A small but fascinating antique shop a few metres down, on the left, offers

insights into Moroccan culture over the last century.

The Rue Semarine eventually forks, a junction heralding the heart of the souk. On the right is a square dominated by spice shops, strung with animals in various stages of desiccation. An entrance on the square's north side, flanked by Berber carpet stores, leads to the former slave market (Marrakesh was an important centre for the trans-Saharan trade). The left fork, **Souk Attarine**, leads to the slipper alley lined by small kiosks crammed with *babouche*. Weak electric bulbs reflect off the brilliant gold thread of wedding slippers. Further on the sound of hammering will guide you into the blacksmith's souk where metal garden furniture and weather cocks are almost as popular as the more traditional ornate window grilles.

The right-hand fork off Semarine passes jewellery and leather souks before arriving at the **Ben Youssef Medrassa** and **Mosque**. When the original 14th-century, Merenid *medrassa* was rebuilt by Abdullah el Ghallib, the Saadian sultan made it the largest Koranic school in Morocco in a deliberate attempt to snub the *imams* of Fez. The tortuous entrance is unusual but succeeds in enhancing the visual impact on entering the main courtyard, where a rectangular marble pool reflects the intricately carved cedar wood and plaster of the walls and the sky above. The open sky is an integral part of Andalusian architecture.

The spacious courtyard leads to a prayer hall whose proportions, balancing detailed carving and zellige decoration, gives an impression of serenity through exquisite, but disciplined beauty.

The Ben Youssef mosque is more interesting for its history than for the mosque that now exists on the site. Rebuilt several times, the current mosque dates back no earlier than the 19th century and is thought to be only half the size of the original. A mosque was first built by the Almoravides in the 12th century and would have been contemporary with the **Koubba el Baroudiyn** (a small ablutions chamber **In the dyers' quarter.**

opposite the mosque), one of the very few surviving examples of Almoravide architecture in Marrakesh. Embodied in the *koubba*'s small carved dome and keyhole arches is the kernel of all Andalusian art that followed, right up until the present day.

The Mouassin mosque: To reach the remaining sights on this tour, it may be easier to return to the Djemaa el Fna. From there, the short street leading past the café Argana connects to a little square. From this approach, a discreet covered alley directly ahead on the left is an often less crowded and more hassle-free entrance to the souk. This is the **Rue Mouassin**.

Follow the road northwards with a final right turn by some high-class jewellery shops to reach the Saadian **Mouassin Mosque** and **Fountain**. The mosque is probably the most impressive in the medina, and dates from the Saadian dynasty. However, little can be seen from the ground as it is heavily surrounded by shops and houses, so enquire in any of the nearby shops for access onto a roof. You will be rewarded by the sight of green tiled roofs and open peaceful courtyards that are hard to imagine in the bustle of the souk below. The fountain, with its plain white arches and discreet carved beam, has been restored; it has an elegant beauty in marked contrast to the heaped brass of the souvenir superstore opposite.

Not to be missed are the **wool and silk dyers**, past the square, at a small junction of alleys, with a convenient but tiny café nearby. It is a constant miracle that the dyers can produce such vibrant colours from their cramped and blackened workshops. Rich iridescent skeins of green, yellow and red silks blaze against the bright blue sky.

Past the wool dyers is a small covered alley identifiable by an old twisted vine. One side of it is dominated by stalls selling thuya wood carvings from Essaouira, but there are also a couple of junk shops and a small shop crammed with folk pottery, mostly from the Rif mountains. This short covered souk links the dyers area to the Souk Attarine,

Reels of finished silk threads.

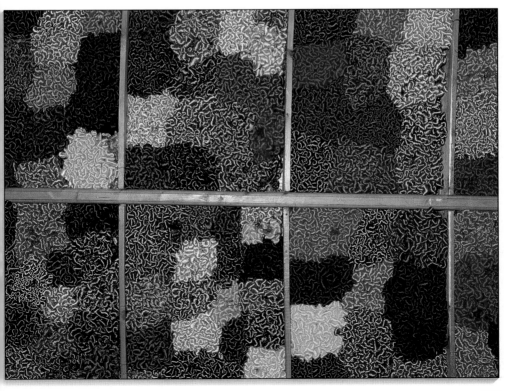

A GARDEN CITY

Some 160 km (100 miles) from the coast and too close to the stony plain to benefit from the cooling altitude of the Atlas, Marrakesh is a veritable furnace in mid-summer. By two in the afternoon the sun's rays are so fierce that the air itself trembles from the onslaught.

For the *Marrakshis*, relief is found in cool, dark interiors, private courtyards and, most pleasingly of all, with a picnic of fruit and water in the city's lush gardens: Jardin Majorelle, to the north of the medina; the expansive Menara Gardens, to the southwest; the Agadal Gardens, an adjunct of the Royal Palace, to the south; and, for any locals willing to risk the wrathful indignation of its watchful gardeners, in the extensive grounds of La Mamounia Hotel.

The gardens of Marrakesh have always surprised and delighted visitors. The British writer Osbert Sitwell, in *Escape with Me*, called Marrakesh "the ideal African city of water-lawns, cool, pillared palaces and orange groves." It was the promise of gardens and flowers that drew Matisse to North Africa – albeit to Tangier rather than Marrakesh. He went in the footsteps of the writer Pierre Loti, who found "nothing but carpets of flowers", and the painter Eugène Delacroix, who remarked on "innumerable flowers of a thousand species forming carpets of the most varied colours".

The image of a carpet, though well-worn, is apt. The favourite theme of carpets all over the Islamic world is the flowering garden. Hung on walls and slipped over couches, rugs are winter reminders of summer's bounty.

Gardens are also earthly intimations of Paradise, the Eden of the after-life described in the Koran as "gardens watered by running streams". Entwined foliage, a constant motif of Islamic decorative art, runs riot over stucco carvings and faience tiling in Moroccan mosques and *medersa*. Islam blossomed in dusty, dry lands where trees, flowers and water were (and are) especially treasured. In the cities, water was introduced as much as possible, in splashing drinking fountains (witness Fez) and pools. Great minds were engaged in solving problems of irrigation. In Marrakesh's El Badi Palace the ornamental pools were raised above the gardens to make watering easier.

Marrakesh's great gardens are 19th or early 20th-century creations, though in most cases they replace earlier gardens which, starved of water during tribal warfare, had withered and died. Originally, they were agricultural estates, where the sultan would reap olives and citrus fruit for profit. On a smaller scale is the city's most recently renovated garden, the Jardin Majorelle, named after its creator, the French painter Jacques Majorelle, who lived in Marrakesh in the 1920s. Lovingly restored by the couturier Yves St Laurent, the garden is a kaleidoscope of tropical colour. Walkways are a dusty pink, flowerpots bright yellow, the ornamental carp in the lily-padded pools a vibrant orange. Most striking of all is the intense cobalt blue of the buildings, a colour traditionally employed to ward off evil spirits but used here to enhance the green of the foliage, a trick which Matisse also learnt in Morocco.

Smaller gardens are found all over Marrakesh, in particular in the old palaces now turned museums, where they offer visitors a refreshing respite from staring into dusty cabinets. The garden in La Bahia, for example, is a walled oasis, where the Grand Vizier's wives and concubines came to stroll and play to the accompaniment of birdsong. As in the sultan's garden in the Oudayas Kasbah in Rabat, the pathways are laid out symmetrically, but plants, flowers and trees intertwine and overarch, creating an enclosed and private world where secret assignations would be veiled by curtains of accanthus and sweet-scented jasmine.

This is no prissy arrangement of neat flower beds and clipped box hedge. Instead it is an intense explosion of perfume (roses, jacaranda, jasmine, orange blossom), juicy fruits (pomegranates, figs, carob, peaches, vines), and the intoxicating pollen from the datura tree, said to drive people mad and known as the "jealous tree". The overriding effect is sensual. It is no accident that the best-loved plants in Morocco are those which release their scent at night, when their heady perfume contributes to the voluptuous courtship of lovers. ∎

which on turning right returns back to the easily recognised Souk Semarine.

The pasha's palace: Also in the northern part of the medina is the **Dar El Glaoui**, part of which today houses the offices of the Delegation du Culture. This was formerly the palace of the Pasha Glaoui who collaborated with the French to rule Morocco. The Glaoui, a Berber clan from the region of Telouet, were the last of the old-style despotic rulers of Morocco. While they never laid claim to the title of sultan it was their power and alliances that allowed the French to subdue the country.

The Glaoui were tribal overlords in the most traditional sense. With their own army they controlled the ancient medina, as they did the whole of the south, with a mixture of terror and charm. On the one hand, they ran hundreds of brothels catering for French legionnaires and had a posse of informers and spies who blackmailed and murdered on their behalf. On the other, they showered mistresses with riches, held lavish banquets and gave away fortunes to the poor. While the Pasha entertained Hollywood film stars, and even attended the Coronation of Queen Elizabeth II, his enemies where tortured and executed in dungeons straight from the pages of a medieval horror.

Caléche rides: The 16 km (10 miles) of Marrakesh's **city walls** are best seen from a *calèche* (fares are posted inside, but it is best to agree a price before setting off) or a hired bicycle. Built originally by the Almoravides as a defence against the Almohads, the walls now have eight working gates, although many more are buried under rubbish or bricked up and built into houses. Worth visiting is the Almoravide **Bab Ed Debbagh**, which gives access to the **tanneries** (just follow your nose). The **Bab Aghmat/Rhemat** is the gate through which the Almohads captured the city after Christian mercenaries betrayed the Almoravides by opening the gate to their attackers.

Outside the southern walls is a fortress called the **Squallet el Mrabit** which once housed a squadron of cavalry to

A morning shave.

help defend the city. Close to the **Bab er Rob**, from where taxis and buses travel to the Ourika Valley and Imlil in the High Atlas, is the much photographed **Bab Agnaou**, a small arch with a carved facade that was once an entrance from the medina into the imperial city.

Great escapes: After a day in the souk, escaping the medina can be a tempting prospect. Tea in the Mamounia gardens is a favourite among visitors, but most *Marrakshis* head for a stroll in the Agadal or Menara gardens. The **Menara** is the smaller though more famous of the two: if, however, you want to see the snow-covered Atlas rising over its pavilion and rectangular pool – a view captured on countless posters and postcards – you must time your visit for sunset in the first few months of the year.

The **Agadal** is much larger and sports several pools but is much less visited because of its greater distance from the centre. The **Majorelle** gardens, in Gueliz, are a delight with more botanical interest. The gardens were built by Louis Majorelle, a French orientalist

painter in the 1920s. A few of his pictures can be seen in the small museum in the gardens.

The city's role as an oasis is brought home on a circuit around the **palmerie** (said to have sprung up from the discarded date stones of the Almohad army besieging the Almoravide city). The palmerie, sandwiched between the Casablanca and Fez roads (signposted "Circuit des Palmeries"), is also home to Marrakesh's rich and famous, who are numerous. Palatial villas set in luxuriant gardens abound, with the occasional tourist café providing mere mortals with a chance of refreshment on their tour round.

It is also in the palmeries that most of the new tourist development is taking place. With Morocco generally experiencing a steady decline in numbers of tourists, the industry is looking to cater for a new class of visitor. As a result, huge luxury hotel complexes offering horse riding, tennis, mountain biking and golf are springing up all over the palm groves.

Marrakesh now boasts three golf courses (the latest being the Amelkis, off the Ouarzazate road from the medina, which opened in October 1995). Elsewhere in the palmeries, restaurants offer fantasy surroundings in which to enjoy *Arabian Nights*-style entertainments, which in one venue includes a laser projected image of a girl floating past on a flying carpet.

All this merely scratches the surface of a city rich in monuments and with many still-inhabited palaces secreted in its medina. And in Marrakesh grand architecture is not a preserve of the past, as the new theatre, under sporadic construction on the Avenue de France, testifies. However, above all, it is the unique atmosphere of the city that is compelling. Marrakesh is a city, where one feels one could fall in love, or be murdered, make a fortune or be lost forever in its winding alleys. It is a city of conspiracy, of magic openly displayed, of pleasure bought, sold and given freely. It is no coincidence that the opening sequence of Carol Reed's *The Third Man* was filmed in the city's medina. It is the perfect place for a mystery.

Left, in the Menara Gardens. **Right**, the annual folklore festival in the grounds of El Badi.

THE SOUTHWEST COAST

In 1949 Orson Welles chose **Essaouira** as a location for his film *Othello*. It lies beneath low Mediterranean-type hills carved by small stony fields dotted with olive and thorny argan trees. After the wide lemon and pink plain west of Marrakesh, or the flat Atlantic coastlands to the town's north, scales suddenly seem small and human. Houses are painted white and blue; there are hanging flower-baskets and a thriving fishing harbour.

Yet the Alantic belts against Essaouira with vigour, and the town's fortified walls, rooted in a ragged outbreak of rocks above a sandy bay, and a crop of rocky islands opposite endow romantic drama. It has long been associated with artists, as murals on the walls testify. In the 1960s the most idealistic of youth cultures congregated here, when Essaouira became a haven for hippies.

Pirate enclave: Until quite recently the town was known by its Spanish or Portuguese name, Mogador. It was founded in the 18th century by Sultan Mohammed ben Abdullah as a free port for Europeans and their Jewish agents engaged in trans-Saharan gold, ivory and slave trading. Before this, it was a pirate enclave. In the 19th century it quickly became a thriving town and many of Morocco's Jews migrated here. In 1860 a traveller and writer called James Richardson recorded that "the population is between thriteen and fifteen thousand souls, including four thousand Jews, and fifty Christians."

Europeans and Jews incurred the dislike of the native race. The law of "protection", under which natives working for European merchants were exempted from Sultanic laws and taxation, was blatantly abused. The merchants and diplomats sold "protection" for large sums of money or goods in kind and he Jewish money-lenders earned high rates of interest on the sums they loaned.

Designed by a European engineer (a captive of the Sultan Mohammed ben Abdullah), Essaouira has wider, more regularly shaped streets than is usual in Moroccan medinas. It also has, on Avenue Oqba ibn Nafi, a clock-tower (a most incongruous feature for Morocco), which houses in its base a late-night cigarette and postcard kiosk.

Place Moulay Hassan, just back from the harbour and the tourist office, is the town's social centre; men congregate outside the **Café de France** or play pool in its once elegant interior, the young gather at Café Sam's Macdonalds and women – without exception veiled – come to sit here in the late afternoon.

An area inside the harbour, heavy with the whiff of smoking charcoal, is occupied by tables and benches. Here, from late morning, fishermen grill and serve sardines, squid and prawns. At midnight the evening's catch from the larger trawlers is loaded on to lorries for transit inland.

Essaouira's main shopping thoroughfares lie behind Place Moulay el Hassan in **Avenue de l'Istiqual** and **Rue Mohammed Zerktouni**. Between **Avenue Oqba ibn Nafi** and **Place Moulay el Hassan** you will find an enclave of

tourist shops and cafés. The **ramparts** (reached via Rue de Souka, past the sign for Hotel Smara) are Essaouira's main attraction. European cannons, several of British manufacture, gifts from the merchants to the Sultan Mohammed ben Abdullah, face the nearby islands, **Isles Purpuraires**, where Juba II established a factory for the manufacture of a purple dye (derived from a shellfish) much in demand in 1st-century Rome. At the end of the 19th century, the islands were used as a quarantine station for pilgrims returning from Mecca who might be importing plague. It is possible to visit the islands by fishing-boat but permission must be gained from Le Grand Governeur in the Province, a formality easily arranged through the tourist office.

In the potently-scented carpenters' souk beneath the ramparts, craftsmen carve everything from small boxes to tables out of cedar and thuya wood. One of the finest woodworkers' souks in Morocco, it supplies shops and bazaars all over the country and abroad.

Essaouira has long attracted European tourists, but so far remains unspoilt. It tends to attract independent holidaymakers, looking for peace and quiet, though coach parties often visit the town during the day. There is one upmarket hotel, **Hotel des Isles** on Boulevard Mohammed V, but for superb Moroccan cooking and a more intimate and characterful atmosphere it is hard to beat **Villa Maroc**, knocked out of two Moroccan houses near the harbour.

Essaouira attracts a tide of French surfers travelling in jeeps and camper vans. In the evening they are especially evident in **Sam's**, the fish restaurant within the harbour enclosure, and **Châlet de la Plage** on the corniche. Both provide surfer-portions. Châlet de la Plage also has a terrace-bar and the bar prefacing the restaurant serves good *tapas*.

Best beaches: An arc of sand lies to the south of town, but further along the coast, off the P8 rolling its way over the foothills of the High Atlas to Agadir, minor roads and tracks lead to what the Moroccans call *plages sauvages*, long

Essaouira's harbour: one of Morocco's busiest.

stretches of white sand-duned beaches thickly fringed by prickly gorse and argan trees and disappearing into thin mists in the distance. Surfers frequent **Cap Sim** and **Diabat**.

Sidi Kaouki, a beach dominated at its northern end by a spectacularly sited *koubba* is an excellent and very accessible alternative. **Cap Tafelney**, a white sandy bay enclosed by hills and sheltering a small community of picturesque fishing huts (some of which sell a frugal selection of sea-damp provisions), can suffer from an off-putting surfeit of washed-up detritus after heavy storms. When the sands are clean, Tafelney offers one of the coastline's longest undisturbed beaches for anyone willing to get away from the tiny tarmaced access point on its northern end.

The road from Essaouira to Agadir is long, winding and remote. It is frequently doused in sea mists, even in mid-summer. The region is thinly populated, though roadside vendors selling local honey and argan oil, a strongly-flavoured cooking oil derived from the thorny argan tree, are fairly common. There are few petrol stations along this stretch, so fill up before you start. Most of the coast, remote and parched, is the preserve of camel drivers and shepherds. It is accessible at **Imessouane**, a tiny fishing harbour, most of its secret beaches can only be discovered on foot.

North of Agadir and high in the mountains, **Imouzzer des Ida Outanane**, with its cascades and flourishing almond orchards, is reached via a torutous road winding its way through a stunning gorge. It is worth discovering – especially as it contains one of Morocco's untouted gems, the inexpensive **Auberge des Cascades**.

Tamri, set in banana plantations, and **Cap Ghir**, the most westerly point of the High Atlas, are quiet, undeveloped places. As the road descends to Agadir, it meets sand-heaped shorelines, blasted by crashing waves, their profiles broken by natural sculptures of sea battered rocks. These are some of Morocco's best beaches, temping escapes from Agadir's commercialised attractions.

Fishermen's tea break.

THE ATLAS MOUNTAINS

Any mountain range 450 miles (700 km) long and with summits over 13,100 ft (4,000 metres) must be counted as a major topographical incident on planet earth. Since the first attempts by Europeans in the early 19th century to follow Arab trade routes across this great barrier, the number of foreign travellers penetrating the Atlas for pleasurable exploratory purposes until World War II probably never exceeded 1,000. The slogan "death to the infidel" applied to all unaccompanied strangers in this "China of the West".

The suggestion of violence goes right back to the fanciful name bestowed by Europeans on these ranges. According to Greek myth, after the Titan Atlas was turned to stone by the cowardly Perseus (who possessed Medusa's head), his burden became a mountain, allegedly supporting the heavens. The story goes that Atlas, under the weight, genuflected towards the setting sun in the northwest part of Africa.

The Atlas mystique lasted even after a prominent pass (Tagharat) and a distinct summit Gourza (10,700 ft/3,280 metres) had been reached by outsiders in 1871. The Hooker-Ball-Maw expedition observed in their report, "The climate is admirable, the natural obstacles of no account, but the traditional policy of the ruling race has passed into the very fibre of the inhabitants, and affords an obstacle all but impassable to ordinary travellers."

These days the Atlas is more accessible and its inhabitants, having developed keen entrepreneurial instincts, are more hospitable towards visitors. Three main roads penetrate the High Atlas from Marrakesh: the Tizi N'Test pass; the S511 through the Western Atlas to Agadir; and the Tichka Pass to Ouarzazate. From the direction of Fez, the P21 quickly climbs into the Middle Atlas, an altogether wider, more expansive mountain range than the Rif to the city's north.

Along all these routes, the contrasts in landscape are spectacular. Descending from the Middle Atlas from the rather bourgeois, almost alpine, environs of Ifrane and Azrou to the desert plain on the way to Midelt and the start of the south, motorists are struck by a pink, blue and gold infinity which looks more like a distant ocean than *terra firma*. Travelling in the other direction on the road from Ouarzazate to Marrakesh, you find views of desert oases dotted with date palms and *ksour* and crowned by snow-covered peaks.

At first sight the Atlas appears to be remote. In fact, one-quarter of Morocco's population lives on ground over 3,300ft (1,000 metres) above sea level; innumerable tiny villages populate the area, inaccessible to the hired Renault or Peugeot. On the major roads, motoring conditions are good but, as the number of dented luxury coaches in Marrakesh testifies, vehicles are often driven perilously fast.

Sampling the Atlas: If you are staying in Marrakesh but not planning to travel in Morocco, it would be a shame not to

Preceding pages: the Dades Valley. Left, the Middle Atlas. Right, a Berber family.

venture into the Atlas for a day or two. The easiest excursion – still recommended, despite now being a tourist draw with a fair share of cafés and souvenir touts – is to the Ourika Valley, about an hour's drive south along the S513, or a 1½ hour's bus journey from the Bab er Rob in Marrakesh. The road, flanked by a string of luxury mountain villas and humble Berber homes, follows the river to **Setti Fatma**, high in the cleft of the valley.

From here a busy mule track cuts deeper south, but the main attraction for most visitors to the village is a series of seven waterfalls on the far side of the river, the first of which is reached after an easy climb through the rocks and trees. In the summer, this is a popular spot for young tourists and *Marrakshis*. There is a small café and swimming in a deep, icy rock pool. Above, wild monkeys stalk the craggy heights and shower walnuts.

The village has several hotels and cafés offering *tajines* and omelettes, but tourism remains low-key and indig-enous; in high summer the valley is a cool and easy escape from Marrakesh's heat and hassle.

Hiking in the Atlas: For those intent on a more serious foray into the Atlas, the Moroccan National Tourist Office publishes free each year a guide covering most of the mountain areas. It lists prices of guides, mules and accommodation, as well as naming recognised mountain lodgings (*gîtes*) and licensed guides. The booklet is available by writing to GTAM, Departement du Tourisme, 64 Avenue Fal Ould Oumeir, Agdal, Rabat. Topographical maps can be harder to come by.

There are a number of Moroccan agencies specialising in group trips to the mountains or desert. They work mostly with foreign agencies but will also take private groups approaching them directly. The range of activities has greatly expanded in recent years and now includes rafting, mountain biking and cross country motorcycling as well as the more usual hiking, camel trekking and horse riding. These agencies are listed

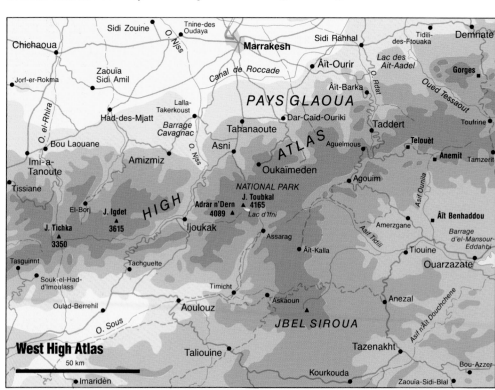

244

in the Moroccan Government booklet on mountain tourism.

TOUBKAL MASSIF: Shimmering in haze barely 60 km (38 miles) from the pink walls of Marrakesh, snow caps the rugged profile of the Toubkal Massif. This craggy mass of peaks and deep valleys contain the highest summits of the Atlas chain. The main springboard for exploring Toubkal is Imlil, 50 km (30 miles) from Marrakesh off the S501, the road through the Tizi N'Test.

Teeming with peasants, animals and lorries belching diesel fumes, the road crosses the hot Haouz plain to **Asni** village, where olive-covered foothills rise. Somewhere in the distance, beyond the terraced crops of maize in the Mizane valley, reigns Toubkal, the highest mountain in North Africa. Asni marks the end of French cuisine and comfortable quarters.

As nothing is done by the clock in country districts, pick-up trucks come and go according to demand along the 11 miles (17 km) between Asni and the Mizane roadhead at **Imlil**. There are a few basic inns, refreshment and food to purchase, but life revolves around a snug mountain hut, with a self-catering kitchen or meals to order from the warden's family. The Old Kasbah, overlooking the valley, has been renovated by an English couple intending to make it a centre for mountain tourism.

For those with boots, a recommended hike aims for the **Tamatert pass** (7,475 ft/2,279 metres, which takes 90 minutes (alternative four-wheel drive piste), then up adjoining scrub ridge to Tanamrout (8,650 ft/2,636 metres, 75 minutes) with its superb panorama of the Toubkal massif. **Sidi Chamarouch**, a pastoral shrine with associated shops catering for pilgrims, lies two hours along the mule trail in the upper Mizane. Like a beacon, its while roof draws many on a day outing; walk or ride a local beast. Mule hire can be expensive, even after haggling, as you pay for the animal's handler as well. Among this huddle of little houses squeezed into a niche at the foot of a rock slope, all Berber life is exposed to public view.

Among the Aspen trees in winter.

A few thousand people come to Imlil in spring and early summer to climb **Toubkal** (13,670 ft/4,167 metres). For a mountain of this height and accessibility to have had its first recorded ascent by a French party under the Marquis de Segonzac not earlier that 1923 testifies to the tribal fortress mentality maintained by the natives well into the 20th century. Visitors also go hiking round the district – there are various five- to 10- day circular tours, staying overnight in remote huts, Berber outposts and open-air bivouacs. Trekking companies predominate in these activities and supervised touring parties are thus spared the hassle of dealing with astute Berbers over porterage, provisions and accommodation. The more self-reliant can always backpack and dispense with the local services on offer.

Allow four to five hours for walking up the Mizane valley to the Toubkal refuge. One-way mule hire costs £6 ($10), local guides for this and the climb on the following day £10 ($17) per day. Locally qualified, they are called *accompagnateurs*, and are registered by the Ministry of Tourism. Several are resident in the Imlil district, although it must be said that their skills can vary from highly competent to downright useless (try and get a recommendation if you can). They all speak French, with a few also able to speak limited Spanish, German or English. If you fail to understand anything else, you should note that mules are not supposed to be ridden, especially up the steep stretches after Sidi Chamharouch; one mule carries the baggage of three trekkers equipped for three to four days. With snow cover on the trail until May, mules stop short of the hut and packs are carried by their handlers.

At the **Toubkal hut** there are spartan facilities: a spring supplies the hut, via a buried pipe, although boiling drinking water is still recommended. Gully water in the stream below flushes the two existing toilets. Refreshments and simple meals can be ordered from the warden. Generally, the hut is overcrowded and resulting bad tempers are common. Camping below the hut is becoming **Tattooed girl near Setti Fatma.**

increasingly popular. There is a plan to clear a proper site for tents, with improved sanitary and rubbish clearing facilities, as well as a long-standing proposal to build an extension to the hut (stalled through lack of funds). The success of either scheme would go some way to alleviating a problem that is rapidly spoiling an area that has already lost its wilderness appeal through the sheer numbers of visitors.

It is sensible to book a place in the hut in advance from Imlil, preferably one day before going up, via a message carried by the in-season shuttle of mules and porters. For all this and a night on a communal paillasse you pay about 3DH. Watch out for extras, such as use of stoves, consumables bought and, of course, tips.

If you are planning to climb Toubkal before mid-May (and you should leave the hut by 6.30 am), apart from stout boots and proper clothing, you may need crampons and ice-axe for complete comfort. Knowing the prevailing conditions, a guide will advise exactly.

As a climb, the ascent is perfectly straightforward, merely a gradual walk up a stony slope, until one reaches the notorious upper scree, where care must be taken as one false move could prove dangerous. Moreover, the path is ruined by careless footwork performed by thousands of tired limbs. Nonetheless the route is graded by Atlas mountaineer Peyron at "*type boulevard*" and, indeed, after about four hours, the summit appears like a big open corral where you half expect to see horses galloping round. In fact, you'll find people stamping feet and trotting round to keep warm, usually the T-shirt and flip-flop brigade.

Imlil to Tacheddirt: A popular excursion for gentle exercise and, if you wish, mule riding, leads from Imlil over the Tamatert pass to **Tacheddirt** in a relaxing 3½ hours. It is a charming settlement epitomising traditional Berber life. There is accommodation in a typical mountain hut with the usual appointments, plus a couple of gites in nearby villages.

Next day, a big climb to the **N'Addi pass** (9,600 ft/2,900 metres) is rewarded

Ait Benhaddou, setting for many a biblical epic.

by views of ravined peaks zebra striped with long streaks of snow. Riding a mule will be allowed only on the easy downslope to the broad pastures of Oukaimeden below. A ski resort during the winter, in spring this site is quiet; its Club Alpine Français hut is like a hotel, with all mod-cons. Equally welcoming is a comfortable hotel called Chez Ju Ju.

A local viewpoint, with orientation table, behind the condominiums commands a wide prospect towards Marrakesh, and there are prehistoric rock engravings along the north side of the pasture plateau. Huge flocks of sheep and goats graze here in early summer, brought up by villagers in the lower valleys. The massive hulk of Angour dominates the scene. While an asphalt road goes back to the city, the proper completion winds westwards through stunted walnut forest and evergreen oak back to the terraced fields of the Mizane and Asni, a five-hour hike.

The Toubkal area is bordered on the west by the S501 Tizi N'Test road. Beyond rises the Western High Atlas,

remote to most tourists but surprisingly densely populated and supporting a thriving agricultural economy. The **Seksawa valley**, its boxy dwellings planted on mountainsides prickling with television aerials, is the principal inroad by transit lorry from Marrakesh. Adventurous tourers bent on exploration away from the crowds will find many diverting sights in this region.

The Tizi N'Test: After Asni, further south on the Tizi N'Test road, the route is tarred to **Ouirgane** (luxury hotel called La Roseraie) and **Ijoukak** (inn). Close by stands the ancient kasbah of **Talat N'Yaccoub**, surrounded by olive groves, and the foaming Nfis river lapping at the foot of its ramparts.

Dominating an adjacent knoll, with the snows of the western monarch Igdet as a backdrop, is the **Agadir N'Gouj**, a former stronghold of the powerful Goundafi tribe, notorious in the 19th century for its dungeons. The location is now regarded as one of the outstanding beauty spots of the Great Atlas chain.

Higher up on the other side of the

Tessaout Gorge, Mgoun Massif.

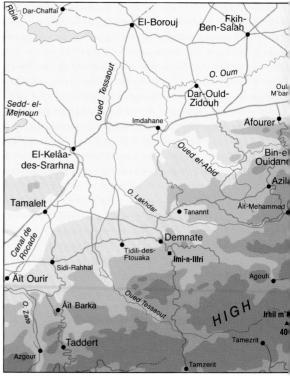

stream is the 12th-century mosque of **Tinmal**, birthplace of the Almohad movement that eventually gave rise to the famous Berber dynasty of the Middle Ages. The mosque has now been largely renovated and is one of the few mosques in Morocco that can be visited by non-Muslims.

The mountain behind the mosque is **Gourza**, climbed by the initial Hooker botanical expedition in 1871. The Test road narrows near the top of the pass but has a good surface afterwards all the way to **Taroudant**. Thorny argan trees take over the vegetation in an otherwise desolate landscape on the Saharan side of the range. Animals, winding along in Indian file, and sentinels watching over groups of dromedaries are some of the images for travellers, but the scene is actually an environmental disaster: vast forests have gone for building materials and firewood.

Here, and similarly along the eastern boundary of the Toubkal massif plainly marked by the Tichka Pass commercial road, the watershed divides the lush from the barren. A quilt of green fields stitched round a few oases occasionally brightens the monotony.

Ait Benhaddou, which regularly functions as a set for Western film epics, is a sort of tumbledown sculpture in rusty brown mud, full of corridors, rooms, storage compartments, walkways and turrets dating from antiquity, in which some Berbers still choose to live. Their lifestyle, governed by relentless wheeling and dealing and dodging authority, is poised on a seesaw of choices and temptations.

The Glaoui, the ruling tribe across the Tichka pass area, was formerly one of the most powerful and belligerent Berber families. They controlled trade from the Sahara to the Mediterranean over the historic Telouet caravan pass, the old salt road, from their kasbahs here. This route provides access for treks into the Central High Atlas. Beyond the Anemiter roadhead the terrain demands toughness and stoicism.

CENTRAL HIGH ATLAS: Base centre on the north side of this sector is the **Bouguemez** (Wgmmaz) **valley**, a broad

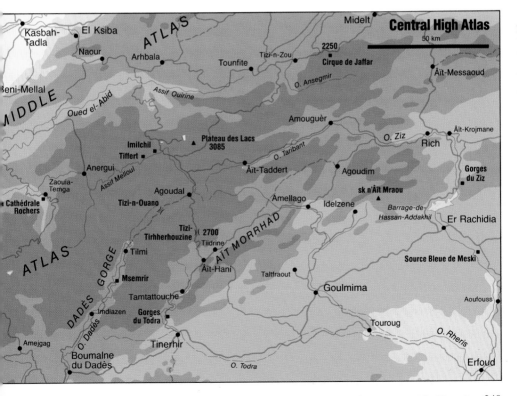

expanse of greensward sprinkled with small villages, with an administrative post at **Tabant**. Once a Shangri La, it can be entered by sturdy vehicles along a lorry track from the market town of Ait Mehammed (near Azilal, the provincial capital) normally without problems after early May but often with difficulty in winter and spring, when heavy snows can block the piste. The new track (turn right just before Ait Mehammed when coming from Azilal) has greatly shortened and eased the journey, and Land Rover taxis ply the route between the market town and the Ait Bouguemez.

An outdoors centre, and guides school has been opened at Tabant by the CFAMM (Centre de Formation aux Metiers de la Montagne). Tabant also provides contact with the local mountain rescue cover and has telephone facilities. Accommodation is provided by a number of *gîtes*, some of which offer facilities such as *hammams*, hot showers and electricity powered by generators or solar panels.

The tremendous barrier ridge of **Irhil Mgoun**, 12 miles (20 km) long, domi-nates the area; it remains a formidable target of endurance until sleeping quarters are established. Relatively easy to reach are the mammoth whalebacks of Azurki 12,100 ft (3,677 metres) and Ouagoulzat, or Wawgoulzat, 12,340 ft (3,736 metres), about five hours apiece.

Mules and porter assistance are *de rigueur* in the Central High Atlas; it is virtually impossible to cover the ground and distances without them. Thus supported, there are fine expeditions to be made to big limestone synclines like **Tignousti** and **Rat**, and cross country and valley riverbed journeys of several days to attractive villages such as **Magdaz**, where the famous poetess Mririda n Ayt Attik was born under the tutelary pyra-mid of Lalla Tazerzamt. The **Tessaout** and **Arous**, spectacular sheer sided gorges, invite wetsuit wanderers and rock climbers, draining south west and north west respectively from Mgoun.

The most frequented canyon trek in the region is the **Mgoun** (Achabou). It winds south from the Central massif to the Dades valley at **El Kelâa des**

Middle Atlas in winter.

M'gounna (Qalaa't Mgouna) on the P32 road. In one place it forces a passage between overhanging rocks for 5 miles (8 km), while the total river distance from El Mrabtin to the Issoumar/ Bou Taghrar dirt road is 30 miles (50 km) (two days).

Supported by mules and porters, supervised parties go from Tabant Bou Guemez over the Ait Imi pass to **El Mrabtin**, an arduous leg even without a rucksack. The best season to tackle it is June to late July when assorted plunges and wading shallows are appropriate for bathing suits and gym shoes. But there are no technical difficulties; pack animals unable to follow through the narrower sections are obliged to detour along a dizzy man made staircase clinging to the canyon wall.

Berbers use the river bottom as a conventional thoroughfare, and you'll stumble upon family groups crouching among the boulders, brewing mint tea. The trek is subject to the level of spate and weather conditions (dangerous in thunderstorms), and a guided tour is possible from El Kelâa in a three- or four-day outing. To quote Peyron once more, "Not all of it is hard work there are moments then the magic of the canyon plays on the mind inducing serenity and reverie."

Another way into the area can be made from **Demnate** (62 miles/100 km from Marrakesh) along the lorry pistes of Tifni, the Outfi pass and Ait Tamlil. Tour operators work most of these valleys, but rarely ascend their great mountains except for the Mgoun summit.

Coming from the south, the valleys off the P32 Dades road from Ouarzazate to Skoura, El Kelâa and Boumalne (the Route des Kasbahs) are harder still, the preserve of seasoned expeditioners accustomed to treeless and waterless wastes. Guiding services are found at El Kelâa Mgouna. Getting a lift to Boutaghrar on the Oued Mgoun cuts out the worst of the walk in.

DADES AND TODRA GORGES: The Sahara side of the Central High Atlas is cut by several gorges of some repute. Two have become well known as scenic routes following recent improvement to

Imilchil: at the brides' festival.

their piste tracks. The Dades, emerging at Boumalne, and the Todra at Tinerhir, both on the P32 road, can be traversed throughout their great length.

The two gorge circuit takes five to six hours, including halts and meal breaks. Protect your backside with an inflatable cushion and dress in safari kit or old togs. Proceeding up the Dades from village to village (whose names are all preceded by the Berber word Ait, meaning "of the people"), the verdant narrow valley meanders.

The road, looping west to avoid obstacles, rejoins the river at **Ait Arbi**, with its charateristic watch towers set among gardens shaded by venerable walnut trees. Dazzlingly bright, the white limestone spurs jut into the valley. The vertiginous incision of the gorge commences outside **Ait Oudinar**.

After a ford bridge to the east bank the piste has been blasted from sheer cliffs. The avuncular native chauffeur who comes with the Boumalne tour rental vehicle takes the hazardous driving ahead with confidence. Crazy sights of

primitive hoeing and ploughing practices ensue as the gorge relents. Near the last ford a glimpse west into the broad Oussikis hollow reveals the density of villages crammed round a jigsaw of simple green patches. The Berbers spend their lives trying to recover and develop arable land.

So to **Msemrir** (40 miles/65 km) with its colourful Saturday market, the historic meeting place between two of the major transhumant tribes, the Haddidou and Merghad, enemies among themselves to a man until they came together under the Yafelmane federation.

The dirt road ahead begins a long crawl to the Ouerz pass. In just over a mile a prominent fork right is reached at point 1996, where there is a survey pillar, signpost and drinking fountain. The piste curves east between stark escarpments to attain the **Ouguerd Zegzaoune** pass in an empty quarter of the "badlands". Even at this height you can be caressed by dust clouds in burning heat and a mirage lurks round every hairpin.

A longer descent and another fork south deposits the vehicle in **Tamtetoucht** on the seasonal Temda stream the chief feeder to the gorge lower down and site of several *marabout* , burial chambers of local saintly persons. The road winds south and in 3 miles (5 km) enters the upper **Todra gorge**. The variable water level at times of flood closes the canyon to vehicles. Parts of the new piste have been raised above the riverbed, first on the west side and latterly in the main gorge on the east side, which starts at a ford just after the tight bend at point 1599.

Palm trees sprout from the stony bed of the gorge. When the river vanishes in the dry season, it is used as a highway by pedestrians and animals. Though less forbidding than the Dades, its rock walls soar 1,300 ft (400 metres) and the defile at its narrowest point is impressive. The Hotel Yasmina is the first of a number of hotels and restaurants in the gorge, preceding a series of pretty Todra villages along the west bank.

Gardens, small fields, date palms and fig trees presage the magnificent oasis of **Tinerhir**, noted for its gold and jewellery workshops, proud castellated

Left, the Todra Gorge. **Right**, powderplay in the Middle Atlas.

buildings and decayed palace (19 miles/ 20 km from Tamtetoucht).

EASTERN HIGH ATLAS: The logical centre for exploring the other, eastern, end of the Atlas is **Beni Mellal.** The nearby reservoir lake of **Bin El Ouidane** is fast becoming a centre for watersports, including some of Morocco's most thrilling rafting. The aptly-named **Cathedral**, a pinnacle of a mountain, surrounded by pine forests, is also a powerful magnet attracting off-road enthusiasts, but it is still waiting to be discovered by trekkers.

However, it is as a departure point for the arduous off road journey to Imilchil, and beyond, that Beni Mellal is of most importance to tourists. Along the secondary 1901 road (hotel at El Ksiba) towards Aghbala, a fork south at Azaghar Fal proceeds to the Abid bridge over the Ouirine river, where the tarmac runs out. In dry weather the continuation piste can be managed by ordinary cars given good ground clearance; tour firms use a variety of 4WD. Drive through sundry villages among oak forests, over several rivers, up to Tassent and along its ravine with tricky zigzags and broken edges, past the old French Army memorial to a moderate descent to **Lake Tislit**, with its twin, Lake Isli, out of sight further to the east. The complete journey takes five hours. The lakes establish a natural boundary between the Central and Eastern massifs. This magnificent high grazing area translates as the Celestial Fields of Berber legend.

The brides' festival: According to the tale, the lakes of Isli (the man) and Tislit (the woman) were formed by the tears of two young people whose wedding was cancelled because of a feud between their families. Today the *moussem* at **Imilchil** (the September gathering of the clans, like a county show) is dominated by a brides' festival held to celebrate the legend. Young men and women dressed in their traditional finery go courting from tent to tent while families barter about the chattels a marriage might produce. It is a unique aspect to a gathering that is otherwise a religious-cum-rural fete noted for its

Legendary Lake Isli.

enormous market. News of the *moussem* has spread world-wide and has consequently transformed the event into an important stopover for 4WD-borne safari mountain tours.

Accommodation in Imilchil itself (the festival is held some kilometres further south of the town) is available in two small unclassified hotels anxious to emulate French standards, plus Berber inns and cafés. The village also runs to a weekly market, stores and a local authority headquarters. There are gentle river walks beside fine turreted buildings with many recent edifices, or longer strolls across miles of pasture between the lakes (piste tracks) among shepherds' huts galore and livestock by the thousands. A small auberge now exists on the shores of Lake Tislit, which is worth noting for is rich, though fragile, aquatic bird habitat.

Local vantage points are **Amalou N'Tiffirt** (8,100 ft/2,470 metres), one hour; and **Bab N'Ouayyad** (9,200 ft/ 2,804 metres), three hours, reminiscent of Striding Edge, on the Lake District's Helvellyn. True summits in the area are merely long hikes. **Msedrid** (10,100 ft/ 3,077 metres) is probably the most frequented and takes two days without 4WD assisted approach.

Tourers on wheels can leave Imilchil by the pulverising trail south to **Agoudal**, one of the highest inhabited villages in Morocco.

Northwest of Agoudal, towards Anergi, over the vast undulating tableland called Kousser, the terrain is cracked by several precipitous watercourses. Discovered by Europeans after 1950, these "secret" canyons have been investigated by a few enterprising explorers. The spectacular **Tiflout** is the master canyon, fed by snaking tributaries of some complexity. This system of ravines introduces another dimension to Atlas exploration. Pot-holing, caving, and rock climbing techniques, sometimes calling for bold swims in squeezes (tunnelled rocks), require equipment and experience.

Astonishingly, these gorges and their mysterious branches have been used for

A bride of Imilchil.

centuries by the Haddidou Berbers as short-cuts during their migrations. Jungle-like creepers, waterfalls bulging over sheer drops into deep pools, and raging torrents can all be experienced. Wood and rock bridges (*passerelles*) must be treated with caution.

One of the main arteries is the fairly Simple **Melloul**, a stretch of 12 miles (20 km) between Anergi and Imilchil populated by cliff dwellers. The others are the **Tiflout** (22 miles/35 km), **Wensa** (9 miles/15 km) and **Sloul** (9 miles/15 km). Approaches and exits add to these distances and represent the serious work.

South of Agoudal the piste crosses over the Tirhizit pass to arrive in the Todra gorge and Tinerhir.

A similar lorry-pounding piste twists east, from the Imilchil/Agoudal track, over the Tioura col to **Ou Tarbat** and down the remorseless Haut Ziz watercourse to the improved stretch after Amouquer and emerges at **Rich**, something of a misnomer, near the P21 road to Midelt.

The extremities of the Eastern High Atlas culminates in the **Jebel Ayyachi** (12,300ft/3,750 metres), whose backbone is double the length of Irhil Mgoun. The **Jaffar Cirque**, named after a local saint, is an inlet with parking places that marks the best departure point for an ascent of the mighty **Ayyachi** (12,300 ft/3,747 metres).

A rutted and often crumbling piste of 15 miles (24 km), known as the axle breaker, extends from **Midelt** (a high market town with several hotels and restaurants), and there is a similar but longer unmade track from Tounfite. Picturesque rock cataracts, the ravined Ijimi valley and clumps of dwarf conifers combine to make the area a popular picnic spot (though take water). Hotels run vehicles here as demands arises.

Snow cover on the mountain is normal until June; on this north side it lies in long trailing ribbons sometimes for weeks later. Most attempts to reach the summit start at dawn from a cosy bivouac at 7,200 ft (2,200 metres), about 30 minutes above the road, and a fit party can attain the summit in five and a half

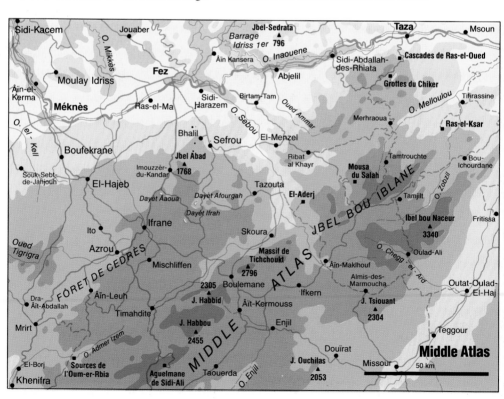

hours. Seen from the north in full winter robe, 25 miles (40 km) long and with a dozen named summits, the mountain is one of the most arresting spectacles in Morocco. A disguised Marquis de Segonzac made the first known ascent in July 1901 by the Ijimi route.

MIDDLE ATLAS: Once regarded as a wasteland these far flung, slatted high lands attach themselves piggyback to the Great Atlas across the wide open spaces of the Moulouya headwaters. The **Zad Pass**, between Midelt and Azrou, is a more precise point of reference. The size of the region can be judged by the perimeter roads, joined at three corners of a triangle formed by Fez, Midelt and Guercif, amounting to roughly 500 miles (800 km).

French administrators of the 1930s were endeared to a number of attractive features on this perimeter, which can be observed for great distances as a limestone escarpment, paralleled internally by successive corrugations or slats. The best of these natural objects have been designated areas for preservation. Al-

most without exception they may be conveniently visited in comfort from reasonable roads.

In the north, near Taza, the Tazzeka touring circuit is a one-day educational course in Moroccan landscape. It covers varied colourful ground of forests and gorges, passes waterfalls, caves and subterranean caverns, skirts sink holes and sunken lakes, and crosses little cols between quaint hamlets along narrow winding corniche roads. Dominating the centre, a television mast on **Jbel Tazzeka** (6,500 ft/1,980 metres) commands extensive views in all directions. The similar but more contrived Kandar Sefrou Sebou circuit is the most popular country district trip outside Fez.

Where the roads from Fez and Meknes converge at **Azrou** one reaches a district created by the French as a summer retreat alongside the most famous cedar forests in Morocco. The purpose-built resort of **Ifrane** (some say, the King's favourite residence) epitomises the idyll of the original scheme.

Extending in patches above and below the Middle Atlas escarpment at 5,200 to 6,900 ft (1,600 to 2,100 metres) over a distance of 62 miles (100 km), a concentration of splendid giant cedars, 200 ft (61 metres) high and mingled with oak, spruce and cork, contain many charming walks between **Ain Leuh** and the **Vallée Des Roches**. Lanes and pistes zigzag through the district, near the P24 Azrou Ifrane road.

Next to a coniferous forest standing in a volcanic depression among beds of limestone, the **Mischliffen** skiing grounds, deserted out of season, emerge as meadows covered with sheep and goats. There are signs of severe overgrazing and cedar stand cemeteries are dotted round the district. Excessive tree felling has been curbed and a programme of reforestation has operated for over half a century.

Nomadic Berber tribes called the Beni Mguild inhabit the forest in spring and summer. As well as tending their animals, they engage in woodland occupations such as making simple furniture and carving trinkets, carried on in large tented encampments.

Giand cedar tree, 200ft high.

THE SOUTH

Nothing north of the Atlas prepares one for "Le Grand Sud" of Morocco, a vast expanse of desert and semi-arid mountains flowing to the Algerian border. There is hardly a road in the region that cannot be described as spectacular. It is a film-maker's dream: wide valleys studded with palm-packed oases, mud-built castles rearing out of the ground, jagged blue mountains stretching across almost every vista.

The people of the south are equally striking: leather-skinned nomads herding flocks; veiled, sombre-clad women evoking Sara and Salome; shy girls flitting among vegetable gardens and disappearing into shadowy black alleys.

Southern Morocco runs westwards from Figuig, on the Algerian border, to Goulimine in the southwest (gateway to the Western Sahara). It is bounded by the Atlas Mountains to the north and by the Algerian border to the south, where it is lapped by the sands of the Sahara. It is a wide expanse: The distance between Figuig and Goulimine is almost 600 miles (1,000 km).

Of immediate interest are the **central valleys**, the Draa, the Dades, Ziz and Tafilalt. The geography of the region is formed by the Anti Atlas, a range of outlying semi-arid mountains that break up the south. In the east, the Saghro wedges the Draa up against the Jebel Aklim Massif; in the north the Dades drains between the Saghro and Atlas proper; eastwards the Tafilalt runs down to its death on the edges of the Grand Erg Occidental.

The Draa is Morocco's longest river, a huge wadi that finds its source in rivers flowing south from the Atlas and is augmented by streams from the Anti-Atlas. It survives the increasing aridity of its southward journey, turns west to form the border with Algeria, and eventually emerges exhausted at Tan Tan on the Atlantic coast.

To the south: From Marrakesh, two passes cross the Atlas. The most spectacular is the **Tizi N'Test** (6,890 ft/

2,100 metres), which leads to Taroudant via more than 62 miles (100 km) of hair-raising bends. The road passes through Ouirgane, a country resort sporting two hotels which make good lunch stops: the more upmarket is the **Roseraie** (run by a one-time manager of Marrakesh's La Mamounia), which is an excellent place for a drink, but never quite lives up to expectations as a place to stay; the other is the **Sanglier Qui Fume**, a characterful if somewhat down-at-heel hunting lodge (decent lunches – on the terrace in summer – with frog legs regularly featuring on the menu).

Further up the pass, beyond **Ijoukak**, is the now almost completely restored 12th-century mosque of **Tinmal**. Open to the public, when not in use for prayers, the mosque marks the birthplace of the Almohads and is roughly contemporary with the Koutoubia in Marrakesh. Nearby are the ruins of the Goundafi Kasbah, a youthful pile less than 100 years old.

The other route south from Marrakesh is over the **Tizi N'Tichka** (7,415

ft/2,260 metres), another stunning drive, albeit more travelled than the Tizi N'Test. The Pasha Glaoui (*see page 52*) once lined the road with 10,000 mounted and armed tribesmen for 62 miles (100 km) of its length, in a display of power intended to intimidate a new Resident General.

Just before the final tortuous climb over increasingly tight switchbacks to the top of the col is **Taddert**, a popular truck stop packed with cafés and grill restaurants. The **Auberge Des Noyers**, a survivor of the Protectorate period, offers a walnut shaded terrace out back, cold beers and rooms.

Deliberately side tracked by the road, built in 1936, the old caravan route passes through **Telouet**, home of the Glaouis and famous for its abandoned Kasbah (deserted after the fall from grace of the self-styled "Sultans of the South"). First visited by a European in 1889 and once host to Wilfred Thesiger on his treks in the Atlas, the huge crumbling ruin is sufficiently intact to give an impression of past splendours.

On your descent from the pass, keep an eye out for the delightful **Chez Mimi** (alas, no longer in residence), a convenient spot for a beer and game of pool on a hot afternoon.

Ouarzazate, the capital of the south, sits astride the Draa, at the end of the Tichka road, dominated by the Atlas filling its northern horizon. It is a crossroads through which everyone must pass, and was originally a base of the French Foreign Legion. It is now a centre of Morocco's increasingly important film-location industry, and is served by a plethora of hotels and an international airport. It is a modern town of little character or interest, but hidden away are a number of things that bring to life its short history. Overlooked by the Club Med is the **Kasbah Taourirt**, whose Glaoui palace, empty and partially open to the public, has some fine painted wooden ceilings. Much of the rest of the kasbah village is still occupied and worth a visit. Just to the west of town is the **Kasbah Tiffoultoute**, now a restaurant with a few rooms offering basic accom-

Southern kasbah.

modation. Yet another Glaoui abode, the kasbah is frequently the setting for fabulous fantasies staged for films and videos. The singer Paula Abdu recently shot a video here.

The Legionnaires have left their mark in the church, which is still maintained by Catholic nuns, and **Chez Dimitri**'s restaurant (good homely casseroles, crêpes Suzette), which was once a wild drinking hole and one of the few civilian establishments outside the garrison. There are numerous hotels of all standards in the town, but the Gazelle is one of the most characterful. Dating from 1962, it offers comfortable, modest rooms arranged around a pleasant garden courtyard behind its popular restaurant.

Scattered around the church and hotel are the bizarre sculptures of the Legion's last remaining representative in the town, an eccentric Austrian who rose to the rank of corporal in the Legion and then chose to stay behind in Ouarzazate as it pulled out, only to blow his own arm off with a grenade.

South of Ouarzazate, the road winds through arid hills, cut by an impressive gorge with a black patina, eventually descending into the oasis of Agdz. Before the descent, a dirt track signposted "**Cascades du Draa**" offers a delightful excursion. Though reached via a terrifyingly steep piste, the destination is an Arcadian-like gorge, boasting waterfalls and swimming pools plus a modest café – an agreeable place to stop.

A small market town, with a carpet-clad square, **Agdz** is surrounded by a sea of palm trees. Left from the square a small road leads to a camp site with a pleasant café. Nearby is a huge rambling kasbah, still occupied and under restoration. The resident family is very friendly and willing to give visitors a tour of their home. If you do nothing else here, climb up to the government **fort** (once a Legion garrison) to admire the view.

South of Agdz, the valley widens considerably. Here the riverbanks are clothed in tall reeds and often brightly decked in newly washed clothes. As the

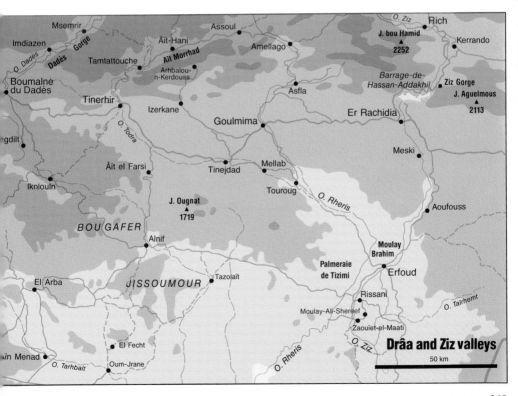

Drâa and Ziz valleys

50 km

towering metropolises of mud multiply, the Sahara begins to make its presence felt, costumes change, and the colourful women of the mountains are replaced by black-swathed negroes. Close to Zagora the changes are increasingly acute, the enclosed villages are more densely packed, reed-made palisades check the increasing quantities of drifting sand, and white-domed *marabouts* stand stark against the brown and ochre of the earth.

A turn-off at **Tansikht** marks the start of the recently tarmaced road to Tazzarine and Alnif, which links up to the road between Erfoud and Rissani in the Tafilalt. Once an arduous two-day drive across a rugged piste, the new road means the crossing from Zagora to Rissani can be made without the need of too much back tracking.

Zagora is the main market of the south. Nomadic Ait Atta, Saharan Berbers who found their way into Morocco in the 17th century, mix with old Arab families who emigrated from the Arabian peninsula eight centuries ago.

Clinging to the side of Jebel Zagora, on the south bank of the river, are the remains of an 11th-century fortress built by the Almoravides, testament to the antiquity of the town despite its dusty modern streets. A signpost declares Timbuktu a mere 52 days' camel journey away. Zagora was once a confluence of trade routes. Camel caravans from the south broke their journey here before making their onward journeys east and north.

Seven and a half miles (12 km) south of Zagora is **Tamgroute**, a small dusty town which has a tiny weekly souk. Tamgroute is dominated by its Naciri (a Sufi brotherhood) **zaouia** that has been a centre of religious learning since the Almoravides spearheaded a wave of religious reawakening in the 11th century. It was also the cradle of the Saadian dynasty (*see page 44*). The *zaouia* incorporates a *medrassa* which, though now a modern school, finds its origins in the 17th century. Alongside the school is a celebrated library (another modern building) which counts among its treas-

The Dades Valley.

ures Islamic commentaries written on gazelle skin dating from before the 13th century. It is open to visitors.

The *zaouia* also attracts the derelict of Moroccan society, people suffering from mental or physical illness, or simply lost souls who find their way to its peace and charity from as far away as Casablanca. The town also supports a **pottery works** famous for a distinctive green glaze derived from a cocktail of ingredients including locally mined magnesium. The co-operative has recently acquired a new gas kiln which should eliminate the unglazed scars caused by stacking the pots one on top of the other in the old charcoal fired oven.

Desert dunes: South of Tamgroute the first sand dune appears, celebrated by **Auberge Rose de Sable**. Owned by an artist couple living in Rabat, and run by their son, the auberge is a delightful gallery of Moroccan contemporary and folk art.

M'hamid marks the end of the road south. Once a Beau Geste outpost, garrisoned by the Legion's camel corps, it was later a target of the Polisario. Sand and date palms crowd the last few kilometres of road before the town, which is rapidly becoming a centre for camel trekking and a pit stop for 4X4 excursions into the desert.

West of M'hamid is a track to **Foum Zguid**. The area between, still with a strong military presence (the Algerian border is never more the a few kilometres away hereabouts), offers a taste of the true Sahara. The Iriqui basin boasts Morocco's most extensive area of dunes, a wide mirage-haunted *playa*, occasionally inundated by freak rains in the surrounding hills. The area, is inhabited by ancient Arabic speaking nomads, descendants of the Bedouin of Arabia, who live amicably alongside Berber Ait Atta tribesmen.

Canyons and roses: East of Ouarzazate is the **Dades valley**, also known as the Valley of Kasbahs. The Dades finds its water high in the Central High Atlas and bursts out of the mountains in one of Morocco's most spectacular canyons, the **Dades Gorge** at whose mouth is the

Crossing the Draa near Zagora.

town of **Boumalne**, a centre for roses and their associated perfume industry (a festival is held each spring to celebrate the opening of the rosebuds). Like its sister, the Todra Gorge, this 1,000 metre (3,280 ft) canyon, sheer in places, becomes a raging torrent in spring when the snow thaws on the Atlas.

The parallel **Todra Gorge** was once populated by Jews, who still remember Todra in a popular Hebrew folksong. Of the two, the Dades, which is longer and in places wider, is probably the more beautiful. Extraordinary rock formations, like elephant hide, look as if they have only recently lost their molten ability to move. For more information about exploring the Todra and Dades gorges, *see pages 109–110.*

The Ziz and the Tafilalt valleys: Beyond **Tinerhir**, the road traverses arid hills to arrive at the modern crossroads town of **Errachidia**, the regional seat of Government. A few kilometres south of here is the Blue Source of **Meski**. Once an idyllic oasis, the clear pools have been cemented and a characterless café has done its best to destroy what charm remains. A little way downstream, young girls, swathed in black, collect water in their copper pots and the landscape opens out into a vista of picturesque villages and hills.

After Meski, the **Ziz** river and the **Tafilalt** appear, a great scar of a valley that cuts through barren hills. The drive to Erfoud is spectacular as the road first descends the plateau to the sheer sided valley floor and then winds it way through a string of villages. The people of the Tafilalt are very different from the communities inhabiting the Dades and the Draa to the west. The home territory of the ruling Alaouite dynasty, the Tafilalt is an isolated Arab community, whose roots in the valley are far older than those of the Berber tribes surrounding them today. Their villages are impenetrable fortresses of covered and winding alleys; they themselves are inward-looking.

Erfoud, another recently developed town – no medina, streets laid out in a grid but pleasant nonetheless, is well

An evening sky near Erg Chebbi, Mourzouga.

prepared to meet the needs of tourists. A base for exploring the Tafilalt, it has several hotels, restaurants, petrol stations and mechanical repair shops.

Rissani, at the end of the Tafilalt, is another great trading crossroads, and home to Morocco's most African market, a continuous melee of haggling and jostling, where enormous trucks compete with laden donkeys. Rissani is said to be one of the world's largest date palmeries, with some 4½ million trees and more than 100 varieties of dates (a date festival is held each autumn to herald the harvest).

Like Tamgroute, the city is also an important religious centre, based on the tomb of Moulay Ali Sherif, the founder of the ruling Alaouite dynasty. Behind are the ruined remains of the Alaouite **Ksar Akbar**. Surrounding Rissani are deep rutted tracks, which turn to mud in rain, linking yet more isolated adobe villages and *zaouia*s dating as far back as the 13th century.

Close to Rissani **Sigilmassa**, founded by a Roman general and a fabulously wealthy town in its heyday in the Middle Ages, is today nothing more than a pile of barely distinguishable rubble, not really meriting a visit.

East of Erfoud and Rissani are the dunes of **Erg Chebbi**, often referred to as **Merzouga** after the small village and military outpost towards their southern limit. The dunes are the highest in Morocco and regularly host film crews shooting on location. On a clear winter's day, it is possible to see the snow-capped Mgoun massif, more than 93 miles (150 km) away, from the summits of the dunes.

At dawn Land Rovers set off in droves from Erfoud's smarter hotels taking tourists to experience a true desert sunrise. If you want to enjoy the dunes in peace, it is advisable to avoid the well-worn track leading to the cluster of small cafés at the dropping point for the tourist convoys. Camping among the dunes is possible, and recommended if you really want to experience the powerful appeal of the desert, but you may be visited by a policemen wanting to check on your

In the grain market at Taroudant.

passport details – Algeria is only a stone's throw away.

Alternatively, the **Kasbah Derkoua**, a few kilometres before the dunes, is a pleasant auberge. Its owner has spent most of his life deep in the desert; the kasbah is a haven of good food, unforced charm and peace.

Eastern outposts: Between Errachidia and the Algerian border crossing at Fuiguig is 250 miles (400 km) of gravel plain desert, with little to relieve the eye, save the occasional palm plantation in the Oued Guir, a scattering of *ksour* and the mountains in the distance. Humanity here is mostly represented by military outposts.

At the end, remote and rarely visited, is **Fuiguig**, which is even more remote from the north, for the road from Oujda is longer and more empty than the one from Errachidia. Like an island in the ocean, Figuig is an oasis of palm dates and gardens. Springs, some hot, feed a maze of irrigation channels. Separate and jealous communities, barricaded within their now crumbling *ksour*, fought each other for lack of other enemies until the French provided them with a common foe.

Fuiguig was once a major staging post on the overland route to Mecca. It supported a significant Jewish population up until the 1950s. Today, traffic to Algeria is much reduced and most of the town's inhabitants are soldiers. Despite all this, Fuiguig has an undeniable charm; it is a haven of calm, a fertile destination after a long journey through a seeming void.

To Taroudant from Ouarzazate: West of the crossroads at Ouarzazate, the P32 climbs between the Anti Atlas and the volcanic peaks of the Jebel Sirwa, which are snow-covered in winter and roasting hot in summer, the home of saffron growing in Morocco and famous for weaving. Along the way the road passes through **Tazenakht**, a market for carpets woven in the surrounding mountains. Further west is **Taliouine**, a snug but essentially one-horse town.

Just before the settlement, a huge rambling ruin appears, another Glaoui

<u>Below</u>, a "Maison Berbère". <u>Opposite</u>, *Lawrence of Arabia* was partly filmed in Morocco.

268

ON LOCATION

If there is one complaint more consistently bellowed at location managers during foreign filming expeditions, it is that there are no hot showers and the food is awful – which, come to think of it, are what constitute most people's idea of a bad holiday. Morocco, however, for all its Islamic customs and African attachment, has satisfied Western expectations of service. For the first half of this century Tangier's international city status opened its doors to a curious assortment of Western influences, including well-known writers and Hollywood stars.

Cary Grant shared nuptial bliss with Hollywood-style Woolworth heiress Barbara Hutton in the Kasbah overlooking Tangier's port (*see page 79*), while Marlene Dietrich marked her US debut in 1930 in a film called simply *Morocco*, in which director Von Sternberg shocked many with Dietrich's lingering screen kiss to another woman before she strode off into the desert dressed in full tuxedo and high heels.

It was after the making of such films as *Our Man in Marrakesh* and *Tangier* that the French set up the Centre Cinématographique Marocain to encourage film-making in Morocco. Until then even the most famous films associated with the country, Bogart's *Casablanca* and the Bob Hope and Bing Crosby comedy *The Road to Morocco* had had to be content with Hollywood versions of desert backdrops and Arabian palaces. The CCM still functions, smoothing the passage of foreign films by recruiting extras, advising on locations and arranging accommodation and props.

But it was David Lean's Oscar-winning *Lawrence of Arabia*, the film that launched the international careers of both Peter O'Toole and Omar Sharif, which really put Morocco on the location managers' maps. It showed that a director could marshal a whole company through many months of arduous conditions on the edge of a desert, with all the paraphernalia and supplies necessary for such a military-style campaign.

Film companies, like tourists, often leave legacies of their encampment, and in the wake of Lean's expeditionary force there emerged a Moroccan legion of extras, assistants, translators, controllers and location gurus who had cut their teeth on *Lawrence*. Lean's film showed off the "real" Morocco in all its Technicolor beauty.

Huge expanses of wide-screen blue sky and rugged splendour, plentiful supplies of Semitic-looking extras and medieval cities, whose trades and traditional ways of life still functioned, tempted an influx of foreign producers. One director, Alberto Negrin, in the film *The Secret of the Sahara*, even used 500 northern Moroccans, with blue eyes, to play French Legionnaires. The location manager on Bertolucci's *The Sheltering Sky* claimed that there was virtually no need to adapt the sites before cameras rolled, as nothing much had changed since 1947 (in fact, for the fly-infested scene in Aïn Korfra, more than 3 million laboratory-bred flies had to be specially imported from Italy).

However, such advantages couldn't tempt David Cronenberg when he directed *Naked Lunch*, the film of William Burroughs's novel set in Tangier. The room in El Muniria Hotel where Burroughs wrote his masterpiece has hardly changed since the 1950s, but Cronenberg recreated the room in a studio set-up, copying the original room right down to the smallest detail.

It is Ouarzazate, once a functional garrison town, which has unwittingly found itself at the centre of film-making; its proximity to both the desert and the imposing Atlas making it a suitable, if remote, choice. The nearby village of Aït-Benhaddou, with its exquisite kasbah, can claim several major screen credits. It was the location for the TV epic *Jesus of Nazareth* and Martin Scorsese's controversial *Last Temptation of Christ*.

The Moroccan government scrutinises scripts before giving the go-ahead to a film. As in any Islamic country, censorship is rigorous. But censorship takes no account of artistic merit. The film *Ishtar*, for example, managed to attract the talents of both Dustin Hoffman and Warren Beatty, but the only fame the actors found in the Moroccan desert was for appearing in one of the most expensive cinema flops of all time – a $45 million loss of face for the two stars. ∎

kasbah. It is still inhabited by descendants of the Glaoui's servants; dozens of noisy children usually swarm round visitors in an over-enthusiastic welcome but they will happily guide you through the ruins. Alongside is a particularly unattractive hotel, which is all cement and no charm despite its fine view. Not far from the town is the much more attractive **Auberge Souktana**, which also offers hiking excursions into the Sirwa hills.

For those with time to spare, but little inclination to hike, a tarmaced road cuts into the Sirwa from Taliouine to **Askaoun**, an uninspiring government centre in the middle of one of the most beautiful and unspoilt parts of the Atlas. From Askaoun a road turns west to **Aoulouz**, back on the P32, while a spectacular track north heads towards the peaks of the Atlas then swings east, away from the Tifnout valley, joining the Tizi N'Tichka road at Agouim. A long and arduous trip, it is not to be counted as an easy excursion in a small hired vehicle.

The journey on to Agadir from Taliouine enters the **Sous** valley, a huge fertile river plain. The walled city of **Taroudant** sits, like a miniature Marrakesh, in the heart of the valley. Centuries ago Taroudant served as a staging post for dynasties on the road to power, and was a temporary seat of government before the capture of Marrakesh itself. In 1912, it was also the stronghold of El Hiba, the "Blue Sultan", whose short-lived revolt against the French protectorate ended in his bloody expulsion at the hands of High Atlas Berbers allied to the colonial power.

Few monuments to the city's rich history now remain apart from the walls, which still follow their Almoravide plan. The **Palais Salem** hotel has become the city's major historical attraction. Converted from the 19th-century palace of the then pasha, the hotel's public rooms maintain some of their original splendour and the ground-floor rooms enclose small, luxuriant gardens of which the towering banana trees form the crowning glory.

Far left, drawing water in Taroudant. **Left,** testing marrows in the market.

Once a quiet, largely tourist-free city, Taroudant has become firmly established on the excursion itineraries from Agadir and so prices and hassle have increased accordingly. Even so its small scale and individualistic crafts make it an enjoyable and easy souk to wander through. There are a couple of notable antique shops whose owners have a fine eye for the unusual and sometimes outright bizarre. Do not expect ancient winding alleys and beautiful old *riads*, however, as much of the medina is made up of dilapidated concrete houses with barely a pavement in sight.

Outside the town, on the road to Amezgou, is the **Gazelle D'Or**, one of the most exclusive hotels in Morocco, if not the world. It is famous for its huge gardens and tasteful interior decor, and was once the home of a French baron. Patronised mostly by wealthy Anglo Saxons, it cultivates an exclusive country club image and regularly attracts international celebrities, including the Duchess of York, who holidayed here with John Bryan before her separation from the Duke. By contrast, inside the medina, is the decidedly eccentric **Hotel Taroudant**, once a famous watering hole of the Legion. It is cheap, friendly and has a reputation for good food, though this can prove unreliable.

South of Taroudant, route 7025 climbs the Anti Atlas massif of Jebel Aklim and the town of **Ighrem**, a small market and administrative centre once noted for its silversmiths.

The road beyond descends spectacularly, through striated hills and huge valleys (dwarfing what villages there are) to **Tata**, an oasis on the shores of the Algerian Sahara. From Tata, the road to Tissint, Foum Zguid and back north, is tarmaced. This eastwards route is rewarded with views of enormous wadis, sometimes filled with black, Bedouin-style tents.

West of Tata, the road arrives at Goulimine, gateway to the deep south (*see page 283*). Alternatively a turn off north, onto the P30, a few kilometres before the town, leads to the resort of Agadir via Tiznit.

Silver, best bought in the south.

AGADIR

The Moroccans shrug, or sneer. Yes, Agadir's okay – for tourists. But it's not *vrai Marocain*; it's a European city. So said a souk trader, and he's partly right. Others – friends, guidebooks – say wisely that you haven't seen Morocco if you stay in Agadir: and that's also true. It lacks the frantic concentration of life and energy that is typically Moroccan. But it's easy to get to, and an ideal base from which to venture into some of Morocco's most spectacular scenery.

A good beach, even the critics have to agree; unmistakably a seaside town: straggling bunting hanging over palm-lined boulevards; roadside trees trimmed into neat cubes; stucco architecture; a couple of 10-storey tower blocks; and even gaunt steel cranes near the beach – all are signs of a town anxious to be seen as an international resort. But there are a lot of resorts in the world with more pretensions – and far worse beaches.

This sounds like damning by faint praise, but there comes a time in many Moroccan itineraries when culture shock has given way to culture fatigue. In that mood, it's possible to find in Agadir a respite from the whirl of typical Moroccan-ness; from colours, sounds and smells, from insistent offers of help and pressure to buy. Of course, that's not a feeling that one boasts about. But it means that it's easy to start feeling affectionate towards the place, as long as you're not stranded there for too long.

A new town: During the night of 29 February 1960, an earthquake destroyed Agadir. The quake wasn't strong, but its epicentre hit the old town right in the kasbah. Agadir had for centuries been a fishing port and a market centre for the valley of the **Oued Souss**, which runs out to sea to the south. But on the morning of 1 March, most of the town was rubble: 3,650 buildings were destroyed, 15,000 people died and 20,000 were homeless. It was here that Save the Children Fund first saw active service in Morocco, one of their longest-running involvements in any country.

Morocco, about to celebrate the fourth anniversary of independence, needed a new centre here. It couldn't be anything but modern. It was bound to be a show-piece for the new state; at the same time it had to serve as port, market place, and industrial and administrative centre.

And so modern Agadir was conceived and built almost in segments. There are the port areas: the fishing port visible from the beach, with an adjacent square crammed with stalls serving the freshly grilled catch of the day, and heavier industrial docks invisible round a headland to the north. There are the poorer residential and industrial quarters to the southwest of the town. Immediately behind the beach, and seaward of the broad dual-carriageway of Boulevard Mohammed V, is the wedge-shaped tourist quarter. Inland of the boulevard is the town's commercial centre – shops, banks and travel agencies.

A beach resort: Six miles (10 km) of broad sandy beach and a claimed 300 days of sunshine every year are a potent combination. The beach – Agadir's chief

boast – is huge. Souvenir sellers' camels lope along the waterline. A *gendarme* on horseback rides the other way. Hundreds of sun-bathers are laid out, either on loungers or on the powder-fine sand, the colour of a murky *café au lait*.

Bathing flags tell you how safe the Atlantic is, but nothing warns you about how cold it is. The beach is between 200 and 400 metres deep and, apart from hired beach umbrellas, without shade.

At the centre of the beach is a ridge of rocks connected to the shore by a spit of sand, like a squat T, uncovered at low tide. This shelters a small area from breakers. It's here that most beach life goes on, with the support of a handful of "beach clubs" in the middle.

Hotels are some distance from the beach: those that aren't guard their own sand jealously, so most visitors, if they want shade or the right to use a toilet, hire a lounger at a beach club (reductions for season ticket holders). If you prefer less developed seaside fun, there is no shortage of less populated sandy coves north or south of Agadir. Moroc-

co's Atlantic coast is undeniably stunning with its succession of ragged cliffs and hundreds of varied beaches, some so large as to be mini-deserts, presaging the Sahara, further south. The wild coastal scenery, variety of seabirds, and in spring, profusion of wild flowers make for delightful, undemanding walks. However, do take plenty of water, it is an arid part of the world.

Most of Agadir's hotels are indistinguishable from those of Europe: standard bedrooms with balconies; "continental" set menus for dinner; chips with everything at a poolside bar. But striking Moroccan decor, Moroccan speciality restaurants and friendly service reflecting old traditions of hospitality combine to make Agadir a bit more than just another sun, sea and sand resort.

It makes financial sense for them to carry on building: it makes even better sense to build more hotels with direct access to the beach. And, as elsewhere in the country, the top-of-the-range hotels are very stylish indeed.

The climate, Agadir's other great ad-

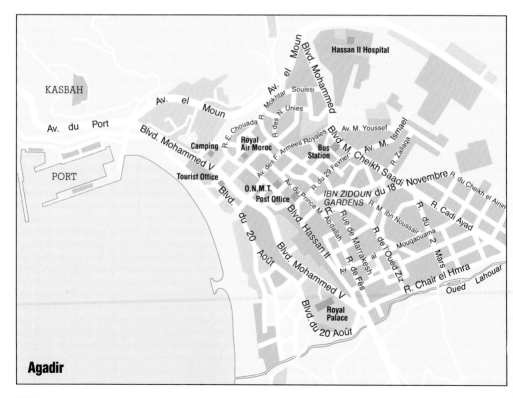

Agadir

vantage, is remarkable. Winter is only slightly cooler and wetter than summer (although it can be much duller). On average, in the whole of the five months from May to September there are between four and five rainy days. During the same months, and even into November, daytime temperatures routinely reach the mid-20s centigrade – cooler than the Greek islands, southern Spain and indeed the rest of Morocco in high summer, but with an advantage over them in the late autumn and spring.

Agadir after dark: So the resort has the right qualifications – but it doesn't create quite enough excitement. Most hotels sit between the **Boulevard Mohammed V** and the narrower but livelier **Boulevard du 20 Août**. It's on the 20 Août that the evening happens. The street is peppered with open-air bar-restaurants displaying illuminated boxes containing menus in French, German, English and Italian.

The atmosphere is animated: people forge friendships over a drink or over a bargain struck in the nearby shops, which are open well into the evenings. But there are long walks between the jolly bits and, apart from hotel discos and folklore evenings, there's not much else to do. If discos are what you want, the Byblos at the Hôtel Dunes d'Or is the best (but also the most expensive) choice.

Shopping scene: There is a *souk* in the industrial quarter, surrounded by a pink battlemented wall, but it's only for those who really know what they want (and the right price). Otherwise, it's less hassle to buy souvenirs from the **Centre de l'Artisanat**, or from **Uniprix**, a cheap fixed-price shop on **Avenue Hassan II**.

There are plenty of other shops in the centre which advertise fixed prices, their bags and trinkets spilling out on to pavements and along trellis-like frameworks, turning shopping walkways into a concrete *souk*, with the same traditions of attention-grabbing and prices high enough to come down if necessary.

There are also several upmarket shops selling designer sportswear, leather luggage, smart clothes and shoes, again at fixed prices. And there's an **English**

Below, Agadir bay from the hill.

language bookshop on the big concrete square of Place Hassan II.

What else to see: You can visit the regional **Centre de l'Artisanat**, west of the centre, where carpets, woodwork, jewellery and pottery are on sale at fixed prices, or direct from craftsmen working in workshop units. Bert Flint has a museum of traditional crafts, including his jewellery collection, in the basement of the municipal theatre.

The only sight with any history behind it is the ruined **Kasbah**, reached by a winding road above the port. There's no need for a guide here (although you'll get one if you're not careful), since so little has survived; but the view is splendid. The old gateway still has an 18th-century Dutch inscription: they were colonists before the French.

The best view of the new **Royal Palace** is from a plane; hope for a clear day as you fly into or out of Agadir. The buildings are reminiscent of Olympic rings in plan; the whole like a fantasy ranch, with green pantiled roofs glinting in the sun. Emerald lawns surround the palace between the southern end of town and the Souss estuary.

Excursions: Most travel agencies will arrange for coach tours to pick up from any hotel. For more independence – and more money – you can hire a car from one of the offices on Mohammed V or Avenue Hassan II. Excursions by Land-Rover or minibus can also be arranged.

Cascading spring waterfalls and lush palm-lined gorges in the **Pays des Ida-Outanane** are reached by a turning eight miles (12 km) north of Agadir; it's signposted **Immouzer des Ida-Outanane**, the main village with a prettily sited hotel between it and the cascades. Seabird watching is possible in the mouth of the **Oued Souss** estuary; but the range of species is better at the lagoon of **Sidi Rabat**.

Longer-range excursions can be made south to **Tafraoute** and north to **Essaouira**, both through superb landscapes; south to **Tiznit**; southeast to **Taroudant**; and a very long day – or, better, two days – to **Marrakesh**.

Right: mending nets in the harbour.

THE DEEP SOUTH

As you leave Agadir to the south, the real Morocco crowds back around the roadside. For the first few miles, you're still in the estuary plains of the Oued Sous: flat fertile land where trees line the road and villages are rows of small, cell-like shops – arcades where metal-workers are next door to butchers.

The road skirts the town of **Inezgane**, southern Morocco's most important fruit and vegetable market, and splits into three in the centre of **Aït Melloul**. One road leads up the Souss river, west-wards to Taroudant and the High Atlas; a second road runs south to Tiznit, and a third via the mountains to Tafraoute.

A trip to Tafraoute: A triangle of roads connects Aït Melloul and Tiznit to Tafraoute, and the fastest way to reach the valleys around Tafraoute is to keep to the wider, straighter road via Tiznit. This is what the coach excursions have to do. But if you have a car and a certain amount of nerve, it's worth travelling on the narrower road.

Both routes pass through mountains, but you'll get to them more quickly by a northern route. The way is full of surprises, such as the curious sight of the town of **Aït Bahia**, a jumbled cluster of low, white, mostly modern buildings, invisible until you top a mountain ridge.

Older villages cling to hillsides, crowd in on top of cols and hillocks: most have *pisé* walls the colour of the mountainside. The slopes are corrugated with terraces ploughed by donkeys driven by black-clad women. Craggy red ochre outcrops at the peaks look like a continuation of the terraces' reinforcing walls: such is the harmony between the unchanging habits of the mountain people and the sombre majesty of the mountains.

The landscape around **Tafraoute** is startling. From crumbly sandstone looms a jutting ridge of pink granite, purple in shadow, the **Djebel Lekst**. Below it, a lush series of palmiers: thousands of date palms spread in the **Vallé des Ameln**, and above them villages in earth colours: umber, pink, red and yellow ochre. The granite behind them looks like a series of cascades, geysers solidi-fying as they fall. This remote area is prosperous: partly due to its fertility but mostly because the majority of menfolk travel to the cities to seek their fortunes. Tafraoute businessmen are among the most successful in Morocco. Sending home money, they build large town-style houses in their home villages, ready for the day when they retire.

Dozens of villages cluster about Tafraoute; they're more fun to explore than the town, whose main square has several souvenir shops, all overlooked by the imitation kasbah which is the Hôtel les Amandiers. Also signposted from the square is the town's best res-taurant, L'Etoile du Sud. The first vil-lages to see are **Oumesnat**, to the north-east of Tafraoute, **Agard Oudad** to the south, and **Adai** to the southwest.

Along the road to Tiznit, on the out-skirts of town, are huge weathered boul-ders of granite, weird contorted shapes in striking contrast to the rigid outlines of the date palms. To the left is a sign

Left, doors are given special significance in the south. **Right**, a determined goat up an argan tree.

post to "*Les Roches Bleus*", huge fauvist boulders painted by Belgian artist Jean Veran. Whether or not you like the art, this is a superb location to explore or to camp out for the night. The grandeur of the mountains and the 1,000-year-old lifestyle are as impressive here as along the northern route. In early spring the hillsides are full of almond blossom; but once out of the mountains, there's a long stretch of pre-Sahara to cover before reaching Tiznit.

Walled city: The four miles (six km) of **Tiznit**'s four-square ramparts look more solid than most: and so they ought, since they're only just over 100 years old. There's only one must inside the walls: the *souk des bijoutiers* (jewellers' market). A short walk from the *mechouar* (main square), grouped around a courtyard, the jewellers work delicate silver filigree into swords and daggers as well as heavy bracelets and necklaces.

Tiznit's walls are *pisé*, built of impacted earth the colour of ginger biscuits. So are most of the walls you find as you continue south into the pre-Sahara and the mountains of the Anti Atlas, which rear abruptly from the plain.

Bleaker terrain: Sharp contoured valleys divide mountainsides covered with green stubble that looks smooth from a distance. They turn out, on closer inspection, to be a mass of knobbly boulders and ground-hugging cactus. Barbary figs (prickly pears) and low, bushy argan trees grow in deeper soil. Argans, native to Morocco, produce a fruit like an olive, which is pressed for oil. The goats like these trees, too; it's not unusual to see them in the spreading branches, nibbling the leaves.

Below the tortuous mountain road, which descends as abruptly as it climbs, the landscape becomes more deserted. This is where the pre-Sahara begins emotionally. In vast open spaces stand swirled mountains like frozen sand dunes: others, with dark patterns, look as if a dry brush laden with dark green paint has been drawn over a light brown background. The sheer extent of these landscapes can be unnerving: there is no human reference point. The abrupt ap- **Oumesnat Village, near Tafraoute.**

pearance of a marching line of pylons can turn the landscape into what seems like a post-industrial wasteland. But it isn't – it's just a desert.

The town of **Goulimine** (some signposts say Guelmim) might not seem like somewhere to write home about. Although the town is an administrative centre, its chief claim to fame is as the venue of a camel and livestock market every Saturday morning. Though this is touted as the place to see "Blue Men", it is really a venue for local farmers who rub shoulders with less rustic salesmen dressed in their Blue Men costumes

The town is also close to a group of oases, and you'll have no trouble finding somebody to take you out to one or all of these. They'll probably offer to introduce you to a blue man, or to a nomad, as well: if you're really "lucky", he might just have some carpets and jewellery with him. Of course, what you believe, who you meet, what you buy, is up to you. Even if you feel pressured, there's a friendly feeling in Goulimine, particularly if you stay there.

The only classified hotel is the Salam, a 2☆B with showers in some rooms. It's a little fly-blown in the dining-room; bedrooms open off an upstairs courtyard with lurid murals, but because there's so little else to do, you can find yourself making friends and spending hours just talking there.

On the road south, the occasional convoy of monstrous trucks heading to the burgeoning city of Layounne and garrisons in Ad-Dakhla, forces oncoming vehicles half off the road. Table-top mountains surrounding Tan Tan look no more substantial than sandcastles.

Tan Tan is made up of custard yellow buildings (the sort of colour that paint manufacturers might call Sahara). The turquoise dome of a mosque stands out, visible from the edges of the basin in which the town stands. There is a military feel: lots of flags, men in uniforms and garrison compounds. There are some hotels, but none of any special note.

The sea is 16 miles (25 km) away at **Tan Tan Plage**: a dusty half-way house, divided into a sardine port (a guarded

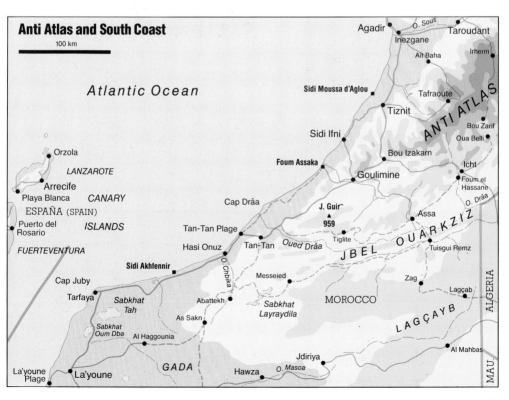

Anti Atlas and South Coast

100 km

private complex) and genteel resort. Small, elaborate seaside bungalows in a *nouvelle*-Moorish style would be better placed next to the Mediterranean. But the wind whips creamy spray from resolutely Atlantic breakers before they hit a crescent beach of sand, layered rock and the odd boulder.

During the week at least, nothing much stirs apart from boys mussel-hunting in rock pools. A 100-bedroom 4☆A hotel, the Ayoub, is under construction.

Police and Polisario: The reason for the military lorries and surfeit of troops from Tan Tan southwards is political. It was from Tan Tan that troops, followed by King Hassan II and 350,000 unarmed Moroccans, marched to claim sovereignty of the then Spanish Sahara in 1975. The anniversary of the *Marche Verte* (Green March) is celebrated as a public holiday every 6 November; posters, postcards and even the crockery of Layounne's Hotel Massira commemorate it in bold green and red.

Consequences for travellers are, nowadays, few and not really irksome.

You are likely to be stopped by the Gendarmerie Royale on either side of Tan Tan, where the white roadside checkpoint buildings are as bare as cells, and the Moroccan flag flapping on its pole is the only sound as a *gendarme* writes down your name, address, car registration, marital status, and the first names of both parents. This rigmarole is much more likely if you're heading south; going north, you're unlikely to be given more than a cursory once-over.

On to Layounne: This is an exhilarating route where the desert meets the sea and where a tarmac road wanders in and out from the coast, occasionally dusted over with blown sand. Between Tan Tan and Tarfaya, crumbling tableland comes to an end, and at once gives way to unstable cliffs. Butterflies play along the edge of the red earth, while pounding Atlantic surf blackens the grey rocks below.

Flocks of seagulls congregate on certain stretches of road: off it are Land-Rovers, swathed in nets and wearing fishing rods like huge antennae, and fishermen casting from the cliffs. At **Heading south.**

times, the road swoops down into a valley of brackish water – a sea inlet, a river outlet, or a salt lake (it's never quite clear which). Here and there are desert cafés: green or white or yellow painted, one-storey concrete cabins whose cheery colours seem to underline their isolation.

A whole village of cafés has grown up in **Sidi Akhfennir**, 63 miles (100 km) north of Tarfaya, at the base of a headland pitted with gaping caves. This is a useful petrol stop: you can rely on petrol around every 100 km from Tan Tan to Layounne. But you can't rely on French or English being spoken: you may need the Arabic for "water" as well as "please" and "thank you" (*see page 312*. At the **Caidat of Sidi Akhfenir** get permission to visit the most notable of the estuaries that bisect the route south. **Khan N'fiss** is a wildlife reserve and unsurpassed wild campsite. The estuary is huge, bounded by emeral-green marshes, silken white dunes and populated by a few fishermen, outnumbered by flocks of flamingoes, cormorants and even the odd osprey. Beyond the dunes on the north bank is a vast beach, wild remote and scattered with flotsam of the Atlantic. There are gulls here and the occasional heron. Harsh, semi-arid plains alternate with shifting sand dunes, looking (deceptively) as cosy as any seaside version.

One potential hazard: In 1987, and again in the late autumn of 1988, huge clouds of locusts descended on southern Morocco (as they did on much of northern Africa). Like pink smoke clouds when they're in motion, and like a rose-coloured carpet as they bask on the road, flying up at approaching vehicles they are extremely unpleasant for drivers. They are also potentially dangerous: you can skid on them, they block up the radiator grille and spatter across the windscreen. If you hit some, drive slowly through, and clear them from the engine and the grille with a stick as soon as the swarm has gone.

Locusts aside, the journey south is eerily quiet. Other vehicles become quite an event; the occasional well-hidden

Dates are harvested in October.

pothole in an otherwise reliable surface is less welcome. North of the little, Spanish-influenced port of **Tarfaya**, the spooky mood is enhanced (or aggravated) by the hulks of abandoned ships and large fishing boats leaning half grounded just offshore. They're too recent to look like wrecks, and some seem as if they're only resting: but they're definitely dead. Nobody will tell, but they're quite probably victims of the Polisario's guerrilla attacks before the desert walls were built.

Denuded bleakness: The animation, size and modernity of **Layounne** are a jolt to the senses after the denuded bleakness of the desert. Passing through two police checkpoints and a huge ornate gateway, and crossing the Green March bridge, the paradox hits you: Layounne has been designed as a city of the desert.

Since the Green March and King Hassan's return visit 10 years later, a lot of money and energy have gone into making the city an emblem of the benefits that Morocco can give to the people of the Sahara. A new hospital and

airport have been built, and public housing and civic buildings are in vernacular style: dome-topped houses, a courthouse like a desert fort.

There is no medina, and the huge modern square – the **Place de l'Allegeance** – is not the focus it sets out to be. The real animation of Layounne is in street after street of shops and daily produce and livestock markets.

For visitors, Layounne puts on its best face in the Hotel Parador: a mock castle enclosing a series of lush courtyards and shallow pools (and one swimming pool); there's Arab decor and green trellises throughout. The alternative is the Hotel Massira – mostly booked out by groups.

Big plans are afoot for the development of tourism in the Sahara, but they still have a way to go. Trips to the "sand sea", an area of shifting dunes, are easy to organise, and are occasionally laid on (together with folklore displays, camel rides and dromedary kebabs) for the cruise passengers from the *MV Orient Express*. Other regular visitors are the expatriate community in the nearby Canary Islands, who use regular flights to Layounne as an easy way of complying with Spanish immigration laws. **Layounne Plage**, 13 miles (20 km) west, is charming chiefly because it's so empty. A trip to Layouune can be fascinating – but come for the pleasure of the trip rather than the town.

Past Layounne, **Ad-Dakhla** is a serious 300 miles (500 km) drive across barely inhabited desert. After so much desolation, this military settlement is metropolis enough, although its few cafés and hotels have little to offer anyone in search of comfort or nightlife. The old Spanish cathedral and square, like that in Layounne, offers a brief cultural respite from the garrison nature of everything else.

The big attraction of the place is its setting of lagoons and beautiful beaches, great places for diving and, at the right time of year, for whale- and sea lion-watching. Ad-Dakhla is also the last staging post for the twice weekly police-organised convoy crossing the border into Mauritania.

Beach pursuit.

REAL BLUE MEN AND FAKE BLUE MEN

Any trip south of Agadir is likely to involve an encounter with *un homme bleu*, a blue man of the Sahara – one of those romantic desert nomads depicted in Hollywood epics as blue-turbaned aristocrats mounted on pure white camels. It was a blue man that swept Kit (played by actress Debra Winger) to safety and desert madness in Bertolucci's film *The Sheltering Sky*.

At least, you might *think* that you're meeting a blue man. In truth, he is probably fake. Southern Morocco only brushes the Sahara, a desert that spans the width of Africa, but Moroccans make the most of it – especially when there are tourists to satisfy. In the town of Goulimine, one of the places where the blue men traditionally came to sell camels, the promise of nomads draws Saturday coach-tours from Agadir, the day when the weekly camel market is held. Most of the traders are, therefore, not real blue men at all, but common or desert townspeople intent on making a profit.

Desert nomads still operating as such are found further south and east, and it should be remembered that all the Soussi tribes have a preference for the colour blue. Real blue men, though fallen upon hard times, are not particularly interested in entertaining tourists, and their pride is legendary. Wyndham Lewis, who visited the region and recorded his adventures in his book *Filibusters in Barbary*, published in 1932, said: "At their feet you may look. A downcast eye, fixed upon the exceedingly filthy blue feet belonging to these lords, will not attract a bullet."

The genuine article belongs to the Taureg tribes, whose roots are spread through Mauritania, the Western Sahara (now part of Morocco), southern Algeria and southwest Libya. Physically, they are unusually tall, handsome, and much more African-looking than the average Moroccan. Their regal demeanour is emphasised by flowing robes. And it is the Taureg men who wear the veil – designed to wrap over the nose and chin, in true desert fashion, to keep out the sand-laden wind.

Traditionally it was the dye in their robes that imbued the skin with an indigo hue, and it is claimed that the origin of these nomads' relationship with the colour lies a long way from the Sahara – Scotland, in fact. In the 15th century an enterprising Scottish cloth merchant is supposed to have travelled to Agadir and introduced a dark-blue coloured calico which was greatly admired. The fact that its dye permeated the skin was the cloth's main attraction. Before buying, a customer would test the cloth between wet thumb and forefinger to ensure the dye came off well.

The Taureg tribes are known for their nobility and historically their social hierarchy was strictly divided into nobles, vassals, serfs and slaves. The Harratin people, still found in the Draa Valley and at similar latitudes across the Maghreb, were once their slaves. It is ironic that many Taureg now do the agricultural work they used to shun.

The Taureg are associated with a rich intellectual heritage, and literature and poetry in particular are valued. The women are known for *guedra*, an erotic dance which they perform on their knees (one theory is that the low tents in which it was staged dictated this position; but it might be that it more readily suggests sexual submission). The shows performed for Westerners' benefit are likely to be fairly sedate affairs, but at one time the *guedra* was the speciality of prostitutes, and might include varying degrees of striptease.

Such vestiges of their culture apart, the nomads' traditional way of life has eroded fast. Causes include the steady decline of the Saharan salt trade and improved methods of transport in the Sahara, the breakdown of the traditional status quo, and severe droughts which have affected the areas of grazing for their goats. At one time the caravans of the Sahara might include tens of thousands of camels. These days you are lucky if you see a even thin trickle of camels trekking through the northern Sahara.

Many nomads have congregated in the towns, picking up odd jobs here and there, abandoning their culture and reluctantly leading a sedentary life. The Maghrebi governments have more pressing problems than the protection of endangered minorities. The blue men of the Sahara have had to be pragmatic to survive. ∎

INSIGHT GUIDES
Travel Tips

Your vacation.

Your vacation after losing your wallet in the ocean.

Lose your cash and it's lost forever. Lose American Express® Travelers Cheques and get them replaced. They can mean the difference between the vacation of your dreams and your worst nightmare. And, they are accepted like cash worldwide. Available at participating banks, credit unions, AAA offices and American Express Travel locations. *Don't take chances. Take American Express Travelers Cheques.*

do more

Travelers Cheques

Getting Acquainted

The Place

Northern Morocco is a natural amphitheatre, with the Rif mountains (to the north) and the Atlas mountains (to the south and east) enclosing the basin of the river Sebou and the *meseta* or table land, which reaches south to Essaouira. The Sebou basin and the meseta are the country's richest and most fertile areas; the Atlantic plains and the lower valley of the Sebou support cereals and vines; higher plateaux around the edge of the meseta are covered by forest and pasture. The river basins and low coastal plains have been the natural settings for Morocco's northern cities: the ports of Casablanca and Rabat; Marrakesh between the meseta and the Atlas mountains; Fez and Méknès on the rich soils south of the Sebou.

The Rif mountains, falling abruptly to the Mediterranean on their northern side, slope more gently towards the Sebou to the west and south. Fields and olive groves surround tiny stone villages: the only towns of any size are industrial and touristic centres on the Mediterranean coast (Tangier, Tetouan, Al Hoceima), or in the foothills (such as the market town of Chaouen). Along the spine of the Rif, hashish is grown: the (illegal) hashish trade centres on Ketama, inland of Al Hoceima.

The Atlas mountains run in parallel ridges across Morocco from southwest to northeast. The Middle Atlas (up to 10,000 ft/3,000 metres) is part flat-topped, part corrugated, damp and green with forests of oak and huge cedars. The western plateaux are interrupted by volcanic scenery. Some of the predominantly Berber population are still nomadic, others raise goats and sheep.

The grand chain of the High Atlas (13,670 ft/4,167 metres at its highest point, the Toubkal) runs for 473 miles (761 km), across virtually the whole width of Morocco. Sandstone and granite peaks, snow-covered until June, contrast with the *pisé* built villages, narrow field-terraces, and the bright green valleys to the west of the Tizi n-Tichka pass. Further east, the mountainsides are largely devoted to goats.

A fault line runs from Agadir to Figuig, splitting the Anti Atlas and High Atlas ranges. At first it follows the val-

Climate Table

MONTH		J	F	M	A	M	J	J	A	S	O	N	D
Agadir	Temp	20	21	23	23	24	25	27	27	27	26	24	21
	Rain	55	33	22	17	7	<1	<1	1	8	14	35	47
	Sun	7.7	8.2	9.3	9.9	10.0	9.6	9.4	8.7	8.6	7.9	7.6	7.2
Casablanca	Temp	17	18	20	21	22	24	26	26	26	24	21	18
	Rain	78	61	54	37	20	3	<1	1	6	28	58	94
	Sun	5.2	6.3	7.3	9.0	9.4	9.7	10.2	9.7	9.1	7.4	5.7	5.3
Fez	Temp	15	18	20	22	26	31	36	36	32	26	20	16
	Rain	80	72	71	64	37	12	1	3	15	36	61	85
	Sun	5.0	6.6	7.1	8.1	8.5	10.0	11.3	10.5	8.6	7.4	5.6	4.3
Marrakesh	Temp	18	20	23	25	29	33	38	37	33	28	23	19
	Rain	29	31	31	33	20	8	2	3	10	17	27	34
	Sun	7.0	7.3	8.2	9.1	9.3	10.7	11.5	10.6	9.7	8.0	7.1	6.7
Melilla	Temp	17	18	19	21	23	26	29	29	27	24	20	18
	Rain	52	30	28	28	38	8	1	1	11	27	33	66
	Sun	5.1	5.5	6.0	6.8	7.9	8.7	9.1	9.4	6.2	5.9	5.0	4.9
Ouarzazate	Temp	17	19	23	26	30	35	39	40	35	27	21	17
	Rain	8	5	15	7	6	5	2	10	21	20	17	19
	Sun	7.4	8.6	9.5	10.2	10.9	11.6	10.0	8.9	8.9	8.4	7.7	7.1
Tarfaya	Temp	20	20	21	21	22	22	23	23	24	23	23	21
	Rain	9	5	3	1	<1	<1	<1	<1	6	1	15	10
	Sun	6.6	6.9	7.7	8.5	7.9	7.8	6.5	7.0	7.2	7.1	5.9	6.6

Key:
Temperature: Average daily maximum (°C)
Bright sunshine: Average daily hours
Rain: Average monthly rainfall (mm)
Source: Meteorological Office Statistics

ley of the river Souss, whose basin is desolate scrub except in the lower valley between Taroudant and Agadir, where early fruits are grown. To the south is the pre-Cambrian bulge of the Anti Atlas. Argan trees and small holdings flourish on the slopes facing west towards the sea. South and east again, the country is no more than desert, scored by oases-dotted river valleys. The pre-Sahara, made up of vast bare rocky plateaux, is swept by dusty winds and occasionally punctuated by flat-topped hillocks or shifting dunes. The Sahara proper is less hospitable still, except at the chains of oases. What were once watercourses are dry for most of the year, except after the occasional desert storm. Trickles of water are more common towards the hazy coast of sands and crumbling cliffs.

The northeastern extreme of the country comprises chiefly plateaux of 1,000 metres or more. In the main they are too dry to cultivate: even the valley of the river Moulouya, running out of the Atlas and east of the Rif, provides only a narrow corridor of cultivated soil. The wealth of the region, dominated by the town of Oujda, comes from the Mediterranean coast, irrigated and dammed, where the climate allows pockets of agriculture and market gardening.

Time Zones

Moroccan time is the same as Greenwich Mean Time; when it is noon in Morocco, it is noon in London, 7am in New York and 8pm in Perth. This does not take into account local seasonal time changes.

Climate

Three types of climate hold sway in three distinct regions: coastal regions have warm dry summers, are wet for the rest of the year and mild in winter: the coast is drier south of Agadir, where it is free of Atlantic depressions in winter. Agadir has a well-protected climate, with a narrow range of temperatures; but in common with the rest of the Atlantic coast, cold offshore water can cause cloud and fog. The mountains get hot, dry summers and very harsh winters; parts of the High Atlas are under snow well into the summer. The remainder of the country has a continental climate, getting hotter and drier in summer to the south, but moderated by the sea to the west. In the inland Sahara very dry, hot summers give way to warm sunny days and cold (sometimes frosty) nights in winter. (*See chart on page 290.*)

The People

The original people of Morocco are the Berbers: predominantly nomadic tribes and famously fierce. But the name Berber itself is thought to be derived from an Arab word for non-Arabs; and from the late 7th century AD, Arabs and Berbers have shared the country and alternately held power – until colonial domination by Europeans. In troubled times, the Berbers retreated to strongholds in the Rif and High Atlas – where they have always been their own masters, and which still remain predominantly Berber today. The Arab population is today concentrated in the north and in the cities: in mountain and country areas three Berber languages are still spoken. But centuries of intermarriage have blurred a distinct Arab/Berber divide.

The population of Morocco is officially estimated at a little over 26 million people, 90 percent of them living north of a line drawn between Tiznit and Oujda. Growth in recent decades has been remarkable: from 6.5 million in 1935, to 12.5 million in 1964, to more than double that today. And it is a young population; four out of 10 Moroccans are said to be under the age of 15.

The Economy

Agriculture: Exports include cereals, dates, figs, olives and almonds, sugarcane, and most notably early fruits: oranges and tomatoes are the best known, but the Souss area has been experimenting with banana growing and the cultivation of roses.

Minerals are dominated by rich reserves of phosphates; some three-quarters of the world's stock. The export of phosphates and its derivatives has historically accounted for over 40 percent of export earnings.

Energy has to be bought: there are some reserves of anthracite, and oil shales are beginning to be exploited, but most oil is imported. Hydro-electric power has contributed less to national needs as northern Africa has become gradually drier. A large lump of the country's foreign exchange comes from wages sent back home by Moroccans living abroad, notably in France and Belgium.

Government

Morocco is a Muslim kingdom governed since 1961 by King Hassan II, son of the late king Mohammed V. It was Mohammed who changed his own title from sultan to king, and reigned when Morocco secured independence from France and Spain in 1956. In 1962, King Hassan put forward a new constitution which described Morocco as a Muslim sovereign state and a social democratic and constitutional monarchy, and which led to parliamentary elections. There have been periods of emergency rule, attempted coups and government by decree. The political structure remains parliamentary, with King Hassan firmly established in power (and much pictured in public places).

Islam & Ramadan

Islam in Morocco is in a strange position: popular unorthodoxy is followed (rather than led) by the state; at the same time, many European habits of government remain. Unlike some Gulf Arab states, there is not much evidence of hard line Islam. Alcohol is not restricted by law. Sunday is the closing day for offices and shops. It is in souks (mainly those in the country) that *djemma* – the word means simply mosque – is observed on Fridays: on that day, country markets will often be closed after noon.

Morocco remains a Muslim country, for all its compromises with Western calendars and customs (a holiday on New Year's Day), and never more obviously than during the holy month of Ramadan. But Islam in the country is a peculiarly Moroccan hybrid – the faith of the Arabs adapted by the tribes of Berbers. There is more emphasis on individuals and saints than rigid Islamic codes would sanction: and that is a direct result of a split between the population in the cities and the country.

Islam in the city is easy to govern. The minarets of the mosques are a constant visible reminder to the populace, and the faithful are loudly called to prayer five times a day. The mosque – and the wisdom and learning traditionally associated with it – are (often literally) central to town and city life. Koranic schools and conclaves of Islamic scholars reinforce orthodoxy, the most important tenet being that there is no God but God and Mohammed is his Prophet. There are no vicars, no intermediaries: in praying five times a day, the Muslim is talking directly to God. At the same time, even without priests, the centres of religious devotion have immense influence – and power. And it is away from this urban structure of influence that part of Moroccan Islam has moved.

The first and most visible element of country Islam in Morocco is the popularity of the *marabout* or local saint – visible, because the countryside of remote areas is dotted with small whitewashed buildings with domed roofs. Each is the tomb of a saint; the tomb itself sometimes known as a *marabout* (otherwise called a *koubba*). Around these local saints, cults of devotion have grown up over centuries – over 1,000 years in the case of Moulay Idriss.

Rich cults have *zaouia* – educational colleges set up next to the marabout in the same way as a mosque set up a *medrassa* – but as an alternative to the city-based orthodox Muslim faith taught at the mosque. And every cult has its *moussem* – the annual festival in honour of the saint (see *Festivals*) – the scale of the festival reflecting the importance of the particular saint.

Ramadan: The ninth month of the Muslim calendar was the one in which God revealed to Mohammed the truths which were written as the Koran. In remembrance of this and in obedience to one of Islam's "five pillars", Muslims must observe a holy fast during the hours of daylight. This means total abstinence from food, drink, tobacco and sex between sunrise and sunset. Moroccans traditionally end the fast with a bowl of *harira* (a rich soup: *see Eating Out* section) and *shebbakiyah* (deep fried, honey smothered pastries) when the mosque lamps signal nightfall. That's followed by an atmosphere

of nocturnal festivity, in the hours when a black thread cannot be distinguished from a white one.

For travellers: The unique atmosphere of Ramadan can be weighed against slight material inconveniences for the traveller (cafés and restaurants are generally closed during the day). Non-Muslims are not required to observe the fast, but abstinence from smoking or eating in public is tactful.

Planning The Trip

What To Bring

Although cash tips are common, certain goods go down well too, with children who have posed for photographs or anyone who has helped you. European or American cigarettes (light tobacco) are worth carrying; so (for children) are coloured ball-point pens or crayons, small notebooks or wrapped sweets. Clothes (e.g. picture T-shirts and Levi's) can occasionally be useful currency when bartering for larger items (such as rugs or killims) in the souks.

Electricity

Most of the country's supply is rated 220 volts, but some places have a 110 volt supply; sockets and plugs are of the continental European type, with two round pins.

What To Wear

Dress for comfort. Light-coloured, lightweight cottons are advisable, and in the south, a sun hat in summer. Hotels are rarely dressy, although some four and many five-star hotels have formal restaurants where men will feel more comfortable in a jacket and tie, and women in a dress. When touring or sightseeing, let tact be a guide: keep skimpy clothes for the beach and remember that jewellery and fine clothes mark the wealthy tourist in a poor country; expensive bags or cameras may also attract more attention than you'd like.

Entry Regulations

Visas & Passports

Holders of full British passports (but *not* a British Visitor's Passport), and holders of valid United States, Canadian, Irish, Australian, New Zealand or Scandinavian passports need no visa for a stay of up to three months. Children under 16 without their own passports must have their photograph stamped in the passport of one of their parents.

Customs

Clothes, jewellery and personal effects including cameras and up to 10 rolls of film can be brought into the country temporarily, without formality. Foodstuffs and medicaments in reasonable quantities for personal use may also be imported. Duty-free allowances for alcohol, tobacco and perfumes are 250 grammes of tobacco *or* 200 cigarettes *or* 50 cigars; one litre of wine; one litre of spirits; a quarter-litre of eau de cologne. To import firearms, a licence is needed from the *Direction de la Sûreté Nationale* in Rabat.

Customs procedure on entry will vary according to point of arrival; baggage is often searched, and will need to be cleared by a customs official before entering the country.

Health

No vaccinations are required by the Moroccan government for entry, unless you have come from a recognised infected area (e.g. a yellow fever, cholera or smallpox zone). For your own safety, however, inoculations against typhoid, polio, cholera, and tetanus are advised by cautious doctors. A course of malaria tablets may also be advisable: these are normally taken for a week before, during, and for four to six weeks after travelling. The risk of malaria is highest in the summer: insect repellent gels or creams are sensible additional precautions.

Some protection against hepatitis may be useful if travelling in country areas. Injections of immuno-globulin give protection for about four weeks: they are no use for long trips, therefore, and should be discussed with a medical advisor. Contact with standing fresh water (swimming or paddling in oases, river valleys and lagoons) may carry the risk of bilharziasis. Rabies is present: take medical advice immediately if you are bitten.

AIDS: The disease can be transmitted either through sexual contact, or through medical treatment using infected needles, blood or blood transfusion equipment. Most Moroccan pharmacies now stock disposable needles, and clinics and hospitals are usually reliable: check with a consulate or embassy if in doubt over treatment. It is possible to buy medical "kits" containing sterile hypodermic needles and plasma which can be carried in case of an emergency.

Humbler ailments are common. A survey conducted by the British consumer magazine *Holiday Which?* found that 29 percent of its readers visiting Morocco had been ill on holiday. This compared with 56 percent in Egypt, 16 percent for Greece and Spain, nine percent in France and three percent in the Netherlands. **Stomach upsets** are top of the list, accounting for 60 percent of holiday illness: diarrhoea remedies or relief will come in handy.

Cutting the risks: avoid food that has been left standing or has been reheated; use bottled water in remote areas. The next most common cause of illness is usually too much heat or sun, especially when combined with alcohol; light cotton clothing, moderate exposure and protective lotions all reduce the risk of sunstroke. (*Also see Emergencies.*)

Money Matters

The Moroccan *dirham* (DH) is nominally divided into 100 *centimes* – but these are sometimes called *francs*. Recent official rates have hovered around £1=13DH and US$1=9DH. Check newspapers for the current rates.

There is one simple rule: Moroccan currency may not be imported or exported. Visitors can import as much foreign currency (in cash or travellers' cheques) as they wish: if the value of currency imported is more than 15,000DH, they must fill out a *déclaration des devises*, which should be carried with them throughout the trip.

It's useful, especially if entering Morocco outside banking hours (e.g. on an evening flight) to have some cash – it will be easier to change at airport exchange kiosks (mostly run by banks), who may refuse travellers' cheques or credit cards.

While in Morocco, travellers' cheques in either pounds or dollars are the safest way of carrying money; though some banks will not handle them, their staff will direct you to those which do (try BMCE and Wafabank). Exchange rates are fixed, whether in banks or hotels. Most major banks do not charge commission. At the end of the trip, the total amount of Moroccan currency you have bought can be changed back, but only if exchange receipts are produced. If you run out of money, it is possible to use major credit cards to obtain money in main banks (e.g. Crédit du Maroc, Banque Populaire or Société Générale Marocaine de Banques). Alternatively, you can telex your bank abroad and arrange for money to be transferred to a Moroccan bank. This takes about 24 hours.

Public Holidays

There are two sets of holidays, religious and secular: the one based on the Muslim (lunar) year, and the other on the Western (Gregorian) calendar. Religious holidays are as follows; for exact dates according to the Western calendar – they get earlier each year by 11 days (12 in a leap year) – consult the Tourist Office.

Muslim holidays
Aid es Seghir (marking the end of Ramadan)
Aid el Kebir (feast of Abraham's sacrifice of a sheep in place of his son)
Muslim New Year
Mouloud (the Prophet's birthday).
These are usually observed by shops and businesses, though these days some shopkeepers are sacrificing piety for prosperity.

State holidays
New Year's Day – 1 January
Manifesto Independence – 11 January
Feast of the Throne – 3 March
Labour Day – 1 May
National Feast – 23 May
Youth Day – 9 July
Allegiance of Oued Edtahab – 14 August
Green March – 6 November
Independence Day – 18 November.

Festivals

Every religious holiday is marked by festivity in Morocco. The other staple of festival life is the *moussem:* a local festival (or pilgrimage) in honour of a saint or holy man. In the country you may occasionally stumble across one of these, a flash of colour and excitement in the daily round of subsistence; men and unmarried girls in costume, a courtyard laid with carpets and rugs, frenzied bands of musicians. But there are several *moussems* which are on a larger scale altogether and worth going out of your way for. Ceremonial dancing and fantasias (displays of horsemanship) may accompany them. There are also folklore and harvest festivals. Most of these are moveable feasts and exact dates should be checked either before you leave or when you arrive.

Tafraoute: an almond blossom festival: February
El Kelâa des Mgouna (Ouarzazate region): festival of roses: May
Goulimine: *moussem:* June/July
Marrakesh: national folklore festival: early to mid-June
Sefrou (Fez region): cherry harvest: June
Asilah: an international music festival, including classical, folk and popular: from the last week in July, for one month.
Setti Fatma (Marrakesh region): *moussem:* August
Imilchil (High Atlas): marriage *moussem* of the Aït Haddidou tribe, a sort of costumed mass pledge: September
Moulay Idriss (Meknes region): this is the country's grandest *moussem* commemorating the founder of Morocco's first Arab dynasty, Idriss I: held throughout September
Fez: *moussem* of Moulay Idriss II, the founder's son: September
Agadir: art and folklore festival: October/November
Erfoud: a date (the fruit!) festival: October

In the fortnight before and after Mouloud, the Prophet's birthday, there are processions and *moussems* in **Meknes**, **Salé** and **Asni** (Marrakesh region).

Getting There

By Air

The national airline, Royal Air Maroc (RAM), has Casablanca airport as its hub. There are flights from London Heathrow and from New York JFK to Tangier, Casablanca, Marrakesh and Agadir

Fez is not served by direct flights from Britain or the USA, but it is from Vienna, Zurich, Toulouse and Rome. The cheapest tickets through RAM are Pex (stay up to two months) and Superpex (stay up to one month). If you cancel either type, you are entitled to only a 50 percent refund and no refund at all when cancelling less than one full day prior to the flight.

GB Airways (tel: 0181-877 4000) in conjunction with British Airways also flies to Morocco. It is worth investigating British Airways' World Offer fares.

With the exception of the company Inspirations (tel: 01293 822244), all British tour operators are currently using scheduled RAM services to Morocco. Consequently there are few cheap charter flights to be found. One of the cheapest sources of non-transferable tickets on RAM is Morocco Bound (Suite 603, Triumph House, 189 Regent Street, London W1. Tel: 0171-734 5307).

If travelling to Tangier, it may be worth investigating flights to Gibraltar or Malaga (from where you must take a bus to the ferry in Algeciras), only a short sea-crossing away (ferries leave throughout the day). See By Sea.

ROYAL AIR MAROC OFFICES

Austria: Opernring 4/1/10, Vienna. Tel: 512 31 51.
Belgium: 46–48 Place de Broukerie 1000. Tel: 219 24 50.
Canada: 1001 de Maisonneuve Ouest, Suite 440, Montreal. Tel: 285 1619.
Denmark: Vester Farimagsgade, 7, 6eme étage 1606, Copenhagen. Tel: 33 32 21 00.
France: 8 Avenue de l'Opera, Paris. Tel: 44 94 13 30.
Germany: Friedenstrasse 9, Frankfurt 9. Tel: 236 220/228/229; Maximiliansplatz 12A, Munich. Tel: 291 604 70.
Great Britain: 205 Regent Street, London W1. Tel: 0171-439 8854.
Greece: 5 Metropoleos Syntagma Square, 10577 Athens. Tel: 32 44 302/303/304/305.
Italy: Via Barbarini 86, Rome. Tel: (06) 474 28 58/487 22 57.
The Netherlands: Leidsestraat 59, Amsterdam. Tel: 624 71 88.
Portugal: 225A Avenida da Liberdade, Lisbon. Tel: 35 21 659.
Spain: Gran Via de Les Corts Catalanes 634, 6th Floor, Barcelona. Tel: 301 8474; Calle Princesa 7, Madrid. Tel: 547 79 05/06/07.
Switzerland: 4 Rue Chantepoulet, Geneva. Tel: 731 5971/5972.
United States: 55 East 59th Street, Suite 17B, New York. Tel: (212) 750 5115.

For Royal Air Maroc offices in Morocco, see page 298.

By Sea

The most logical point of entry by sea is from **Algeciras** in southern Spain across the Strait of Gibraltar to **Tangier** (around 2½ hours) or the Spanish duty-free territory of **Ceuta** (around 90 minutes). Tangier is better connected to public transport in Morocco; the Ceuta crossings are up to four times more frequent, and convenient for drivers who aren't daunted by arriving in kif-touting Tetouan. These short hops are the best bet for those in cars, since there are sailings throughout the day: on all the longer routes you will probably need a reservation. Where possible, avoid all routes in July and August, when migrant workers clog ports. Passport control takes place on board the boat. You must have your passport stamped before disembarking.

There are also hydrofoil services to Tangier from **Algeciras**, **Gibraltar**, and **Tarifa** (Spain's southernmost town). Hydrofoils don't run if the sea's too rough; nor do they run on Sundays. Spanish car ferries run from Almeria and Malaga to the Spanish duty-free port of Melilla (6½ and 7 hours respectively). Finally, there are car ferries run by the Compagnie Marocaine de Navigation from Sète, in southern France, to Tangier or via the Balearic islands to Nador; the Tangier crossing takes 38 hours, so it's not for bad sailors or anyone in a hurry.

By Rail

Trains leave London Victoria and connect via the Algeciras ferry with Tangier, Rabat and Casablanca, by way of Paris (change to Gare d'Austerlitz in Paris). The total journey time, London to Tangier, is around 48 hours. Travellers aged 26 and under can save by buying youth or student fares.

By Road

Two options: drive through France to catch the ferry at Sète, or through France and Spain to take one of the Algeciras ferries. Generally, travelling to Morocco by car is expensive (allow for toll fees in France and Spain as well as ferries, petrol and overnight accommodation). For travel through France you will need Green Card insurance, and for Spain a bail bond, both issued by your regular insurer. Few British insurers are prepared to cover cars in Morocco. Your best bet is to purchase insurance when you arrive: see Assurances aux Frontieres in Tangier's harbour. You will also need to take your Vehicle Registration Document.

Coach as far as **Algeciras** is the least comfortable way to make the trip (around 48 hours from London).

Special Facilities

Doing Business

Business customs are a mixture of Arab and European; the French influence remains in many of the country's industrial concerns. Personal contacts and hospitality are important; urgency and on the spot decision-making are not. Intermediaries who have set up business deals or contacts may expect commissions as a matter of course; businessmen should be careful in such cases, since to suggest that such conduct is less than honest could give offence. Signs of impatience are also considered rude: the best signs of a successful deal are meetings with a series of executives from the same company. Promotional literature, if any, should be supplied in French. Useful addresses for businessmen include:

Chambre de Commerce et d'Industrie de Casablanca: 98 Boulevard Mohanned V, Casablanca. Tel: (02) 221524.
Office for Industrial Development (ODI): 10 Zankat Ghandi, PO Box 211, Rabat. Tel: (07) 768460. Telex: 731053.

British businesses should contact

the Department of Trade and Industry for useful information in the publication *Hints to Exporters: Morocco*, available from the DTI, Export Department, C/O Westex Ltd, 7 St Andrews Way,, Devon Road, Bromley by Bow, London E3 3PA, tel: 0171-510 0171.

Gays

Morocco no longer offers visitors the free and easy attitude it once did towards homosexuality. Tangier in particular has been officially cleaned up. What the Moroccan law describes as an "unnatural act" between two persons of the same sex is now punishable by imprisonment (six months to three years) and by fines. The British embassy in Rabat stresses this. Despite all this, and regional taboos, male gay sex is still available, and in some cities (Marrakesh, for example) young male hustler-prostitutes are becoming more evident.

In common with the whole of Africa, the risks of sexually-transmitted diseases (including AIDS) must be considered (although there are few figures available). In general, Marrakesh is associated with French homosexuals, and Tangier attracts an English gay community.

Disabled

No official register exists of facilities within Morocco for people with disabilities. Relatively few hotels are overtly suitable for wheelchair access, particularly those converted from older buildings such as palaces. That said, the Moroccans' attitude to disability is extremely solicitous. UK tour operators able to cater for disabled travellers are Cadogan Travel, Horizon Holidays and Kuoni Travel.

Students

There are few official discounts available to students in Morocco. Chief benefits of student status are the use of an Inter Rail pass on the railways. There are also discount fares for students from Royal Air Maroc. Domestic discount fares can be booked in advance from RAM offices (but not on spec at the airport) on proof of student status. Some international discounts are also available: check your local office for details

Practical Tips

Security & Crime

Crime against tourists is not common, but neither is it unknown. In a survey published by the British consumer magazine *Holiday Which?*, it was found that 4.3 percent of visitors to Morocco had been victims of theft: smaller than 1 in 24. But any guide in the packed souks of Fez and Marrakesh will advise you to hold tightly to your bag. Violent attacks or muggings were still less common – less than one percent were affected. Nevertheless, both types of crime were found to be more common in African countries – including Morocco – than in Europe or America. What tends to be most intimidating, especially in the imperial cities, is harassment from *faux-guides* (literally, false guides) who try to force their services on you. The best way to deal with them if you don't want their help is to decline firmly but with good humour. Above all, don't become agitated – it only prompts abuse. (*Also see "Guides"* under *Orientation.*)

Emergency telephone numbers: Police: 19.

Fire services/ambulance: 15.

Elementary precautions: Avoid wearing jewellery, or carrying too much money in the streets: use hotel safe deposit boxes. If you're on the move, prefer a secure pocket or money belt to a shoulder bag for valuables; if you wear a bag, sling the strap over the head, not just the shoulder.

If you are attacked, don't put up a fight: better to lose money than risk being hurt. If driving, don't leave bags visible in the car, always lock your vehicle and leave it empty overnight. Better still, do as the locals do and leave it where an all-night *gardien* can watch over it (5DH upwards).

Left luggage: For a small charge, luggage may be left at railway stations or offices of the Compagnie Transport Marocain (CTM): it should be safe.

Loss Of Belongings

If belongings have been stolen, a police report must be made. Do not be put off by hotel staff; insurance companies invariably require a local police report before they will entertain a claim for theft. If tour company representatives are on hand, they may be able to help, and should certainly be informed. If your belongings do not arrive at the airport, it is the responsibility of the airline: ask for a Property Irregularity Form to fill in. Many travel insurance policies will then allow reasonable expenses on clothes and other essentials.

Medical Services

There are private clinics in all main towns, and government hospitals in many. Consulates may be able to give advice about English-speaking doctors; or tour companies' representatives (and noticeboards) at hotels. All services will be charged for immediately, except in cases of need or emergency: if your travel insurance is not explicit on the point of medical treatment, and you have to pay, ask for and keep receipts.

Pharmacies in towns sell many kinds of medicines and contraceptives (but not tampons or sanitary towels – these may be available from general stores in town). Medicines are expensive: aspirin, insect bite cream and stomach settlers are best bought at home. There is a late night pharmacy in each major town: it's often in the town hall (*Municipalité*).

Metric measures are used throughout Morocco: distances are in kilometres, quantities in litres and weights in grammes or kilogrammes.

To convert	multipy by
Kilometres to miles	0.621
Metres to feet	3.28
Kilograms to pounds	2.204
Grams to ounces	0.035

Hours vary slightly, but the timetable is based around a two-hour rest in the middle of the day. Standard hours for: **Banks**: Monday–Friday 8.30–11.30am and 2.30–4.30pm.

Offices: Monday–Friday 8.30am–noon 2.30–6pm.

Post offices: Monday–Saturday 8.30am–2pm (at least: the bigger the town, the longer they open). Telephone services, at the same offices, often open in the evenings (the biggest are open 24 hours).

Shops: Monday–Saturday 8.30am–noon and 2–6pm. Many shops stay open much later than this; some close on Friday (the Muslim equivalent of the sabbath) and some are open on Sunday.

Media

Newspapers & Magazines

The main newspapers in Morocco are: *L'Opinion* (printed in French, circulation 60,000); *Le Matin* (in French, circulation 55,000); *Maroc Soir* (in French, circulation 35,000); *Al Alam* (in Arabic, circulation 30,000). The principal business magazine is *La Vie Economique*, a French language financial and economic weekly with a circulation varying between 2,500 and 5,000.

Enjeux, a current affairs, pro-government magazine, is a monthly put out by the publishers of *Le Matin*, and *Lamalif* is an arts magazine with left/centre viewpoint.

English newspapers are available in cities and resort hotels, as are most European papers, the *International Herald Tribune* and many magazines.

Radio & Television

The television service of *Radiodiffusion Télévision Marocain* is government-run, along with the associated *radio* channel: both are fairly dull. There is also the privately-run 2M, generally considered better, which is funded by subscription. Satellite television is widely available, both in the home and in hotels.

A radio station based in Tangier, *Radio Méditerranée-Internationale*, broadcasts to Algeria, Tunisia, Spain and the South of France as well. All carry advertising. The British World Service from the BBC broadcasts between 6am and midnight (try 16.94 m, 17.70 MHz). Details of BBC times and wavelengths are available from the British Council in Rabat.

Post & Telecoms

Post offices (PTT) deal with postage, poste restante, telephone and telegraph services. Since privatisation of the telephone service, it has become increasingly easy to make international calls from phone boxes in the street: arm yourself with plenty of 5DH coins or purchase a *telecarte* from a nearby *tabac* (make sure a booth that takes phone cards is at hand). Also increasingly common are private telephone and fax shops, which charge slightly more than you would pay in a public booth. Calls are also possible from any post office, but you may have to wait – and wait. Calls from a hotel mean that waiting is more comfortable, but make sure that you are clear about the rate being charged before you go ahead.

Dial 00 for an international call, wait for a second dial tone, then dial the country code. The codes are as follows:

Australia: (00 61)
Austria: (00 43)
Belgium: (00 32)
Canada: (00 1)
Denmark: (00 45)
France: (00 33)
Germany: (00 49)
Great Britain: (00 44 1)
Ireland: (00 353)
Italy: (00 39)
New Zealand: (00 64)
Portugal: (00 351)
Spain: (00 34)
Switzerland: (00 41)
United States: (00 1)

Local calls can sometimes be made from cafés and small grocers. Cafés will add a nominal charge to the bill for this service.

Telephone codes in Morocco:

02: Zone of Casablanca
03: Zone of Settat (includes Azzemour, Azilal, Beni Mellal, El Jadida, Ksiba, Mohammedia).
04: Zone of Marrakesh (includes Demnate, El Kelaa Mgouna, Essaouira, Ouarzazate, Oukaimeden, Safi, Tinerhir, Zagora).
05: Zone of Fez (includes Erfound, Er Rachidia, Guercif, Ifrane, Khenifra, Meknes, Moulay Idriss, Rissani, Sefrou).
06: Zone of Oujda (includes Figuig, Nador and Saidia).
07: Zone of Rabat (includes Khenitra,

Moulay Bousselham, Ouezzane, Skhirate, Souk el Arba, Temara).
08: Zone of Laayoune (includes Agadir, Guelmime, Sidi Ifni, Tafraoute, Tan-Tan, Taroudant and Tiznit).
09: Zone of Tangier (includes Al Hoceima, Azilah, Chaouen, Larache, Tetouan).

Tourist Offices

Outside Morocco

Australia: C/o Consulate of Morocco, 11 West Street North, Sydney, NSW 2060. Tel: 957 6717/922 4999.
Belgium: 66 Rue du Marché aux Herbes, 1000 Brussels. Tel: 512 2182.
Canada: Place Montreal Trust, 1800 MicGill College, Suite 2450, Montreal. Tel: 48428111.
France: 161 Rue Saint Honoré, Place du Théâtre Francais, 0075 Paris. Tel: 42 60 63 50.
Germany: Graf Adolf Strasse 59, 4000 Dusseldorf 1. Tel: 911370552.
Great Britain: 205 Regent Street, London W1R 7DE. Tel: 0171-437 0073.
Italy: Via Larga 23, 20122 Milan. Tel: 58303633.
Japan: Owariya Building 4F, 8 Banchi LP. Chome, Kandacho Chiyoda KU, Tokyo 101. Tel: 81 03 325 17781.
Portugal: Rua ArtiLharia, 1, 7985 Lisbon. Tel: 3885871.
Spain: Calle Ventura Rodriguez, 24, 28008 Madrid. Tel: 5427431.
United States: 420 East 46th Street, Suite 1201, New York 10017. Tel: 5572520/21/22.

In Morocco

National Tourist Offices (Office Nationale Marocain du Tourisme, ONMT: headquarters in Rabat) are often complemented by a municipal *Syndicat d'Initiatif*. Both can give plans, maps, advice and provide guides, but the ONMT are usually better staffed, with more guides on hand. Most are open Monday to Saturday mornings from 8am.

Agadir: Place Prince Heritier Sidi Mohammed (off street: on first floor level of paved square opposite post office). Tel: (08) 840307.
Casablanca: 55 Rue Omar Slaoui. Tel: (02) 271177.
Fez: Place de la Résistance, Boulevard Moulay Youssef. Tel: (05) 623460/626279.
Marrakesh: Place Abd el Moumen Ben

Ali, Boulevard Mohammed V. Tel: (04) 436239.

Meknes: Place Administrative. Tel: (05) 524426.

Ouarzazate: Avendue Mohammed V. Tel: (04) 882485.

Oujda: Place du 16 Août. Tel: (06) 685361.

Rabat: 22 Avenue al Jazair (Ave d'Algier). Tel: (07) 730562.

Tangier: 29 Boulevard Pasteur. Tel: (09) 948661.

Tetouan: 30 Avenue Mohammed V. Tel: (09) 961915.

Algeria: 12 Rue d'Azrou, Rabat. Tel: (07) 767858/767668.

Canada: 13 Bis Rue Jaffar al-Sadak, Agdal, Rabat. Tel: (07) 772880.

France: 3 Rue Sahrioun (Agdal). Tel: (07) 777822

Germany: 7 Zankat Mednine, Rabat. Tel: (7) 769692.

Great Britain: 17 Boulevard de la Tour Hassan, Rabat. Tel: (07) 720905/06. There is also a consul in Tangier, Tel: (09) 941557.

Italy: 2 Rue Idriss el Azhar, Rabat. Tel: (07) 766598.

The Netherlands: 40 Rue de Tunis, Rabat. Tel: (07) 733512/3.

Spain: 13 Zankat Mednine, Rabat. Tel: (07) 708989/707980.

United States: 2 Avenue de Marrakech, Rabat. Tel: (07) 762265.

Getting Around

On Arrival

When you arrive you will be given an official form to fill in stating profession, addresses in Morocco and length of stay. Each time you register at a hotel you are required to fill in a similar form which is submitted to the police.

An international health and inoculation certificate is needed to bring pets into the country.

Orientation

Reaching a Moroccan town or city is often a bewildering experience. The largest are divided into the old and new towns. The old town – or *medina* – is the traditional quarter. Often surrounded by ramparts and entered through grand gateways, it will contain a disorientating maze of narrow streets and *souks* running between squares. It may also contain the fortified *kasbah* – ramparts within ramparts. At the other extreme is the *nouvelle ville* – usually planned and laid out by the French, with grand, straight avenues connecting roundabouts. The grandest avenue is often named after Mohammed V, and it's usually here or in the main square of the new town that you'll find the tourist office (*addresses, page 296*). This is the place to find an official guide (*see below*): the quickest and simplest method of orientation. On the roads, there are few problems with navigation: signposts are clear, and the long roads have few turnings. It's worth taking local advice about the state of mountain or desert roads at any time of year, but particularly in the mountains during winter.

Guides – Official & Otherwise

The experience of arriving in an unfamiliar town or city is inevitably accompanied by the offer of a guide's services. The guide may be a small grubby boy, a genuine student or a professional hustler; and he will be persistent, rarely taking your first no for an answer. If you've decided you need a guide, such meetings can be fruitful, as long as you explicitly agree on a fee in advance (10–15 dirhams an hour is fairly standard, and perhaps round it up a little when you've finished).

The proper rate for official guides can be difficult to discover. The Fez tourist office displays a tariff which is five years out of date and refuses to give you a straight answer about what the rate should be. Generally 20 dirhams an hour is more than ample.

Whether your guide is official or not, he/she will try to lure you into the bazaars, where guides earn commission on what their charges spend. If you are not interested in buying goods, point this out before beginning your tour and remain resolute.

Maps

The most accessible and reliable maps produced by European companies are: Hallwag (1:1,000,000); Lascelles (1:800,000); Michelin No. 969, Maroc Nord et Centre (1:1,000,000). Also very good is the companion fold-out map to *Insight Pocket Guide: Morocco*, which contains town plans of major towns as well as a clear country map. Tyre companies in Morocco sometimes sell road maps, or try a *librairie* in major towns. Serviceable town and city plans are available free of charge from the National Tourist Office (available in advance from the Moroccan National Tourist Offices abroad). Large scale topographical maps of the Atlas are difficult to obtain. In Morocco try the shop at 31 Avenue Hassan I, Rabat. Main agent in the UK is West Col Productions, Goring, Reading Berks. RG89AA. In the US: Michael Chessler Books, PO Box 2436, Evergreen, CO80 439-2436. Maps of Toubkal National Park are available at Imlil and Asni.

Reservations

At busy times (Easter, Christmas and mid-summer) it is sensible to book ahead from one hotel to the next: telephone charges will normally be added to your bill. Flights must be reconfirmed at least 72 hours in advance; contact an airport desk or Royal Air Maroc office, or let a travel agent or hotel member of staff do it on your behalf.

Airport/City Links

There are taxi services between international airports and their respective towns. With the exception of Casablanca, distances are small, so in theory taxi fares should be low. There are official fare tables published, but you're unlikely to see them around the airport: most of the *grands taxis* on the airport run will be unmetered, and drivers may want to haggle over fares. Use the guide prices below as a rough estimate. **Casablanca** airport is 19 miles (30 km) south of the city: the taxi fare will be 140 dirhams. **Agadir** airport is 13 miles (22 km) south of town, and the taxi fare is around 80 dirhams; **Fez** airport is 6 miles (10 km) south of the town (taxi around 100 dirhams); **Marra-**

kesh airport is 4 miles (6 km) south-west of the city (taxi around 80 dirhams); **Tangier** airport is 9 miles (15 km) southwest of the city (taxi up to 100 dirhams). In the day there are also bus services from the airports at Casa-blanca, Agadir, Marrakesh and Tangier.

Internal Flights

There are internal flights between most cities, even as far south as Layoune and Dakhla. The advantages of flying are clear cut: speed and reli-ability. The chief drawback is equally obvious: cost. The best reason to use an internal flight would be to complete the lion's share of a long circuit. For example, the single journey from Tan-gier to Marrakesh costs around 685 dirhams (first class: 820 dirhams), which is three or four times the bus or train fare. But the journey time is two instead of 10 hours.

Royal Air Maroc Offices

IN MOROCCO

Agadir: Avenue General Kettani. Tel: (08) 84 07 93.
Casablanca: 44 Avenue de l'Armee Royale. Tel: (02) 31 11 22.
Fez: 54 Avenue Hassan II. Tel: (05) 62 55 16/17.
Marrakesh: 197 Avenue Mohamed V. Tel: (04) 43 62 05/44 64 44.

Ouarzazate: 1 Boulevard Mohammed V. Tel: (04) 885 080.
Oujda: Hotel Oujda, Boulevard Moha-med V. Tel: (06) 68 39 09.
Rabat: 9 Rue Aboufaris Almarini. Tel: (07) 70 97 00.
Tangier: 1 Place de France. Tel: (09) 93 55 01/01/03.
Tan Tan: Avenue de la Ligue Arabe. Tel: (08) 87 72 59.
Tetouan: 5 Avenue Mohamed V. Tel: (09) 96 12 60/96 16 10.

City Transport

In cities take *petits taxis*: small saloon cars, theoretically metered, and with a different livery (and often different rates) in each town. They'll take up to three people. They are very cheap, but it's wise to ask the fare before you get in: and there's no harm in politely but firmly disputing an exorbitant fare at the end of a journey. In the end, as with so much in Morocco, the price depends on the agreement of the driver and the driven.

In **Marrakesh** (and also in Taroudant), an alternative means of urban transport are the glossy horse-drawn *calèches*, with large wheels, loud horns and folding leather cano-pies. These can be as cheap as taxis (not much more than the bus if there are two or three of you) for three or four people, though increasingly exor-

bitant prices prevail when tourists are many. Official rates are posted inside the vehicle, but congratulate yourself if you manage to pay no more than what they recommend. City buses are occa-sionally useful and always cheap (but usually crowded).

Local Transport

The choice in local transport is be-tween trains, buses and taxis. **Railway lines** are confined to the major cities; the network extends south to Marra-kesh, and links up with Safi, El Jadida, Casablanca, Rabat, Tangier, Fez, Meknes and Oujda. First-class and second-class in *autorail* trains have air-conditioning. Groups of 10 or more receive a discount of 20 to 30 percent: travellers under the age of 26 can use Eurotrain or Inter-Rail passes on Mo-roccan trains. In any case, prices are cheap (for example, Tangier to Rabat costs around 80DH one way). Plan your journey in advance (timetables are available from stations and tourist offices and published in daily newspa-pers). It can be worth travelling first-class at busy times and over popular routes, especially if you are not joining the train at the start of a journey. Train stations are usually found near the centre of the *ville nouvelle*. Be sure to get out at the right station: for exam-ple, in Rabat you will probably want

Distances in Kilometres From City To City

	AGADIR	BENI MELLAL	CASABLANCA	CHAOUEN	EL JADIDA	ER RACHIDIA	ESSAOUIRA	FEZ	LAAYOUNE	MARRAKESH	MEKNES	OUARZAZATE	OUJDA	RABAT	TANGIER	TAZA	TETOUAN	TIZNIT
AGADIR																		
BENI MELLAL	467																	
CASABLANCA	511	210																
CHAOUEN	841	480	330															
EL JADIDA	417	271	99	429														
ER RACHIDIA	681	375	545	548	606													
ESSAOUIRA	173	370	351	681	252	745												
FEZ	756	289	289	225	388	364	640											
LAAYOUNE	849	1116	1160	1490	1066	1330	822	1396										
MARRAKESH	273	194	238	568	197	510	176	483	922									
MEKNES	740	278	229	202	328	346	580	60	1389	467								
OUARZAZATE	375	398	442	772	399	306	380	687	1024	204	652							
OUJDA	1099	632	632	499	731	514	983	343	1748	826	403	820						
RABAT	602	260	91	239	190	482	442	198	1251	321	138	528	541					
TANGIER	880	538	369	118	468	608	720	303	1529	598	267	811	609	278				
TAZA	876	409	409	345	508	484	760	120	1525	603	180	790	223	318	423			
TETOUAN	892	536	358	61	484	604	736	281	1541	615	258	820	555	294	57	370		
TIZNIT	93	560	604	934	510	774	266	849	556	366	833	468	1192	699	973	969	985	

Rabat Ville, not Rabat Agdal (a pleasant suburb); likewise you will need Meknes, not Meknes amir Abdelkader.

Bus travel is the cheapest way to get around, and there's no better way to get to know Morocco in detail. There is a national network, CTM, which runs comfortable air-conditioned buses; a network between Casablanca, Agadir and the south, SATAS; and a lot of small local companies who may or may not run according to a timetable. Allow plenty of time to travel by bus: all of them stop frequently. Fares are usually some 20 percent cheaper than trains. Comfortable express coaches run by ONCF (the railway company) ply the southwest and northern coasts (where the railway doesn't run): these cost 50 percent more than standard bus fares.

Most large cities have acquired a new, centralised bus station in the last few years. These are equipped with efficient information centres that can advise on routes, etc. In **Fez**, all buses now leave from the station below Borj Nord. In **Meknes**, most buses leave and depart from the station ouside Bab Khemis, but limited delivery and pick-up continues at Bab Mansour

Grands taxis are large cars, usually Mercedes, which rattle along with up to six passengers on routes from town to town, charging a fixed price. They will leave when they are full: it's possible to charter an entire taxi, but make sure you know the going rate. The fare is liable to be a third as much again as a bus, but the journey is likely to take half the time, or less. In remote or desert areas, Land Rovers often replace taxis, and open trucks act as local buses.

Private Transport

Car: Drivers must be over 21, and be fully insured against claims by third parties. The insurance is automatic on renting a car. If taking your own vehicle, the European insurance Green Card is required and you will also need the registration document. If your own particular company doesn't issue Green Card insurance for Morocco (few do) you will need to purchase it in Morocco (*see Getting There*). Your own national licence is valid, but it does no harm to carry an International Driving Permit as well (it has French and Arabic translations; available from motoring organisa-

tions). An international customs carnet is required for caravans.

The rules of the road are to drive on the right, and give priority to the right (the same system as the French *priorité à droite*). This means that traffic going on to a roundabout has priority over the traffic already engaged. Major roads are well surfaced, minor ones good with lapses (some treacherous potholes) and mountain roads often not as bad as you'll have been led to expect. A toll-funded motorway is gradually being built between Casablanca and Tangier. So far it has reached Kenitra. Tolls are extremely low, at least by European standards.

Beware of other drivers: the driving test in Morocco is notoriously open to corruption.

Fuel (*essence* or, more likely, *super* for petrol/gas; *gas-oil* for diesel) is available in towns of even modest size, but fill up before striking out on a long journey away from main roads. An increasing number of petrol stations sell lead-free (*sans plomb*) especially Afriquia. Petrol gets cheaper to the south, but costs around 7 dirhams a litre on average (a little over £2 per gallon). Parking in towns of any size is likely to cost a few dirhams, collected by an official attendant, who may offer car cleaning services – at a price.

Hiring a car: The major international hire companies are all represented in Morocco and it is possible to make arrangements to pick up a vehicle at any of the airports. In the cities there are always several local companies, who will undercut the rates of the major companies considerably, possibly by as much as half. This will be useful for short rentals (which are proportionately more expensive): but for a rental lasting the whole trip, it may be cheaper to organise a car in advance on a special **holiday tariff** – either through a travel agent or direct with one of the major companies.

Car hire prices are usually quoted exclusive of a 19 percent government tax: be sure this has been added to the price which is agreed. A week's inclusive hire of a basic car (Renault 4) can be had for about 2,800 dirhams (around £200) from small local companies out of season. Booked from London, prices from specialist brokers start at roughly the same level, but prices from the majors start at around

£300. Remember that the large international companies are likely to have a better network of offices if anything goes wrong with the car. For gruelling itineraries with a lot of mountain driving, consider hiring cars from group B (Fiat Uno) or C (Renault 5): they feel a bit more secure on tight corners. Land-Rovers for more adventurous routes can be hired locally, often supplied with a chauffeur.

Agadir
Avis: Avenue Hassan II. Tel: (08) 840345
Budget: Avenue Mohammed V. Tel: (08) 840762
Hertz: Bungalow Marhaba, Avenue Mohammed V. Tel: (08) 840939.

Casablanca
Avis: 19 Avenue des FAR. Tel: (02) 311135
Budget: 71 Rue Provins. Tel: (02) 301480.
Hertz: 25 Rue de Foucald. Tel: (02) 312223/294413.

Fez
Avis: 50 Boulevard Chefchaouni. Tel: (05) 626746
Budget: (05) 620919
Hertz: 1 Boulevard Lalla Meryem. Tel: (05) 622812.

Marrakesh
Avis: 137 Avenue Mohammed V. Tel: (04) 433723
Budget: 213 Avenue Mohammed V. Tel: (04) 434604.
Hertz: 157 Boulevard Mohammed V. Tel: (04) 434680

Tangier
Adil: 84 Boulevard Mohammed V. Tel: (09) 942267/945231
Avis: 54 Boulevard Pasteur. Tel: (09) 933031
Budget: 79 Avenue du Prince Moulay Abdellah. Tel: (09) 937994
Cady: 3 Avenue Allal Ben Abdellah. Tel: (09) 934151.
Hertz: 36 Avenue Mohammed V. Tel: (09) 933322/934179.

On Foot & By Thumb

With public transport so cheap, and distances so vast, walking and hitch-hiking by visitors aren't that common. Arranging lifts with other tourists is sometimes easier at campsites. Tourists are more likely to be a source of rides – for other visitors or for Moroccans. If you accept a ride from a Moroccan driver, or ride on a truck, you may be asked for money: if you're using the only means of transport around, this is fair enough. But watch out for exorbitant "fares", and don't pay until you arrive at your destination (or you may be left stranded).

Complaints

In cities, contact the tourist office, the *Sûreté* or *Gendarmerie*; even the hotel may be able to help resolve problems. On the road, if you're following a major route, the chances of a *Gendarmerie* road block are high; this can be a good place to air problems (as long as everybody remains reasonably calm). In remote areas, travelling off roads or in the desert, the intrepid traveller will be literally beyond help: remember this before setting out.

Extensions Of Stay

Contact the local police department well in advance if your stay is likely to exceed 90 days. Extensions may be difficult: proof of funds is often required, and the purpose of an extended visit will be requested. It will be easier, at least in the north, simply to leave Morocco inside the 90 day period, and re-enter.

On Departure

Moroccan money cannot in theory, be exported. If, on departure, you want to reconvert your dirhams into hard currency, you must show your reciept/s for the original exchange.

Where To Stay

Hotels

Most Moroccan hotels are classified, and their rates set, by the Federation of Hotel Association and approved by the Ministry of Tourism. The only exceptions, free to set their own prices, are unclassified hotels, usually simple central establishments without ensuite baths or showers, probably in the medina (sometimes the local *hammam*/steam bath takes the place of hotel baths). It's worth noting that some hotels, while charging the official rate for their standard rooms, will quietly slip you into a superior room – away from the road, or with an extra sitting-room – which is undeniably more pleasant, but can end up much more expensive. Check the rate when you arrive. Local tourist offices are prepared to investigate inflated prices.

Categories of hotels range from 5-star to 1-star, with A and B distinctions in each classification except for the top one, where 5-star indicates those with the very best amenities. A 4-star A hotel is superior to a 4-star B. There are also unclassified hotels.

Generally, the standard of facilities for each star rating are as follows (prices are a rough guide and refer to the price of a double with bath, dependant on location and season). Five-star hotels (800–1,650DH are truly luxurious and in some cases their tariffs are on a par with those in luxury hotels in Europe. Morocco's top 5-star hotels, renowned for their character and style, are La Mamounia in Marrakesh, Palais Jamai in Fez, El Minzah in Tangier and, the most exclusive of all, La Gazelle d'Or in Taroudant.

Four-star establishments are usually very good indeed, but much less refined (about 396–1,138DH for a double). You can expect decent plumbing, a good swimming-pool (sometimes heated in winter), often a night-club, but not always tennis courts (rarely in 4-star B hotels). In warmer regions nearly all 4-star hotels have air-conditioning. Their disadvantage is that they tend to lack character.

In a 3-star hotel (around 143–475DH for a double), guests can expect a reasonable restaurant and bar, private facilities in all rooms and often a swimming-pool. Sometimes they are not as modern as 4-star hotels, but tend to be efficiently run.

Two-star hotels (about 146–226DH for a double) have private facilities in most rooms, sometimes a modest bar and restaurant, but rarely a pool.

One-star hotels vary tremendously. Nowadays most have at least some rooms with showers. Decor may be bright and pleasant; it may be downright shabby. Occasionally one will also find a restaurant or even a bar, but never a swimming-pool. Expect to pay about 89–160DH for a double, sometimes less.

Unclassified hotels vary more widely than any other category. They range from flea-pits costing less than 20DH to modest "hotels" containing a few rooms with private shower at 70–100DH. Even in this category, you may find a bar – for example, in El Muniria Hotel in Tangier.

As a rule, breakfast is provided only in better class hotels.

It is sensible to book ahead during busy periods (for example, Easter, Christmas and high summer). There are several specialist companies in London who will tailor make an itinerary and take care of all the bookings: see section on *Attractions*.

There are **campsites** all over the country, especially along the coast: they act as meeting places for budget travellers, both Moroccan and visiting. Prices start at around 8DH per night for one person and a tent. You may be able to hire a tent if you don't possess one. Security can be a problem: don't leave valuables unattended. There are half a dozen **youth hostels**, all but one in cities: Casablanca, Fez, Marrakesh, Meknes and Rabat. The sixth is at Asni in the High Atlas, a popular hiking base. Here is a list of recommended hotels; the National Tourist Office can provide a comprehensive booklet containing all graded hotels.

Agadir

There are probably more large hotels and holiday clubs in Agadir than in any other Moroccan resort, but in summer they tend to be booked up by package tour groups. Most are on Boulevard Mohammed V, which runs parallel to (though not alongside) the beach; smaller establishments occupy side-streets.

Hotel Sahara: ☆☆☆☆ A; Avenue Mohammed V. The largest and most resplendent of the monster-size hotels, with every amenity, including air-conditioning in all rooms, swimming-pool, sauna, cinema and tennis courts, night-club with resident band. But a fair way from the sea. Tel: (08) 840660/840125, fax: (08) 840738.

Hotel les Almohades: ☆☆☆☆ B; Quarti des Dunes. Closer to the sea than most hotels, with all amenities. Tel: (08) 840233, fax: (08) 840130.

Club les Dunes d'Or: Cité Balneaire. A huge club complex, but popular and lively. Amenities run to a cinema, but not air-conditioning in the rooms. Tel: (08) 840150/840396.

Hotel Club Salam: Boulevard Mohammed V. Club-style hotel with tennis courts, swimming-pool and night-club. Efficiently-run. Lots of organised entertainment. Tel: (08) 840184/840108, fax: (08) 840821.

Hotel Miramar: ☆☆☆ B; Boulevard Mohammed V. Comfortable small hotel (just 12 rooms) with bar and reताurant. Situated above the harbour. Tel: (08) 840770.

Hotel Petit Suede: ☆☆ B; Avenue General Kettani. Comfortable and adequate, but only a third of the rooms have showers. Tel: (08) 840779/840057.

Hotel Diaf: ☆ B; Rue Allal ben Abdellah. Modest, clean, friendly. A few rooms have showers. Tel: (08) 825852.

Hotel Mohammed V: ☆☆ A; Place Marche Verte. Part of the large hotel complex occupying most of the beach. In summer it is generally booked by package tour companies. Tennis courts and swimming-pool. Tel: (09) 982371.

Hotel Karim: ☆☆ B; 27 Avenue Hassan II. Unexceptional hotel, but with bar and restaurant. Shower or bathroom in most rooms. Tel: (09) 982184.

Hotel National: ☆☆ B; 23 Rue de Tetouan. Small but adequate. Most rooms have bathrooms. Tel: (09) 982141.

Hotel Florido: unclassified; Place du Rif. Distinctive-looking hotel over a lively café. The star-shaped motif outside was the emblem of Abd el Krim's Rifian republic. Relatively clean (for the price); spacious rooms, some with balconies. Noise can be a problem.

Asilah

Hotel Al Khaima: ☆☆☆ A; 2k Route de Tanger. Asilah is becoming increasingly popular with tour operators and this hotel caters to many of them. It is almost two miles out of town, on the Tangier road. Swimming-pool, bar and disco, and close to the beach. Windsurfing and horse-riding available. Tel: (09) 917428.

Hotel Oued el Makhazine: ☆ A; Avenue du Melilla;. Comfortable and

pleasant, with sea views and bar. Tel: (09) 917500.

Hotel Asilah: ☆ B; 1 Avenue Hassan II. Simple, but clean and friendly. Tel: (09) 917286.

Hotel Marhaba: unclassified; 9 Rue Zallakah. Clean, with central position.

Asni

Grand Hotel du Toubkal: ☆☆☆ A. Comfortable base for exploring the Toubkal National Park. Restaurant, bar and, in summer, a swimming-pool; central heating (valuable out of season). Rooms at the rear enjoy good views. Tel: 3 via the operator.

Azrou

Hotel Panorama: ☆☆☆ B. Fairly charmless hotel, but with restaurant, bar and central heating. Tel: (05) 562010.

Azrou Hotel: ☆ A; Route de Khenifra. Small, pleasant and lively. Restaurant, bar and central heating. Tel: (05) 562116.

Hotel des Cèdres: ☆ A; Place Mohammed V. Another congenial small hotel, with licensed restaurant and central heating. Tel: (05) 562326.

Beni Mellal

Hotel Ouzoud: ☆☆☆☆ B; Route de Marrakech. Large modern hotel which, along with Hotel Chems, serves as a stop-over for tour groups visiting Marrakesh. Most amenities, including tennis-courts and swimming-pool. Tel: (03) 483752/483753.

Hotel Chems: ☆☆☆☆ B; Route de Marrakech. Well-appointed but lacking in character. Tel: (03) 483008.

Hotel Gharnata: ☆☆ B; Boulevard Mohammed V. Comfortable modern hotel with central location. Tel: (03) 483482.

Hotel du Vieux Moulin: ☆ A; Boulevard Mohammed V. Welcoming auberge, with decent restaurant. Tel: (03) 482788.

Casablanca

Plenty of ☆☆☆☆☆ luxury hotels, including:

Hotel Hyatt Regency: Place Mohammed V. Tel: (02) 261234.

Holiday Inn: Avenue Hassan II. Tel: (02) 294949/293434.

Hotel Safir: Avenue des F.A.R. Tel: (02) 311212.

Sheraton: Avenue des F.A.R. Tel: (02) 317878.

Hotel Royal Mansour: 27 Avenue des F.A.R. Tel: (02) 311130/311212. This hotel has more character than the international chains.

Hotel Riad Salam: Boulevard de la Corniche. Tel: (02) 391361. The only luxury hotel overlooking the rather grim beach and conveniently placed for the Royal Anfa Golf Club.

Cheaper recommendations include:

Hotel Plaza: ☆☆☆ A; 18 Boulevard Houphouet Boigny. Small, well-run hotel with restaurant and bar. Tel: (02) 221262/220226.

Hotel Rialto: ☆ A; 9 Rue Claude. Basic but all rooms have bath or shower. Tel: (02) 275122.

Hotel du Louvre: ☆ B; 36 Rue Nationale. Tel: (02) 273747.

Chaouen

Parador: ☆☆☆☆ B; Outa el Hamam. Old-style Spanish parador with swimming-pool, bar and view. Tel: (09) 986324/986136.

Hotel Asma: ☆☆☆ A; Boulevard Sidi Abelhamid. Ugly and modern, but with most amenities and a great view. Tel: (09) 986002/986265.

Hotel Magou: ☆☆ B; 23 Rue Moulay Idriss. Comfortable small hotel with restaurant and bar. Tel: (09) 986257.

Hotel Rif: ☆☆ B; 39 Tarik Ibn Ziad. Congenial hotel with restaurant and bar. A few rooms have showers. Tel: (09) 986207.

El Jadida

Club Salam des Doukkala: ☆☆☆☆ B; Rue de la Ligue Arabe. Sporty beach club hotel; 82 rooms. Tel: (03) 340802.

Hotel le Palais Andalous: ☆☆☆ A; Boulevard Docteur de Lanouy. A converted palace with much charm and reasonable rates. Tel: (03) 343906/343745.

Hotel de Provence: ☆☆ B; 42 Avenue Fkih Er Rafi. Pleasant hotel run by an Englishman, a few rooms with bathrooms. A bar, of course; and a good restaurant. Tel: (03) 342347/344112.

Hotel de Bruxelles: ☆ B; 40 Avenue Ibn Khaldoun. Good value hotel. All rooms have showers and balconies. Tel: (03) 342072.

Erfoud

Hotel Salam: ☆☆☆☆ A; Route de Rissani. A luxurious older-style hotel with much dignity, overlooking the palmerie. Swimming pool. Tel: (05) 576665/576424.

Hotel Sijilmassa: ✰✰✰✰ B; this PLM hotel is not particularly attractive, but it does have most amenities, with the exception of a night-club. Tel: (05) 576522.

Hotel Tafilalet: ✰✰✰ B; Avenue Moulay Ismail. Efficient if unexceptional hotel with swimming-pool. Restaurant only tolerable. Tel: (05) 576535/576036.

Er Rachidia

Hotel Rissani: ✰✰✰✰ B; Route d'Erfoud. Member of the PLM chain. As the most luxurious hotel in town and the only one with a decent swimming-pool, it serves as a stop-over for passing coach tours. Views over Oued Ziz. Tel: (05) 572186.

Hotel Oasis: ✰✰✰ A: 4 Rue Abou Abdellah. Bar and restaurant. Tel: (05) 572519.

Hotel Meski: ✰✰ B: Avenue Moulay Ali Cherif. Unpromising exterior leading to a warren of large, if austere, rooms. Restaurant, but no bar. Swimming-pool of sorts, but very murky. Tel: (05) 572065.

Hotel Renaissance: unclassified; 19 Rue Moulay Youssef. Modest, but well-run and clean. Tel: (05) 572633.

Essaouira

Hotel des Iles: ✰✰✰ A; Boulevard Mohammed V. Well-run, if fairly dull hotel. Popular with the British; 77 rooms. Tel: (04) 472329.

Hotel Tafoukt: ✰✰✰ A; 98 Boulevard Mohammed V, situated south of town on the road running parallel with the coast. Congenial, with licensed restaurant. Tel: (04) 784504/784505.

Villa Maroc: ✰✰✰ B; 10 Rue Abdellah Ben Yacine. English-run, stylish and comfortable. Moroccan meals cooked to order. Open fires out of season. Be sure to make reservations. Prices above average for the category. Tel: (04) 473147.

Hotel Sahara: ✰✰ A; Avenue Okba Ibn Nafaa. Fairly large and very efficient. Tel: (04) 472292.

Hotel des Remparts: unclassified; Rue Ibn Rochd. Recently repainted and under some restoration, Des Remparts is still basic but more comfortable than it was. Rooms are arranged around a central courtyard. Dramatic views from a roof terrace.

Auberge Tangaro: 4 miles (6 km) south of Essaouira. Split-level room, romantic location, but no electricity (candles suffice). Half-board terms. Tel: (04) 784784. .

Fez

Hotel Palais Jamai: ✰✰✰✰✰; Bab Guissa. Nineteenth-century palace with beautiful gardens and views of Fez; superb cuisine; 115 rooms, 25 suites. It is worth spending extra for a medina view. Stay here if you possibly can. Double rooms from 1,150 DH. Tel: (05) 634331/32/33, fax: (05) 635096.

Hotel Merinides: ✰✰✰✰✰; Avenue Borj du Nord. Flashily restored since being burnt down in riots. High above the medina, with fabulous views. Tel: (05) 6646040, fax: (05) 645225.

Sheraton: ✰✰✰✰; Avenue des F.A.R. As regards atmosphere, this new town hotel is not a patch on Palais Jamai, but better service. Tennis courts. Tel: (05) 930905.

Jnan Palace: ✰✰✰✰✰; Avenue Ahmed Chaouki. Flashy new hotel set in extensive grounds in the *nouvelle ville*. All facilities, including well-equipped business centre. Probably a better choice for a confrece than for a holiday. Tel (05) 65 39 65.

Hotel Salam Zalagh: ✰✰✰ A; Rue Mohammed Diouri. Medium-sized hotel with a good reputation. Pool and nightclub. Tel: (05) 622810/625531.

Hotel de la Paix: ✰✰✰ A; 44 Avenue Hassan II. Popular hotel off the main drag in the new town. A few rooms have air-conditioning. Tel: (05) 625072.

Moussafir: ✰✰✰; Plaza de la Estacíon. In the nouvelle ville, this is one in a chain of comfortable, good-value railway hotels. Attractive decor, garden and swimming pool. A good option, especially if you are travelling by train. Book.

Splendid Hotel: ✰✰✰ A; 9 Rue Abdelkrim el Khattabi. Good value hotel with air-conditioning (welcome feature in Fez in summer), pool and popular bar. Tel: (05) 622148/626770.

Hotel Batha: ✰✰✰ B; Place Batha. Excellent position near Bab Boujeloud, gateway to Fez el Bali. Slightly run down for a modern hotel. Pool which is in shadow most of the day Tel: (05) 636437.

Hotel Amor: ✰✰ B; 31 Rue Arabie Saoudite. Out of the clutch of hotels close to the railway station Amor is one of the most comfortable. Good value. Tel: (05) 623304/622724.

Ifrane

Hotel Michlieffen: ✰✰✰✰✰; flashy luxury but at a high price. Tel: (05) 566607.

Grand Hotel: ✰✰ A; Avenue de la Marche Verte. Models itself on a Swiss chalet. Restaurant and bar. Tel: (05) 556614.

Hotel Perce Neige: PP A. Rue des Asphodelles. Smaller hotel with bar and restaurant. Tel: (05) 566404.

Immouzer Des Ida Outanane

(Agadir region)

Hotel des Cascades: ✰✰✰ B; small hotel in superb site by pretty waterfalls; 14 rooms. Tel: 16 via the operator.

Ketama

Hotel Tidighine: ✰✰✰ A; a government-run hotel with swimming-pool and tennis courts, but even here you may not be free from kif-touting locals. Tel: 16 via the operator.

Larache

Hotel Riad: ✰✰ B; Rue Mohammed ben Abdellah; charm and comfort in this old hotel. Tel: (09) 912626.

Hotel España: ✰ A; 6 Avenue Hassan II; down-at-heel, but inexpensive and not too bad. Tel: (09) 913195.

Layounne

Hotel Parador: ✰✰✰✰✰; Rue Okba ibn Nafaa. Central, with bedrooms giving on to lush courtyards, good food; 31 rooms. Tel: (08) 894500.

Marrakesh

If you arrive in Marrakesh during busy times (such as Easter) without a hotel booking and have difficulty finding a room, your best bet is to try the streets off Avenue Mohammed V in Gueliz (the New Town), where two- and three-star hotels abound.

Hotel La Mamounia: ✰✰✰✰✰; Avenue Bab Jdid. Former palace close to the medina: expensive but truly luxurious; renowned for its superb gardens; 180 rooms, 48 suites. Double room from DH 1,250. Tel: (04) 448981, fax: (04) 44 49 40.

Palmeraie Golf Palace: ✰✰✰✰✰; New luxury hotel (eight restaurants, five swimming pools, horse riding, fitness centre, etc) attached to superb 18-hole golf course designed by Robert Trent Jones. Tel: (04) 30 10 10; fax (04) 30 50 50.

Hotel Es Sadi: ☆☆☆☆☆; Avenue Quadissia (in the upmarket Hivernage area west of the Koutoubia); not half as flashy as the Mamounia, but slightly more affordable and very popular nonetheless. All amenities, including tennis courts. Tel: (04) 448811/447010, fax: (04) 447644.

Hotel Tichka: ☆☆☆☆ A; Route de Casablanca. Uninteresting location but a designer's treat, with a fine pool; 140 rooms. Tel: (04) 448710.

Hotel Tichka Garden: ☆☆☆☆ A; Circuit de la Palmerie (off the Fez road). A luxury hotel-cum-sports club, counting golf, mountain biking, and tennis among its activities. On a more intimate scale that the Club Med-style resorts. Tel (04) 30 90 99

Hotel Le Marrackech: ☆☆☆☆ A; Place de la Liberté. Large hotel, conveniently located on the edge of the medina, near Bab Larissa. Reasonable rates with most amenities. Tel: (04) 434351.

Hotel Tafilalet: ☆☆☆☆; Route de Casablanca. Polished, personal service, a little way out of town; 84 rooms. Tel: (04) 434518.

Hotel Imilchil: ☆☆☆ A; Avenue Echouhada. Moroccan decor, pool but no bar at this good value hotel; 96 rooms. Tel: (04) 447653.

Hotel Islane: ☆☆ A; Clean, friendly and pleasant. Good position close to the Koutoubia. Accepts credit cards. Tel: (04) 440081.

Hotel de Foucald: ☆☆ B; Avenue El Mouahidine. Boasts a popular licensed restaurant, medina location and friendly atmosphere. It is a favourite among hikers and adventure travellers. Tel: 445499.

Hotel CTM: ☆ A; Djemma el Fna. Right at the heart of Marrakesh. Basic and a bit shabby, but with reasonable bathrooms and interior courtyard. Terrace has excellent view of the Djemma el Fna. Very popular. Tel: (04) 442325.

Hotel Ali: unclassified; Rue Moulay Ismail. Along with the CTM hotel, most popular amongst backpackers. Cheap and cheerful, with a decent restaurant and buffet on its well-placed terrace in summer. Tel: (04) 444979.

Riad Mia Remmal Metzger: Kaat Benahid Derb Bounouar, 12. Tel: (04) 427851. Delightful *riad* run as informal Bed & Breakfast by artist. Good alternative for those willing to trade hotel services for immersion in cultural medina life.

Mdiq

Hotel Golden Beach: ☆☆☆☆ B; Route de Sebta. One of several club-style hotels that are spreading along the white, if narrow sands between Ceuta and Tetouan. Tel: (09) 975077.

Holiday Club Mdiq: Route de Sebta. Package-tour establishment right on the beach. Rooms are basic but adequate. Sport facilities, including windsurfing, riding, tennis and waterskiing. Tel: (09) 975223.

Meknes

Hotel Transatlantique: ☆☆☆☆☆; Rue El Merinyine. This is a long established luxury-class hotel. Tel: (05) 525050/51.

Hotel Rif: ☆☆☆☆ A; Rue Zankat Accra. Much less refined than Transatlantique, but congenial and popular, with most amenities. Tel: (05) 522591/92/93/94.

Hotel Volubilis: ☆☆☆ A; 45 Avenues des F.A.R. Medium-sized hotel running to a bar and nightclub. Tel: (05) 520102.

Hotel Modern: ☆☆ A: 54 Avenue Allal Ben Abdellah. Adequate establishment. All rooms have bath or shower. Restaurant. Tel: (05) 521743.

Hotel Continental: ☆ A; 42 Avenue des F.A.R. Roomy old-fashioned hotel. Tel: (05) 525471.

Hotel Excelsior: P A; 57 Avenue des F.A.R. Reasonable hotel. Most rooms have showers, a few have baths. Tel: (05) 521900.

Ouarzazate

Hotel Riad Salem: ☆☆☆☆ A; Avenue Mohammed V. Out of a number of luxury hotels in Ouarzazate (including two owned by the French chain PLM), this is supposed to be the best. Medium-sized with tennis courts and large swimming-pool, and round the corner from the less pricey Hotel Salam Tichka. Pleasant setting. Tel: (04) 883355.

Hotel Tichka: ☆☆☆ A; Avenue Mohammed V. 113 rooms; tennis, pool, nightclub, in *ksour* style. Tel: (04) 882393; fax: (04) 882766.

Hotel La Gazelle: ☆☆ B; Avenue Mohammed V. Well-established and popular with restaurant and bar. Swimming-pool. A short walk from the centre. No air-conditioning. Tel: (04) 882151.

Hotel Essalem: unclassified; Avenue Mohammed V (directly opposite the best restaurant in town, Chez Dimitri). Basic, but reasonably clean, with a courtyard interior. Some rooms have showers and views of the snow-capped Atlas.

Ouirgane

Residence de la Roseraie: ☆☆☆☆ A; folded into the mountains, with rose garden, swimming-pool, stunning views, bungalows and apartments; 9 rooms, 16 suites. Tel: (04) 439128; fax: 439130.

Hotel Le Sanglier Qui Fume: ☆☆ B; if you cannot afford La Roseraie, this hotel will do. It has plenty of character, a restaurant and bar, a swimming-pool.

Oujda

Hotel Terminus: ☆☆☆☆ A; Place de l'Unité Africaine. Modern hotel close to the station. Very comfortable rooms with air-conditioning. Swimming-pool and tennis courts. Rooms at the front can be noisy due to the constant stream of newly-weds that come to have their photographs taken in the forecourt. Reasonable rates. Tel: (06) 683211/2.

Hotel Lutetia: ☆ A; 44 Boulevard Hassan Loukili. Well-run and quite comfortable, though no restaurant. Tel: (06) 683365.

Hotel Royal: ☆ A; 13 Boulevard Mohammed Zerktouni. Most rooms have bath or shower. Clean and adequate. Tel: (06) 682556.

Oukaimeden

CAF Refuge: Offers very reasonable dormitory accommodation, with discounts for affiliated associations. Justly popular restaurant and very cheap bar. Crowded during the skiing season, it is a recommended base for Atlas hiking at other times of the year. Tel: 04) 319036.

Hotel Auberge Chez Juju: Small, comfortable alternative, again with bar and restaurant. Tel: (04) 319005.

Ourika

Ourika Hotel: ☆☆☆☆ B; the one hotel approaching luxury in this popular

Atlas valley just south of Marrakesh. Restaurant, bar and swimming-pool. Tel: (04) 433993.

Hotel Auberge Ramuntcho: ☆☆ A; Restaurant and bar. Tel: 446312

Rabat

Hyatt Regency: ☆☆☆☆☆; everything one would expect from a Hyatt Regency hotel, plus a cinema. Situated in Souissi. Links with the superb Royal Dar-es-Salem golf club. Tel: (07) 771234.

La Tour Hassan: ☆☆☆☆☆; Avenue Abderrahmen Annegai. Central, traditional style hotel with facilities kept up to modern standards; 150 rooms. Tel: (07) 721401.

Hotel Safir: ☆☆☆☆ A; Place Sidi Makhlouf. Large, flashy hotel between the medina and Hassan Tower, overlooking the river. Most amenities. Tel: (07) 734747.

Hotel Chellah: ☆☆☆☆ A; 2 Rue d'Ifni. A quiet location near the archaeological museum. Pleasant and comfortable. Tel: (07) 764052.

Hotel Balima: ☆☆☆ B; Avenue Mohammed V. Old-style hotel close to the railway station. Well-maintained, with bar, restaurant (of sorts) and nightclub. Although its standing has long been surpassed by bigger, more modern hotels, its outside café is still a lively meeting place in summer. Tel: (07) 707967.

Hotel Majestic: ☆ B; 121 Avenue Hassan II. Reasonable. Most rooms have shower or bath. Tel: (07) 722997.

Sidi Harazem

Hotel Sidi Harazem: ☆☆☆ A; ugly hotel dominating the springs; reasonable comfort, but wiser to choose a good hotel in Fez. Tel: (05) 690057.

Tafraoute

Hotel aux Amandiers: ☆☆☆☆ B; ochre-coloured, kasbah style, above the town square: atmosphere and setting striking, decor a little worn; 62 rooms. Tel: (08) 800008.

Tangier

Hotel el Minzah: ☆☆☆☆☆; 85 Rue de la Liberté. Smart but relaxed hotel with Moorish decor. It overlooks the Strait of Gibraltar; 100 rooms. Tel: (09) 935885.

Hotel Rif: ☆☆☆☆ A; 152 Avenue des F.A.R. Modern but characterful, and still frequented by Tangier's literati. Pleasant garden and pool. Central location. Tel: (09) 935908/9.

Hotel Solazur: ☆☆☆☆ B; Avenue des F.A.R. To everyone's surprise, this was where the late Malcolm Forbes housed his guests for his 70th birthday party in 1989. Even a special face-lift for the occasion couldn't transform what is basically a functional package-tour establishment. But offers most amenities and overlooks the beach. Tel: (09) 946897.

Tanjah Flandria: ☆☆☆☆ B; 6 Boulevard Mohammed V. Popular town-centre hotel with swimming-pool. Tel: (09) 933279.

Hotel Rembrandt: ☆☆☆ A; Avenue Mohammed V. Classy old-style hotel that has recently been renovated. Tel: (09) 937870.

Hotel Chellah: ☆☆☆ A; Rue Alal ben Abdellah. Large but decent hotel with pool. Tel: (09) 943388.

Hotel Djenina: ☆☆ B; 8 Rue Grotins. Small and comfortable, with bar, restaurant. Tel: (09) 942244.

Hotel Continental: ☆ A; 36 Rue Dar el Baroud. Old hotel behind the harbour. What it lacks in modern comforts it makes up in atmosphere. Tel: (09) 931024.

Hotel Miramar: ☆ B; Avenue des F.A.R. Well-run modest hotel with restaurant, bar. Tel: (09) 938948.

Hotel el Muniria: unclassified; Rue Magellan. Pleasant English-owned hotel, with literary associations. William Burroughs wrote *The Naked Lunch* in room 9. Groovy bar which is sometimes packed and sometimes empty. Some rooms have showers. If you want breakfast, you have to ask for it. Tel: (09) 935337.

Tan Tan

Hotel Royal, with its pool, restaurant and bar, is the most comfortable choice – it may still be occupied by the military. Alternatives include:

Hotel Ayoub: ☆☆☆☆ A; promises luxury – but may not be finished yet.

Hotel Etoile du Sahara: ☆ A; 17 Rue el Fida. Decent enough, with restaurant. Some rooms have showers.

Taroudant

Gazelle d'Or: ☆☆☆☆☆; 3 kilometres from town, a sybarite's dream; pool, tented restaurant and bungalows under the High Atlas. It shot to fame in 1992 when it was revealed that the then married Duchess of York had stayed here – but not with the Duke. Just 30 rooms. Tel: (08) 852039/852048.

Hotel Palais Salam: ☆☆☆☆ A; a palace built in to the city walls, with luxuriant banana palms. Thoughtful service, mediocre food; 75 rooms, 38 suites. Tel: (08) 852312/852130.

Hotel Saadiens: ☆☆ A; Borj Annassim. Newish hotel unlicensed but with attached pastry shop and swimming pool. Good value for money and very clean, if a little lacking in atmosphere. Tel: (08) 852589.

Tetouan

Hotel Safir: ☆☆☆☆ A; Route de Sebta. Large modern hotel on the Ceuta (Sebta) road. Tennis courts, pool and night-club. Tel: (09) 970144.

Paris Hotel: ☆☆ A: Rue Chakib Arsalane. Good position, but not worthy of its two stars. If you don't like the room they show you, ask to see a better one. Tel: (09) 966750.

Hotel National: ☆ A; 8 Rue Mohammed ben Larbi Torres. Pleasant, comfortable and with character. Bar. Tel: (09) 963290.

Volubilis

The Volubilis Inn: ☆☆☆☆. Comfortable modern hotel in wonderful rural setting near the ruins and the town of Moulay Idriss. Pool and terrace overlooking the ruins. Tel: (5) 544369.

Zagora

Hotel Tinsouline: ☆☆☆☆ B; desert's edge hotel, unpretentious, with good food and swimming-pool; 90 rooms. Tel: (04) 842224.

La Fibule du Draa: ☆☆☆☆ B. Popular, with views and most amenities. Tel: (04) 847318.

Eating Out

The following are the staples of Moroccan menus.

Brochettes: cubes of meat on kebabs, most often made from lamb or liver.

Cous-cous: a huge bowl of steamed semolina grains with vegetables and meat – usually mutton or chicken. It's supposed to be eaten by hand, but spoons are usually provided for Westerners, which is just as well. More of a domestic meal than a meal eaten out – at least as far as the Moroccans are concerned.

Fish: This usually goes under its French names – *loup de mer* (perch), *rouget* (red mullet), *merlan* (whiting), *thon* (tuna). In stews, baked or grilled, they are most usual (not unnaturally) on the coast.

Fruit: good quality fresh fruit is everywhere: dates, grapes, melons, peaches, oranges, cherries or bananas. Fruits that you can peel are the least likely to damage your health. One more fruit, rarely on menus but often sold in the streets, is the sweet and juicy cactus fruit, known as prickly pear or Barbary fig; it's good for settling upset stomachs.

Harira: thick, spicy, sometimes creamy soup, based on lamb and pulses. It's often offered as a starter, but beware: it is enough to be a meal in itself.

Kefta: meatballs flavoured with coriander and cumin.

Khobz: bread for mopping up *harira* or *tajines*, the traditional flat round loaves are ideal. Fairly dry, with a grainy texture. Left-over bread is used in making sweets.

M'choui: whole lamb, spit or oven roasted. *M'choui* is are usually found only on special occasions – at festivals, say – or in the more "traditional" restaurants.

Merguez: spicy beef or lamb sausages, often served with *harissa*, a fiery pepper condiment.

Pastilla: spiced pigeon meat encased in flaky, *warkha* pastry, often dusted with sugar or cinnamon – a traditional delicacy. Sweet versions are also found.

Poulet: chicken – whether cooked with lemon and saffron or olives, or with dates and nuts, or just plain roasted – is common to humble and sophisticated (or expensive) menus.

Tajine: stew – meat or fish, often with fruit and nuts, slowly cooked over charcoal on a bed of oil, vegetables, fruits and spices in an earthenware pot. One of Morocco's most visible dishes (because of the distinctive conical topped dish in which it is served).

Moroccan-style meals are available in most four and five-star hotels, in traditionally furnished restaurants. In cities such as Fez and Marrakesh, there are several restaurants in the medina which specialise in Moroccan meals combined with a floor show. These are mainly the preserve of the tourist trade, since Moroccans tend not to eat out or, if they do, they prefer French or Italian restaurants for the change.

The design of a Moroccan dining-room is similar everywhere. Low banquette seats against the wall, and even lower tables, are the norm in both restaurants and private homes. The classic Moroccan meal is eaten with two fingers and thumb of the right hand – but hotels and restaurants may not insist! When tea or coffee is served, it is a sign that the meal is at an end: you should prepare to leave after three cups or so.

You will probably need to book such meals in advance (even in your hotel): occasionally you may need to be part of a group to order a certain dish. If you're looking for a good restaurant, rely on word of mouth from other visitors rather than the recommendations of guides: the restaurants themselves pay a hefty commission to the guides.

European style meals are served in three, four and five-star hotels, and in several city restaurants. Especially in Agadir, but also elsewhere, the number of pizza and spaghetti restaurants is rising. But there will always be cheap roadside or medina cafés – pick the cleanest and busiest.

Restaurants
AGADIR

Agadir likes to think of itself as a cosmopolitan resort, and this is reflected in the restaurants – sadly rather too many pizza, burger and pasta establishments, most of which are on Boulevard du 20 Août. The restaurant in Al Madina Palace and the Marrakesh Restaurant in the Agadir Beach Club Hotle are at the top end of the quality scale, with Moroccan and international cuisine accompanied by a floor show.

The restaurant in **Hotel Miramar**, overlooking the harbour end of the beach, is well regarded (expect homely French cooking).

There are also some good fish places. Try **Restaurant du Port** – unsurprisingly, at the port entrance – or, more basic, take a seat at one of the makeshift stalls inside the harbour. A plate of fried squid, prawns and sardines costs about 35 dirhams. They serve from late moring through to the evening. On weekends, another possibility is to drive to Aouir, north of Agadir, where the rooftop restaurants specialise in tasty *tajines*.

ASILAH

Of all the small fish restaurants just outside the medina, **Pepe's** is one of the best. Simply cooked sardines, squid, swordfish, prawns, sole, is served with bread and salads. Pavement tables provide a good view of the evening promenade. A more upmarket choice is **Garcia's**.

CASABLANCA

The city may not have much to recommend it from the point of sight-seeing but it has good restaurants. These include:

The outstanding **A Ma Bretagne**, Ain Diab (corniche south of town). Tel: (02) 366226.

The expensive **Al Mounia**, 95 Rue du Prince Moulay Abdallah, off the Boulevard de Paris (Tel: 02-222669); and **Sijilmassa**, Rue de Biarritz. Their Moroccan character extends to providing floor shows.

Less expensive **Ouarzazate**, Rue Mohammed el Qorri, off Boulevard Mohammed V; and **Bahja**, Rue Colbert, off Boulevard Mohammed V. **Restaurant du Port de Pêche** (through the port entrance), tel: 02-318561, and **Ostrea** (also in the port), tel: 02-441319) are good fish restaurants, with moderately expensive prices. For fine Spanish food, try **Le Chalutier**, Centre 2000, tel: (02) 203455.

ESSAOUIRA

Expect to find both these restaurants busy with French surfers:

Chez Sam's, inside harbour perimeter, i.e. through the gate. Excellent seafood and lively atmosphere.

Châlet de la Plage, large portions of good French food at reasonable prices. It is possible just to drink at the bar and eat *tapas* – particularly useful when the few other bars in the town have closed.

FEZ

L'Anmbra, 47 Route d'Immouzer. Tel: (05) 641687. Has an international reputation and is famous for its Moroccan specialities, particularly *pastilla*. Essential to book in advance.

Hotel Palais Jamai, Fez's most stunning hotel, contained in a former palace, has a very good Moroccan restaurant. To book, tel: (05) 634331.

Dar Saada, 21 Souk Attarine, near the Attarine Medrassa, tel: (05) 637370; and **Palais de Fez**, opposite the Kairouyine Mosque, 16 Boutouil, tel: (05) 634707 are downmarket alternatives; but their locations are reflected in their overwhelmingly tourist clientele.

Rather more interesting is **Firdaous** at Bab Guissa (near Palais Jamai), which offers floor show and quite good food at reasonable prices.

As a change from Moroccan cuisine, **Young Tse** (Avenue Salaoui, tel: [05] 623681) is a popular Chinese restaurant; and there is **Vittorio's**, an excellent Pizzeria/Italian at 31 Rue Jabir, just off Mohammed V.

MARRAKESH

Marrakesh's good choice of restaurants reflects the presence of a wealthy expatriate community and its attraction to large numbers of high-spending visitors.

Yacout, 79 Sidi Ahmed Soussi, is at the top end of the price spectrum (approximately £30 per head). The newest and most fashionable restaurant in town (it attracts international names). Classic Moroccan dishes, superbly cooked and presented; a terrific ambience; and exquisite decor. It is necessary to book, tel: (04) 641903.

La Palais Gharnatta, 56 Derb el Arfa, Riad Zitoun Jdid. Tel: (04) 440614. Superb Moroccan food in traditional riad. Family-run. Offers the most value of the up-market restaurants. Book in advance.

Douriya, Place des Ferblantiers. Tel: (04) 442806. Prettily furnished house in the medina. Choice of two menus. Prices rather high for middling quality.

Restaurant Chez Gérard, corner of Avenue Echchouhada and Rue de Paris. Tel: (04) 437755. Good French option.

Restaurant de France on Place Djemma el Fna. So-so Moroccan food and traditional decor beyond the very popular bar. Relatively inexpensive,

popular with tourists, and not necessary to book.

Restaurant Foucald, Rue el Mouahidine, is a Moroccan restaurant again popular with tourists – possibly because it serves large portions!

Le Jacaranda, 32 Boulevard Mohammed Zerktouni. Tel: (04) 447215. Good French option. Stylish setting.

Le Pavilion, Bab Doukala, 47 Derb Zaouia. Tel: (04) 443747. Beautifully decorated restaurant offering up-market French food in an orientalist setting. Book in advance. Closed Tuesday.

Petit Poucet, 56 Avenue Mohammed V, Gueliz. Tel: (04) 432614. Still the restaurant most frequented by European residents. French cuisine.

Le Cantanzaro, Rue Tarik ibn Ziad. Tel: (04) 433731. Good, if pricey, pizzeria.

The Moroccan restaurants in **La Mamounia** and **Tichka** hotels are excellent – and expensive. In the former, expect to pay over £50 per head.

In contrast to the more expensive restaurants listed is a humble and anonymous café close to the Café de France on Djemma el Fna. It can be identified by two vast cauldrons, containing *harira* and vegetable soups, on its raised terrace. The food is fresh and delicious. Inside, standards of hygiene may make nervous diners blanch, but trade is reassuringly brisk!

MEKNES

Hotel Transatlantique, Rue El Merinyine. Tel: (05) 520002. This is a long established luxury-class hotel; it serves old-fashioned Moroccan food at its best. Expensive.

Hacienda, about 2 miles (3 km) outside Meknes on the Fez road. Tel: (05) 521091. A good French restaurant, with bar, dancing and al *fresco* dining.

OUARZAZATE

Chez Dimitri, on Boulevard Mohammed V, looks from the outside like an upmarket café. Serves throughout the day and evening. It has a French Foreign Legion feel: large old-fashioned bar, wooden tables and chairs, old military memorabilia on the walls. Its namesake, Dimitri, died in 1991 but his son has now taken over. At dinner there is usually a *table d'hôte* menu as well as *à la carte*. Choices include hearty casseroles, comprising rabbit or lamb. Extremely reasonable prices and obliging staff.

Hotel La Gazelle, at the western end of town, is a very adequate alternative to Chez Dimitri.

OUIRGANE

La Roseraie is open to non-residents. **Au Sanglier qui Fume**, a roadside auberge, which serves homely French cooking. Lunch is served in the garden in summer.

OURIKA

L'Auberge de Ramuntcho, Aghbalou. Tel: (02) 114373. Sophisticated alternative to the simple cafés and grill bars.

RABAT

L'Oasis, off the Place Pietry (site of the flower market); and **Le Mont Doré** in l'Ocean (next to the medina) are inexpensive traditional restaurants.

Alternatively **La Pagode** (tel: 763383), behind the railway station, and **Le Dragon d'Or**, out of town, next to the Supermarche Souissi on Lotissement ben Abdallah, are good Chinese restaurants.

For pizza and Italian food: **Sorrento** in the Place de Bourgogne; and the very popular **La Mamma** behind Hotel Balima of Boulevard Mohammed V.

TANGIER

Tangier, perhaps as a legacy from its international days, is well served by restaurants. It also has numerous good *tapas* and sandwich bars. Among the *tapas*, try **172**, on Avenue F.A.R.

Restaurant Hammadi (end of Rue Italie) provides reasonable Moroccan cooking in kitsch surroundings. As this is the only Moroccan restaurant in town (outside El Minzah Hotel) customers are generally tourists.

Le Marquis, Rue Tolstoy; **Nautilus**, Rue Velasquez; **Guitta's** (famous in the international era), Place Kuwait: all recommended, but expensive French restaurants.

Couer de Tanger (Boulevard Pasteur) is another good French option.

For a change from Moroccan or French food, there are **Pagode**, an excelent Chinese restaurant; and **San Remo-Chez Toni** in Rue Murillo (Italian). You might also try **Osso Bucco**, Rue Moulay Abdellah, which offers good Moroccan and international dishes at moderate prices.

Good restaurants close to Tangier

include the fish restaurant **Lâchari**, overlooking the river at Ksar es Seghir, along the coast road east of Tangier; and **Eucalyptus**, on the Mountain road to Cap Spartel.

TAROUDANT

La Gazelle d'Or contains another of Morocco's very best traditional restaurants. The hotel is situated in extensive grounds outside town. But even the simplest lunch will cost 300DH a head. Tel: (08) 852039. Closed: during July and August.

Drinking Notes

Mint tea (*thé à la menthe*) and mineral water are the most common beverages in Morocco. There is more or less ceremony attached to the making and pouring of it, depending on whether you are drinking in a home, a shop or a hotel. But the basic brew is consistent – green or black tea, sugar and mint, poured from a height into small glasses. Light, thin and refreshing on the first cup, it can quickly become slightly astringent, and is often gulped down quickly.

Coffee: Turkish coffee is the traditional type of coffee – drunk at any time during the day. *Café au lait* (with milk), *coffee cussé* (with a dash of milk), and *lait cussé* (mainly milk) can all be ordered in the cafés.

Islam and alcohol are strictly speaking incompatible: hence the popularity of Moroccan mineral water, still or sparkling (*gazeuse*, or use the brand names *Oulmés*, or *Sidi Harazem*, which come from sources close to Fez). It may be difficult to find anywhere serving alcohol in remote areas, especially during Ramadan, or on religious holidays.

However, you can usually buy Moroccan **wine** and **beer** in restaurants used by tourists. Robust red wines such as Cabernet, make a good accompaniment to a spicy meal (40–60 dirhams). Other recommendations are Oustalet (inexpensive rosé), Gris de Boulouane (excellent rosé), Special Coquillage (popular white) and Guerrouane (good red).

Local beer is good – Flag Pils and Flag Spéciale (15–20 dirhams). The price of spirits is outrageous – easily 25 dirhams for a single measure (but it is larger than a British single), more

for a simple cocktail. Visit the duty free shop on your way, and bring your own.

Attractions

City

The great imperial cities all glory in vestiges of their splendid past. But all mosques and many *zaouias* (the centres of a saint's cult) are closed to non-Muslims, which means that the number of monuments you can actually visit is reduced. But the ornate gateways (*babs*) into the walled medinas, and the decorated towers (*minarets*) of the mosques are impossible to miss.

The *kasbah* is worth a visit, and the shade of luxuriant gardens usually a relief after a few hours' heavy sightseeing. Palaces and mansions in many cities have been converted to luxurious hotels, or to galleries and museums (see below); and it's usually possible to visit a mausoleum or *medersa* (former lodging-houses for students at the mosque-universities, and often elaborately decorated). Officially-run monuments charge 10 dirhams per person (apart from Volubilis, which is 20); smaller sights and *medersa* are supervised by a *gardien*, who will expect a tip of a few dirhams.

Imperial Cities: Essential Sights

The unmissable city highlights.
Fez: Kairouyine Mosque; its university is older than those of Oxford and Bologna; Medrassa Bou Inania, Medrassa Seffarine; Zaouia Moulay Idriss, one of the holiest shrines in Morocco; Place Nejjarine, with its ornately portalled *fondouk* (an ancient inn-cum-warehouse) and tiled fountain; Place Seffarine; the tanneries.
Marrakesh: Koutoubia minaret; the Saadian tombs, and Medrassa ben Youssef, the latter two fabulously rich in decoration; El Badi and El Bahia palaces.
Meknes: Bab Mansour, one of North Africa's finest gateways; the mausoleum-mosque of Moulay Ismail (open

to non-Muslims); the Medrassa Bou Inania.
Rabat: Tour Hassan; Mohammed V mausoleum; Kasbah des Oudayas; the Roman remains and Islamic necropolis of Chella; the Archaeological Museum.

Arts, Crafts & Museums

Art, craft or folklore museums usually occupy converted palaces or mansions (smaller towns also sometimes have museums containing craft displays).

Despite their superb settings, they rarely have much to offer in the way of supporting literature.
Fez: Museum of Moroccan arts, Dar Batha Palace; Weapons Museum, in the fort overlooking the city, Borj Nord.
Marrakesh: Moroccan Arts Museum, in the Dar Si Said palace.
Meknes: Museum of Moroccan Arts, in the Dar Jamai palace
Rabat: National Archaeological Museum, near the Royal Palace; Museum of Moroccan Arts, in the Oudayas Kasbah; Museum of Handicrafts, rue des Consuls.
Tangier: Museum of Antiquities in the palace of the kasbah.

Souks

A major part of city sightseeing is bound to be wandering through a city's souks. Keep a hand on your bag, and see the section on shopping for buying advice. A visit to the *Maison* or *Centre de l'Artisanat* is somewhere between museum-going and shopping. In each regional centre is a handicrafts co-operative, where as well as craftsmen in small workshops, there will be a crafts shop with fixed prices (it's also possible to buy from the artisans themselves; they may or may not be prepared to haggle). Occasionally there is a craft college attached to the centre.

Hammam

If there comes a time when you are hot and bothered and there is no bath in which to relax, a visit to the *hammam* could be the answer. Most towns (of any size larger than village) have one: a public steam bath, part of Islam's requirement of cleanliness, and Morocco's answer to the sauna (without the birch twigs).

A *hammam* is usually open to women during the day, to men from six or seven in the evening, though arrangements differ from place to place. In a fairly shy atmosphere (nobody strips completely, but you will be stared at rather than expelled for doing so) bathers line the edge of a steam room; after as much steam as they can take, it's time for a cold water dousing, usually from buckets (more modern *hammams*, e.g. in hotels, use cold showers). An attendant will physically "scrub" you with pumice and a black, tar-like soap. In the men's *hammams* massage is often also provided. In the traditional *hammams* the cost is between two and five dirhams. Unfortunately, some male *hammams* prohibit non-Muslims.

A good sweat sounds like the last thing one wants after a sticky day, it clears the pores and relaxes the body – and nobody is likely to hassle you. The same is true (at least for men) while sitting in the barber's chair for a *wet shave*. There is an extraordinary number of barbers in the larger towns, packed with fathers and sons waiting for a cut and other customers swathed in pints of foam. Barbers will also tidy eyebrows and nasal hair. They are good places in which to meet ordinary Moroccans.

For other leisure pursuits, see section on *Sports*.

Country

There is, of course, an infinite number of touring routes and excursions throughout Morocco that could be contrived: and the main text of this book should help in the planning of a suitable itinerary. Below, however, are lists of the must-see excursions and routes radiating from the most popular holiday centres.

FROM AGADIR

The mountain villages and scenery around **Tafraoute**, 95 miles (150 km) southeast; the old Portuguese fishing port of **Essaouira**, 112 miles (180 km) north.

FROM MARRAKESH

The pass roads through the High Atlas of **Tizi n-Test** (to the south) and **Tizi n-Tichka** (to the southeast); the highest peak of Morocco, **Jebel Toubkal**, due south, visible for miles around, and climbable from Imlil; the **southern valleys** of oases and kasbahs, east and south of Marrakesh and reached via

Ouarzazate 126 miles/204 km from Marrakesh – specifically the **Draa** valley, the **Dadès** valley and the **Todra** gorge; the really dedicated will press further east into the Sahara to the **Tafilalt** to watch sunrise over the dunes. Via Beni-Mellal 125 miles (200 km northeast), you can reach the reservoir at **Bin el Ouidane** and the waterfalls (*cascades*) at **Ouzoud**.

FROM MEKNES OR FEZ

The cedar forests around **Azrou** and **Ifrane** (50 miles/80 km and 37 miles/60 km south of Fez); the **Kandar massif** (19 miles/30 km south of Fez); the holy city of **Moulay Idriss** and the nearby Roman ruins of **Volubilis** (19 miles/30 km north of Meknes); the end of the Middle Atlas mountains to **Taza**, and further east, the end of the Rif at the **Beni-Snassen** mountains.

FROM RABAT

Head inland! There are only coastal towns to visit closer than Meknes: **Salé**, Rabat's other half; **Casablanca** (56 miles/90 km) and **El Jadida** (117 miles/187 km).

FROM TANGIER

The large market town of **Tetouan** and the pretty white houses at **Chaouen** and **Ouezzane** are in the foothills of the Rif. **Asilah** is a good place to head on the west coast. You might also contemplate a day trip to **Gibraltar**.

FURTHER AFIELD

Hiking into the mountains and riding into the desert can both be arranged with relative ease. English speaking travel agencies arrange Land Rover "safaris" deep into the desert, along prearranged routes, and these obviously have considerable attractions over random forays, especially since reliable maps are hard to come by. Hiking in the High Atlas is well catered for, with mules, guides and mountain huts – the latter maintained by the French Alpine Club (CAF). First base is at Imlil, two hours from Marrakesh (you can take a bus as far as Asni then buy a place in a truck or taxi for the remaining 11 miles/17 km). Again, specialised tour operators can provide guaranteed expertise, as well as a bit of security for your adventure. But there's no reason to ignore independent possibilities, at least if it's sum-

mer and you're reasonably fit. The Toubkal National Park is well charted (IGN maps available from either Imlil or Rabat), the terrain not difficult (except for coping with the loose scree underfoot). All in all, very little specialist equipment is necessary.

Tour Packages

Package travel to Morocco divides into the mass market – chiefly packages to the coastal resorts, Fez or Marrakesh – and the specialist, either up-market (tailor-made itineraries and specialist hobby holidays) or budget (adventure holidays, treks or expeditions). Tour operators operating from the UK are listed below.

Tour Operators
General

Based on information and telephone numbers supplied by the Moroccan National Tourist Office in London:

Abercrombie & Kent: up-market hotels in Tangier, Mohammedia, Marrakesh, Fez, Taroudant and Ourigane. Tel: 0171-730 9600.

Cadogan Travel: good hotels in Agadir, Tangier, Marrakesh; Imperial Cities tour. Tel: (01703) 332661.

Cosmos Tourama: Tangier, and Moroccan Adventure tour. Tel: 0181-464 3477.

Club Mediterranée: Club holidays in Agadir, Marrakesh and Ouarzazate. Tel: 0171-581 1161.

Hayes & Jarvis: Imperial Cities Tour; Agadir and Marrakesh. Tel: 0181-748 0088.

Inspirations: Packages to Tangier, Asilah, Agadir and Marrakesh. Tel: (01293) 822244.

Travelscene: Tel: 0181-427 4445.

Specialist Companies

You can expect these companies to offer a wider choice of packages, more local knowledge, to tailor itineraries (and to charge more than the above).

British Museum Tours: Occasional escorted tours of the imperial cities. Tel: 0171-323 8895.

Creative Leisure Management: Agadir, Tangier, Marrakesh, Ouarzazate, Fez, Rabat, Mohammedia, Casablanca, El Jadida, Essaouira, Taroudant; golf, shooting, trekking and birdwatching holidays. Tel: 0171-235 0123/2110.

Golf International: Caters to the growing interest in golfing holidays in Morocco. Tel: 0181-452 4263.

Morocco Bound: Imperial Cities tour; Great South tour; Grand Tour; Agadir, Marrakesh, Casablanca, El Jadida, Essaouira, Layoune, Mohammedia, Ouirgane, Taroudant, Rabat, Tangier, Fes, Meknes, Smir-Restinga, Al Hoceima, Ouarzazate, Zagora; fly-drive tour. A good source of discount tickets on Royal Air Maroc. Tel: 0171-734 5307.

Rambler's Holidays Ltd: Walking through the foothills of the Atlas. Springboard Marrakesh. Tel: 01707-331133.

The Best of Morocco: Imperial Cities tour; Great South and Kasbahs tour; Discovery of Morocco tour; Agadir, Casablanca, Essaouira, Fez, Marrakesh, Mohammedia, Ouarzazate, Taroudant, Tangier. Tel: (01380) 828533.

Adventure & Expeditions

Africa Explored, tel: (01633) 880224.

Encounter Overland, tel: 0171-370 6951. Trans-Sahara and Trans-Africa trips.

Exodus Expeditions, tel: 0181-675 5550. Provides the most complete adventure programme in Morocco of any British agency.

Explore Worldwide, tel: (01252) 319448.

Guerba Expeditions, tel: (01373) 826611.

Worldwide Journeys and Expeditions, tel: 0171-381 8638.

American Express Agencies

American Express is represented by Voyages Schwartz in Morocco. These English speaking travel agencies can be useful for anyone, but particularly those carrying an Amex card or travellers' cheques. Cardmembers can also use the offices for drawing cash in emergencies, mail forwarding and poste restante.

Agadir: 87 Place du Marché Municipale. Tel: (08) 820252.

Casablanca: 112 Rue du Prince Moulay Abdallah. Tel: (02) 273133.

Marrakesh: Rue Mauritania, Immeuble Moutaoukil. Tel: (04) 433022.

Tangier: 54 Boulevard Pasteur. Tel: (09) 933459.

Resort nightlife is restricted to Tangier, Casablanca and its outskirts (Ain Diab and Mohammedia) and Agadir (where it is, in fact, fairly subdued). The most exciting city at night, and with the most Moroccan feel, must be Marrakesh, but Tangier still has claim to being the late-night town.

Bars

Bars are a late 20th century addition to Moroccan nightlife, and not always a happy one. It's as though they are symbols of the clash between Moroccan Islam, with its traditional rule of total abstinence from alcohol, and Moroccan modernity, with its liberal, urban, Westernised way of thinking. They can be loud and intimidating or furtive and uneasy. **Hotel bars** are a different matter, and can be insular.

Nightclubs & Discos

Nightclubs (often with belly dancing) and **discos** in tourist centres and cities are aimed at the tourists and the Westernised urban population and visiting Gulf Arabs intent on letting their hair down. Many are in hotels.

Gambling

There are **casinos** in Marrakesh (in the Hivernage district of the new town) and in the resort area of Mohammedia, just north of Casablanca.

Folklore & Fantasias

In *medina* restaurants or on main roads out of town, the most common evening entertainment is a combination of a typically Moroccan meal with a display of folklore: folk music and dancing, or (in the open countryside) an equestrian fantasia. Although these evenings often have a rather "packaged" feel, they can be genuinely spectacular – especially the fantasias. There may, of course, be the chance of coming across real festivals (while touring, for example), where the excitement is more spontaneous. The early evening in any town or city is vibrant as everyone comes out after an afternoon siesta. Evening street life is notably exciting in Marrakesh, where the celebrated *Djemaa el Fna* whirls with people; dancers, snake charmers, traders, beggars and musicians and tourists. Have plenty of change in your pocket

while you watch the performers: a contribution is expected from everyone, visitors above all – and especially from all photographers.

In Morocco touting is an everyday occupation; selling is a polished and sinuous art form, the rigmaroles of buying can be prolonged, even wearisome. One thing is worse: attempting *not* to buy articles is completely exhausting.

Dealing with it: The only rule about bargaining for something you really want is to know the price you are prepared to pay, and start well under it (at, say, half or a third). Tactics and strategies on both sides (incredulous laughter, walking towards the door), and bids, which come gradually closer, will probably end with the buyer paying a little more than his original maximum; part of the seller's art is to determine how much more.

Fixed prices: The first priority, then, is to ascertain a fair market price for goods on offer. This is often possible in the state-run Handicraft Centres (*Centre* or *Maison de l'Artisanat*) in major towns. The quality of goods here is underwritten by the government, and there is always a shop with fixed prices on display. These will be higher than the prices that should be possible through bargaining, but the lack of hustle and pressure mean that some people are bound to prefer shopping here.

The Moroccan authorities, as well as the traders themselves, recognise that bargaining makes many visitors nervous; and many of the souks, as well as city shops, are beginning to display *prix fixes*, for everything from room-sized carpets to small brass trinkets. Although haggling is not about to die, these are depressing sights.

What To Buy

The traditional crafts of Morocco still make the best bargains. First and most prominent of the handicraft traditions are **carpets**, hand knotted and a few cases, still coloured with vegetable dyes. Designs (apart from the Turkish inspired patterns of Rabat carpets) are predominantly traditional to Berber tribes. Their use of colours and schemes of stylised illustration are supposed to enable experts to pin down not only the area but sometimes the individual tribe or even family that made them. Top quality carpets sell for thousands of dirhams (compare shop prices in Europe and the US); more affordable and more easily portable are Berber rugs, kilims or blankets. For Berber patterns, try the small country souks around Marrakesh.

Leather goods are widespread: from unpolished leather bags and belts, through the distinctive pointed slippers known as *babouches*, to ornate *pouffes*, studded and dyed. Some leather goods are finished in a style closer to Italian designer luggage – in all cases, price should go hand in hand with quality, so check the hide and workmanship before buying. Printed boxes and bookbindings are often on show, but, with their shiny tooling, have become the victims of their imitators and too often look merely tacky.

Jewellery is available everywhere, although the most exciting place to buy it is Tiznit, with its famous silversmiths' souk. Dull silver is the basic material: heavy but beautifully decorated bracelets, delicate filigree rings, chunky necklaces of semi-precious stones (or occasionally of plastic, for the unwary), are most common. Slightly more unusual, and sometimes antique, are decorated daggers, scabbards, or Koran boxes, covered in silver-wire decoration. Whatever the piece, the fastenings are often a weak point. Beware, too, of silver-plating masking what the Moroccans call *b'shi-b'shi* – meaning rubbish.

Marquetry is another traditional craft: wooden furniture, ornaments, chess-sets, and small wooden boxes made in cedar, thuya, and oak. Many wooden goods are inlaid with contrasting veneers or mother of pearl. Often the quality of finish is less than ideal: hinges or joints are points to watch. The woodworkers' *ateliers* at Essaouira are an ideal place to buy (and to watch the manufacture).

Pottery ranges from the rough earthenware of household pots and crocks to gaudy (and predominantly tourist-orientated) designs in the main towns and markets.

Whether you're looking for egg-cups or Berber carpets, it's worth visiting craft museums to determine what is traditional, and what is tat. In the end,

however, visitors will end up buying what they like and paying what they think it's worth.

Where To Shop

The following list contains the more upmarket places to shop (many include antiques). For cheaper souvenirs and gifts there is a host of bazaars, all selling much the same merchandise.

CASABLANCA

Art de fez, 6 Rue General Laperine.

FEZ

Au Petit Bazaar de Bon Accueil, 35 Talaa Seghira, Fez el Bali.
Boutique Majid, Abdelmajid Rais el Fenni, 66 Rue des Chrétiens.

MARRAKESH

Bazaar du Sud, 117 Souk des Tapis.
Chez Alaoui, Souk Shouari.
Chez le Brodeuses Arab, 12 Rue Rahba Lakdima.
Coopartim, Ensemble Artisinal, Ave Mohammed V.
Fondouk el Fatmi, Bab Ftouh
Fondouk el Quarzazi, Bab Ftouh.
La Lampe d'Aladdin, 99 and 70 bis Rue Semmarine.
Mamounia Arts, 47 Rue Dar el Bacha, Bab Doukkala.
Maison d'été, 17 Rue de Yougoslavie. Pretty furnishings and ornaments.
Moroccan Arts, 67 Sabeb Mouley Hadj, El Ksour.
L'Oiseau Bleu, 3 Rue Tarik Ibn Ziad.
L'Orientaliste, 15 Rue de la Liberté. Antiques and fine crafts.

RABAT

Gallerie Cheremetieff, 16 bis Rue Annaba.

TANGIER

Adolfo de Velasco, 28 Boulevard Mohammed V. Antiques and fine crafts.
Arditti, 87 Rue de la Liberté.
Bazaar Sebou, 18 Rue Sebou.
Boutique Majid, 66 Rue des Chrétiens.

Export Procedures

Beware of buying anything that can't be carried away. Many traders will offer export facilities (e.g. for large carpets) and, although there are no customs formalities to be met, the shipping of goods could take months. There is little comeback against a souk trader

who has been paid in cash and fails to deliver. However, paying by credit card is getting easier, and the networks of the card companies may well provide a back-up. Always ask for a detailed invoice.

Complaints

Complaints can be taken to the local police. A complaints book is supposed to be kept by every classified hotel, specifically for tourists' complaints (albeit usually complaints about accommodation, as might be expected). Copies of complaints are then forwarded to the headquarters of the tourist office in Rabat. The *Syndicat d'initiatif* or ONMT offices should also be able to help in passing on complaints, or advising on any appropriate action.

Sports
Golf

It is said to be King Hassan's enthusiasm for golf which has led to courses sprouting near major cities and resort throughout the country. The main golf tournament is the Hassan II trophy, held in November at the Royal Dar es-Salam in Rabat. The Moroccan Open is held in January. Lessons and caddies are available at all courses. Some courses require a handicap card.

Agadir: Royal Golf d'Agadir, 9 holes. Built in 1955. Tel: (08) 241278.
Golf les Dunes, 27 holes. Built in 1992. Course comprises: Tamarisk (9), par 36; Eucalyptus (9), par 36; Oued (9), par 36. Tel: (08) 834690.
Ben Slimane (near Casablanca): Royal Golfe de Bani Slimane, 9 holes. Built in 1992. Tel: (03) 328793.
Casablanca: Royal Golf d'Anfa, 9 holes. Built in 1945. Tel: (02) 365355.
Royal Golf Mohammedia. Tel: (03) 324656.
El Jadida: Royal Golf d'El Jadida, 18 holes. Built in 1993. Tel: (03) 352251.
Meknes: Royal Golf de Meknes, 9 holes. Built in 1943. Tel: (05) 530753.
Marrakesh: Royal Golf de Marrakech, 18 holes, par 72. Built in 1923. Tel: (04) 444341.
Palmerie Golf, 18 holes. Built in 1993. Tel (04) 301010.
Amelkis: 18 holes. Built in 1995.
Mohammedia: Royal Golf de Mohammedia, 18 holes, par 72. Built in 1925.
Ouarzazate: Royal Golf de Ouarzazate,

18 holes. Built in 1993. Tel: (04) 882653.

Rabat: Royal dar-es-Salam, 45 holes. Built in 1971. Course comprises: Red (18), par 73; Blue (18), par 72; Green (9), par 32. tel: (07) 755864.

Tangier: Royal Golf de Tanger, 18 holes, par 70. Built in 1914. Tel: (09) 944484

Tetouan: Royal Golf Cabo Negro, 18 holes. Refurbished. Tel: (09) 978303.

Hunting

From the first Sunday in October, on Sundays and public holidays until January or early spring, it's open season on game birds and wild boars. In the Arbaoua Game Reserve, most notably, but elsewhere too, abundance of wildlife has led to the government licensing shooting. Victims include quail (season closes late January); snipe woodcocks, pigeons and turtle doves (there is a separate season in May and June for the doves); and partridges, Iducks, rabbits and hares (season closes early January). The season for wild boar runs until mid-February, on Thursdays as well as Sundays and holidays; but hunting is only allowed with beaters. **Licensing** is strictly controlled, and hunting without a licence is an offence. It is theoretically possible to organise the temporary import of one's own guns, but it is more convenient to leave to an expert the formalities and the procurement of a local shooting licence (which, in 1990, cost visitors 300DH and nationals 100DH, or 500DH and 100DH for boar). The specialist company in Morocco is Sochatour, who co-operate with the Ministry of Agriculture and the *Administration des Eaux et Forêts*. Sochatour, 72 Boulevard Zerktouni, Casablanca. Tel: (02) 277513.

Fishing

Trout fishing is popular in Morocco: to the extent that the rivers and lakes that are easily reached have been overfished. The fly fisher's choice is extreme: fishing in isolated streams and pools of the Middle and High Atlas, or casting into custom-stocked lakes (most of them in the Middle Atlas) where the permits are expensive and the catch weighed before leaving.

Coarse fishing: Lakes and reservoirs of the Middle Atlas are the most popular setting for coarse fishing;

around Azrou, Ifrane and Immouzer du Khandar in particular, and in the reservoir of Ben el Ouidane. Species include some of the world's largest pike, as well as black bass and perch.

Permits are required for trout and coarse fishing; these are usually available locally (through hotels or tourist offices) or from the *Administration des Eaux et Forêts*, 11 Rue Revoil, Rabat (Tel: 725335). The Adm*inistration* also sets the fishing seasons year by year.

Sea fishing is rich, too, and does not require a permit. From massive sea bass off Dakhla and Layounne in the south, to the summer visits of tuna north of Casablanca, and swordfish off Tangier or lobster and langouste in Rabat and Agadir, fish are populous and varied. Bream, mackerel and sardines are common also. The Mediterranean and the South Atlantic coasts are the most fruitful: deep sea fishing from boats is relatively easy to arrange, and spearfishing with aqualung is possible with a permit.

Hiking

Several adventure tour operators run hiking holidays in the Atlas and Anti-Atlas mountains. These come with experienced guides and porters. However, it is possible to devise your own hikes *in situ*, especially in the Toubkal National Park south of Marrakesh. Unless you are a very experienced (and properly equipped) mountain hiker, hire a local guide and pack mules and follow the standard routes. The price of such services, including accommodation and sometimes food, are set and published, though they may be negotiable when business is quiet. Good springboards, where hiking has been turned into an important local industry, are Imlil (a few kilometres from Asni), Oukaimedan, and Tabant. Basic accommodation on hikes is found in mountain refuges or in the homes of locals.

For further information on hiking in Morocco, contact Centre d'Information sur la Montagne, Ministry of Tourism, 64 Avenue Fal Ould Oumeir, Agdal, Rabat, tel: (07) 770686, fax: (07) 770629. They will send you the latest copy of GTAM (*la Grande Traversee des Atlas Marocains*), which includes information on guides, services (local accommodation, transport and tariffs).

White-Water Rafting

In spring, when the snows melt, and in late autumn, when rains fall, the rivers of the High and Middle Atlas quickly swell. Good rafting is to be had on the Dades and Ourika rivers in the High Atlas, and (more demanding) the Oum er Rbia River in the Middle Atlas. Several adventure tour operators are now including rafting in their programmes, along with mountain biking. If you want to join an organised rafting programme while in Morocco, contact:

Dynamic Tours, 34 Boulevard Zerktouni, 11th Floor, Casablanca. Tel: (02) 229935.

Sport Travel, 8 bis Rue Abou Bakr, Seddaq, Marrakesh. Tel: (04) 436158.

Ribat Tours, 3 Avenue Moulay Youssef, Rabat. Tel: (07) 760305.

Tizi Randonne, 42 Avenue de l'Istiqlal, Kenitra. Tel: (07) 374009.

For general information, contact the Federation Royale Marocaine de Canoe-kayak, Centre National des Sports, BP 332, Avenue Ibnou Sina, Rabat. Tel: (07) 754424.

Skiing

The peculiarity of the High Atlas climate enables the tourist board to boast of Marrakesh being a base from which you can go skiing in the morning and sunbathe in the afternoon. The ski resort of Oukaimeden (altitude 8,700 ft; 2,650 metres), around an hour's drive south of Marrakesh, expects snow from December to April – but the snow is not to be relied on. The skiing is stiff; skis and boots can be hired. The other resort, Mischliffen, is on a volcanic crater, reached through cedar forests from Azrou or Ifrane – the setting rather than the skiing is the attraction. There are plans afoot to develop Ketama in the Rif as "the Moroccan Switzerland". In the meantime, or at least until Ketama loses its reputation as the Moroccan drug capital, the casual visitor might care to think twice about sampling the (undeniably attractive) slopes of Mount Tidighine in the Rif mountains.

Bird Watching

Some of the migratory birds lucky enough to have avoided death by shotguns are rare and beautiful: Morocco lies under one of the two major migratory routes for European birds wintering in Africa. Storks, ibis, and flamingoes are seen in the wetlands of river estuaries and coastal lagoons. Eagles and falcons sometimes wheel high in a semi-desert sky. Several tour companies offer specialised bird-watching holidays; their expertise will help determine the place and time to go. Mid-October is one of the best times.

Particularly good areas include: **Oualidia**, where the lagoons and salt pans attract flamingo, black-winged stilt, avocet, Audoin's and Slender-billed gulls; the islands off **Essaouira**, where a colony of Eleonora's falcon breed, Pale Crag Martin and osprey; the **Sous valley** for Moussier's redstart, bush and great grey shrike, Lanner falcon and chanting goshawk; the **Anti-Atlas** for long-legged buzzards, cream-coloured courser and black wheatear; **Djebel Sarho** for desert sparrow, trumpeter bullfinch, brown-necked raven, mouring and rat-rumped wheatear and larks.

Other Sports

Tennis, and (along the coast) watersports are easy to find in most tourist areas, through hotels. One of the most popular activities, though, is riding – whether it is mule-trekking in the rugged terrain of the mountains, or galloping on horseback along the sandy beaches of the coast.

For most sports, it is easy (with the help of the Moroccan Tourist Office) to find a specialist who will sell (or arrange for you) an inclusive holiday. It is, of course, possible – and certainly cheaper – to arrange for a few days' sport *in situ* when you arrive.

Language

Getting By

Arabic is the official first language of the kingdom, although many people speak dialects of the **Berber** language, especially in and south of the High Atlas. Moroccan Arabic is unlike other forms of Arabic, so Arabic phrase books are not a good investment (although classical Arabic speakers will be understood). The easiest way to communicate for most Westerners is to use **French**, the second language, commonly used alongside Arabic on signposts, menus and in shops. The average Moroccan puts the average visitor to shame in his command of second, third and fourth languages. English, German or Spanish will be understood in many hotels or markets – or wherever tourists are found.

It's very useful to have a few words of Arabic as a matter of courtesy, and to establish friendly relations. A few useful words are listed below; an accent shows the stressed syllable.

Pronunciation

í	as in	see
ya	as in	Soraya
ai	as in	eye
ay	as in	may
aw	as in	away
kh	as in the Scottish	loch
gh	as in the Parisian	r
dh	as in	the

Double consonants: try to pronounce them twice as long.
An apostrophe ' indicates a glottal stop.

Greetings

Hello/*Márhaba, ahlan*
(reply)/*Marhba, ahlan*
Greetings/*As-salám aláykum* (peace be with you)
(reply)/*Waláykum as-salám* (and to you peace)

Welcome/*Áhlan wasáhlan*
(reply)/*Áhlan wasáhlan*
Good morning/*Sabáh al-kháyr*
(reply)/*Sabáh al-kháyr*
Good evening/*Masá al-kháyr*
(reply)/*Masá al-kháyr*
Good night/*Tisbáh al-kháyr* (wake up well)
(reply)/*Tisbáh al-kháyr*
Good bye/*Máa Saláma*
How are you?/*Káyf hálak?* (to a man)/*Káyf hálik?* (to a woman)
Well, fine/*Al-hámdu li-llá*
Please/*min fádlak* (to a man)/*min fádlik* (to a woman)
After you *Tafáddal* (to a man)/*Tafáddali* (to a woman)/*Afáddalu* (to more than one)
Excuse me/*Samáhli*
Sorry/*Áfwan* or *mutaásif* (for a man)/*Áfwan* or *mutaásifa* (for a woman)
Thank you (very much)/*Shúkran* (*jazilan*)
Thank you, I am grateful/*M'tshakkrine*
Thanks be to God/*Al-hámdu li-llá*
God willing (hopefully)/*Inshá allá*
Yes/*Náam* or *áiwa*
No/*La*
Congratulations!/*Mabrúck!*
(reply)/*Alláh yubárak fik*

Useful Phrases

What is your name?/*Sh'nnu ismak?* (to a man)/*Sh'nnu ismik?* (to a woman)
My name is.../*Ismi...*
Where are you from?/*Min wáyn inta?* (for a man)/*Min wáyn inti?* (for a woman)
I am from:
England/*Ána min Ingíltra*
Germany/*Ána min Almánia*
the United States/*Ána min Amérika*
Australia/*Ána min Ustrália*
Do you speak
English?/*Tkellem Inglisia?*
I speak:
English/*Kan tkellem Inglesa*
German/*Almámi*
French/*Fransáwi*
I do not speak Arabic/*Ma kan tkellemichi Arbia*
I do not understand/*Ma báfham*
What does this mean?/*Shka te aní?*
Repeat, once more/*Sh'hal*
Do you have...?/*Ándkum...?*
Is there any...?/*kayn...?*
There isn't any.../*Ma kaynsh*
Never mind/*Ma'alésh*
It is forbidden.../*Mamnú'a*
Is it allowed...?/*Masmúh...?*

What is this?/*Sh'nnu hádha?*
I want/*Baghi*
I do not want/*Ma Baghish*
Wait/*Istánna* (to a man)/*Istánni* (to a woman)
Hurry up/*Yalla/bi súra'a*
Slow down/*Shwáyya*
Finished/*Baraka*
Go away!/*Imshi!*
What time is it?/*Adáysh as-sáa?/kam as-sáa?*
How long, how many hours?/*Sha'al?*

Vocabulary

GENERAL

embassy/*sifára*
post office/*máktab al-baríd*
stamps/*tawábi'a*
bank/*bank*
hotel/*otél/fúnduq*
museum/*máthaf*
ticket/*tadakir*
ruins/*athár*
passport/*jiwáz as-sáfar*
good/*m'zyan*
not good, bad/*mashi m'zyan*
open/*maftúh*
closed/*múghlk*
today/*al-yáum*
tonight/*Al barah ghadda*
tomorrow/*búkra*

EATING/DRINKING OUT

restaurant/*máta'am*
food/*ákl*
fish/*sámak/hout*
meat/*láhma*
milk/*halíb*
bread/*khúbz*
salad/*saláta*
delicious/*záki*
coffee/*káhwa*
tea/*shái*
cup/*kass*
with sugar/*bi súkkar*
without sugar/*bla sukkar*
wine/*sh'rab*
beer/*bíra*
mineral water/*mái ma'adaniya*
glass/*kass*
bottle/*karaa*
I am a vegetarian/*Ána nabbáti* (for a man)/*nabbátiya* (for a woman)
the bill/*al-hisáb*

GETTING AROUND

Where...?/*Wáyn...?*
downtown/*wást al bálad*
street/*shária*
Amir Mohammed Street/*Shária al-amir*

Mohammed
car/*sayára*
taxi/*táxi*
shared taxi/*servís*
bus/*tobis*
airplane/*tayára*
airport/*matár*
station/*mahátta*
to/*íla*
from/*min*
right/*yamín*
left/*shimál*
straight/*dúghri*
behind/*wára*
near/*karíb*
far away/*ba'id*
petrol, super/*benzín, benzín khas*

NUMBERS

zero	*sifir*
one	*wáhad*
two	*itnín*
three	*taláta*
four	*árba'a*
five	*khámsa*
six	*sítta*
seven	*sába'a*
eight	*tamánia*
nine	*tísa'a*
ten	*áshara*
eleven	*hidáshar*
twelve	*itnáshar*

SHOPPING

market/*súq*
shop/*dukkán*
money/*fulús*
cheap/*rakhís*
expensive (very)/*gháli (jídan)*
receipt, invoice/*fatúra, wásl*
How much does it cost?/*Adáysh?/bi-kam?*
What would you like?/*Sh'nou khsek?*
I like this/*Baghi hádha*
I do not like this/*Ma baghish hádha*
Can I see this?/*Mumkin ashúf hádha?*
Give me/*A'atíni*
How many?/*Kam?*

LOOKING FOR A ROOM

a free room/*ghúrfa fádia*
single room/*ghúrfa munfárida*
double room/*ghúrfa muzdáwija*
hot water/*mái skhoon*
bathroom, toilet/*hammám, tuwalét*
shower/*dúsh*
towel/*foota*
How much does the room cost per night?/*Sha'al al bit allayla?*

EMERGENCIES

I need help/*Bídi musáada*
doctor/*doctór/tabíb/hakím*
hospital/*mustáshfa*
pharmacy/*saidalíya*
I am ill, sick/*Ána marídh* (for a man)/*Ána marídha* (for a woman)
diarrhoea/*ishál*
operation/*amalíya*
police/*shúrta*
lawyer/*muhámmi*
I want to see/*Ba'ghi anshoof*

Glossary

agadir/fortified granary
agdal/garden
Aid el Kebir/feast day celebrating Abraham's Sacrifice of the Lamb
Aid es Seghir/feast day held after the first sighting of the moon after Ramadan
El Andalus/Muslim Spain
aït/community
bab/gate
baraka/blessing, often thought magical
bled el makhzen/land of government
bled es siba/land of dissidence
caid/district judge
djemma/assembly, but also mosque
djinn/spirit
Fassi/person from Fez
fondouk/lodging house with stables
Gnouai/a black African tribe in the south
Hadith/the written traditions of Islam
Hadj/the pilgrimage to Mecca
hammam/steam bath
horm/sanctuary
imam/prayer leader
jebel/mountain
koubba/white, domed building containing the tomb of a saint
ksar (ksour)/fortified *pisé* building or community (plural)
l'tam/veil
Maghreb/collective name for Morocco, Algeria and Tunisia
makhzen/government
marabout/saint
Marrakshi/person from Marrakesh
mechouar/square, assembly area
medrass (medersa)/Islamic college and living quarters for students (plural)
medina/old town
mellah/Jewish quarter
mihrab/niche indicating direction of Mecca in mosque
minaret/tower of mosque
Moriscos/Muslim refugees from Spain in 15th century

*moujehaddin/*Islamic soldiers engaged in Holy war

*Moulay/*indicates descendancy from the Prophet

*Mouloud/*Prophet's Birthday

*moussem/*religious festival

*msalla/*prayer area

*muezzin/*caller to prayer

*oued/*river

*pisé/*mud and rubble

*quibla/*direction of Mecca in a mosque

*Shia/*branch of Islam which recognises Ali as the successor to Mohammed

*shouaf/*fortune teller

*shereef/*ruler who is descendant of Prophet

*stucco/*elaborate plaster work

*Sufi/*religious mystic

*Sunni/*orthodox Muslim

*tizi/*mountain pass

*tabia/*mud used in *pisé* architecture

*zaouia/*religious fraternity

*zellige/*elaborate tile mosaics

Days of the Week

Often used to identify towns and villages, which are named after the day of their weekly *souk*: thus Souk-Tnine is the town which has a market on Monday. On many road signs, the day is mentioned where the map or guidebook omits to mention it. The days are numbered from Sunday, with the exception of Friday, the day of Muslim worship, which has no number.

El had the first day: Sunday

Et tnine the second day: Monday

Et tleta the third day: Tuesday

El arba the fourth day: Wednesday

El khemis the fifth day: Thursday

Ej djeema day of mosque or assembly: Friday

Es sebt the sixth day: Saturday

Further Knowledge

Books

History

Morocco by Neville Barbour. London: Thames & Hudson, 1965. The standard historical work from the Phoenicians to the 1960s.

Lords of the Atlas, by Gavin Maxwell. London: Century, 1983. Compelling story of the Glaoui dynasty in the last two centuries.

The Conquest of Morocco, by Douglas Porch. London: Jonathan Cape, 1986. French colonial adventurism and Moroccan history at the turn of the century.

Fiction

The Spider's House, by Paul Bowles. London: Arena Publishing. Good introduction to the work of a writer working in and out of Moroccan traditions, translating and fictionalising. This is a novel set against daily life in Fez.

For Bread Alone by Mohamed Choukri. Grafton, 1987. Autobiography of a man who grew up poor and illiterate. Translated into English from classical Arabic by Paul Bowles.

Hideous Kinky by Esther Freud. London: Hamish Hamilton, 1993. Comic novel about a young girl's adventures with her hippie mother in Morocco in the 1960s.

The Lemon and **Love with a few Hairs** Mohammed Mrabet. Al Saqi Books. Fiction by one of the leading Moroccan novelists.

The Sand Child by Tahar Ben Jellouan. Quartet. Novel by foremost Moroccan novelist, which won the French Prix Groncourt.

Food and Cooking

Taste of Morocco, by Robert Carrier. Century, 1988. Excellent introduction to food and recipes, plus social customs. Sumptuous photographs.

Good from Morocco, by Paula Wolfert. John Murray, 1989. Comprehensive introduction to Moroccon cuisine; a diverting read.

Travel Literature

Morocco: The Traveller's Companion by Margaret and Robin Bidwell. I.B. Tauris, 1992. An anthology of extracts by famous and obscure writers.

The Voices of Marrakesh by E. Canetti. London: Marion Boyars. Impressions by Nobel Prize winner.

Tangier: City of the Dream by Iain Finlayson. Harper Collins, 1992. A gripping account of Tangier in its louche heyday.

The Dream at the End of the World by Michelle Green. Bloomsbury, 1992. Gossipy account of epatriate life in Tangier.

Morocco That Was, by Walter Harris. London: Eland Books, 1983 (first published 1921). Accounts of the end of feudal Morocco and the beginning of French rule from London *Times* correspondent who died in 1933.

A Year in Marrakesh, by Peter Mayne. Eland Books, 1984. Engrossing, personal account superbly written.

By Bus to the Sahara, by Gordon West. London: Black Swan. A journey through Morocco during the 1930s, calling at the palaces of various Moroccan caids, including El Glaoui, Pasha of Marrakesh.

General

Morocco, by Rom and Swaan Landau. London: Elek Books, 1967. Worth tracking down for photographs, which include mosque interiors.

The World of Islam: Faith, People, Culture, edited by Bernard Lewis. Thames and Hudson. Excellent general introduction to the Islamic world, lavishly illustrated.

The Moors: a comprehensive description by Budgett Meakin. London: Sonnenschein, 1902. Comprehensive indeed, long certainly, with a good claim to be the first guide book to Morocco.

Women

Beyond the Veil, by Fatima Mernissi. London: Al Saqi Books. Classic polemic on women's position in Islam by Moroccan feminist educated in Morocco and America.

Photographic/Art Books

Matisse in Morocco, by Jack Cowart; Pierre Schneider; John Elderfield; Albert Kostenevich; Laura Coyle. Thames and Hudson, 1990. Stunning record of Matisse's two fruitful trips to Tangier in 1912.

Living in Morocco: Design from Casablanca to Marrakesh by Lisl (photographs) and Landt Dennis. Thames and Hudson, 1992. Sumptuous exploration of Moroccan arts and crafts and their application in interior design.

Berbers of the Atlas by Alan Keohane. London: Hamish Hamilton. Impressive photographic study.

Films

There is little state support or interest in Moroccan film-making, most energy being employed in promoting Morocco's advantages as a film-location. But the following films are worth catching.

Hamid Benani's *Traces* (1970). About an orphaned boy adopted by a strict Muslim father.

Souhel Ben Barka's *A Thousand and One Hands* (1972) about the problems of dyeworkers; *The Petrol War Won't Happen* (1975); and *Amok* (1982).

Moumen Smihi's *El Chergui* (1975) is about a young wife's problems.

Ahmed el Maanouni's *Oh, the Days* (1978) is concerned with harsh peasant life and the lure of France.

Mohammed Reggab's *The Hairdresser from a Poor District* (1982); Abderrahmane Tazi's *The Great Voyage* (1981).

Moustafa Derkaoui's *The Beautiful Days of Scheherazade* (1982).

Jilali Ferhti's *Reed Dolls* (1981) about the plight of a widowed woman.

Other Insight Guides

Other *Insight Guides* highlighting destinations in this region:

Insight Guide: Tunisia explores the country's heady mix of African, Arab and European cultures.

Insight Pocket Guides: Morocco and *Tunisia*. Hand-made itineraries extracting the best of these astonishinly beautiful countries.

Photography by
Associated Press 53, 54, 61
David Beatty 1, 2, 6/7, 12/13 14/15,
18/19, 20/21, 22, 24, 25, 26, 71,
73, 106/107, 142/143, 146, 178/
179, 187, 188, 189, 231, 245, 250,
260, 261, 266, 267, 268, 280, 282,
285
Bodo Bondzio 127
Columbia Pictures 269
Dominique Dallet 230
Steinar Haugberg 70, 99, 108/109,
183, 192, 194, 195
Holiday Which? 112, 125, 140, 145,
158, 258/259, 277, 284
Alan Keohane cover, 102, 104, 105,
248L, 254
Alain Le Garsmeur 31, 35, 38/39, 44,
46L&R, 47, 49, 50L& R, 52, 55, 75,
76, 77, 78
Louvre Museum 28/29
Mary Evans Picture Library 33, 74
Middle East Pictures 3, 30, 32, 34,
36, 43, 66, 67, 72, 80/81, 82/83,
84, 85, 86, 87, 92, 94, 110/111,
126, 134, 164/165, 166, 172, 196,
265, 274
Kim Naylor 62, 90, 93, 121L&R, 124,
136R, 138, 184, 186, 190, 193, 197
Polly Phillimore 208L, 210, 211, 212
Jorg Reuther 135, 137
Jens Schuman 42, 88/89, 96/97,
133, 157L, 162, 170, 172, 176/177,
203R, 223, 224L, 226, 247, 251,
255, 270R
Spectrum Colour Library 105, 116,
117, 150, 151, 272/273, 278
Topham Picture Library 48, 51, 58, 59,
60, 63, 64, 79, 239
Bill Wassman 18/19, 91, 120, 122,
130, 136L, 147, 157R, 159,
198/199, 203L, 204, 227, 234/235,
242, 246, 252, 253, 254, 264
Phil Wood 163L, 163R, 169, 174,
222R, 225, 228, 229,262L, 264, 286
Fritz Wolfgang 9, 23, 27, 37, 45, 56,
57, 65, 68/69, 95, 98, 100/101,
119, 123, 128/129, 131, 132L&R,
139, 144, 148/149, 153, 154, 156,
161, 167, 175, 180, 182, 191, 200,
201, 206, 208R, 209, 213, 214, 216/
217, 218, 224R, 232, 236, 237, 238,
240, 243, 257, 270L, 271, 275, 281,
287, 288

Maps Berndtson & Berndtson

Visual Consultant V. Barl

Index